TOP HOODLUM

**FRANK COSTELLO
Prime Minister
of the Mafia**

ALSO BY ANTHONY M. DESTEFANO

Top Hoodlum:
Frank Costello, Prime Minister of the Mafia

The Big Heist:
The Real Story of the Lufthansa Heist, the Mafia, and Murder

Mob Killer:
The Bloody Rampage of Charles Carneglia, Mafia Hit Man

The King of the Godfathers:
Joseph Massino and the Fall of the Bonanno Crime Family

TOP HOODLUM

FRANK COSTELLO
Prime Minister
of the Mafia

ANTHONY M. DESTEFANO

CITADEL PRESS
Kensington Publishing Corp.
www.kensingtonbooks.com

CITADEL PRESS BOOKS are published by

Kensington Publishing Corp.
119 West 40th Street
New York, NY 10018

All Kensington titles, imprints, and distributed lines are available at special quantity discounts for bulk purchases for sales promotions, premiums, fund-raising, educational, or institutional use.

Special book excerpts or customized printings can also be created to fit specific needs. For details, write or phone the office of the Kensington sales manager: Kensington Publishing Corp., 119 West 40th Street, New York, NY 10018, attn: Sales Department; phone 1-800-221-2647.

CITADEL PRESS and the Citadel logo are Reg. U.S. Pat. & TM Off.

ISBN-13: 978-0-8065-3869-3
ISBN-10: 0-8065-3869-4

First Citadel hardcover printing: July 2018

10 9 8 7 6 5 4 3 2 1

Printed in the United States of America

Library of Congress CIP data is available.

First electronic edition: July 2018

ISBN-13: 978-0-8065-3871-6
ISBN-10: 0-8065-3871-6

CONTENTS

Life can only be understood backwards;
but it must be lived forwards
—SØREN KIERKEGAARD

PROLOGUE

THE HUNDREDS OF THOUSANDS OF DRIVERS who travel each day along the Grand Central Parkway in the Borough of Queens in New York City likely never give much notice to the small urban cemetery of St. Michael's. Crammed into less than 100 acres, the burial ground sits back off the highway and is partially obscured by roadway abutments, fences, and trees. Started by an Episcopal church in Manhattan in 1852, St. Michael's is non-denominational. Its burials reflect the history of the city's migration stream: many of the older graves are for Polish, German, and Italian families, the newer ones are for interments of Greeks, Eastern Europeans, and Asians.

On an unseasonably warm and sunny day recently, I pulled onto Astoria Boulevard and made my way to the cemetery's front gate. St. Michael's doesn't have many notable burials, certainly nothing like the more historically significant cemeteries of Green-Wood in Brooklyn and Woodlawn in the Bronx. But one mausoleum right by the entrance is of great importance in the history of the American Mafia, and I was going to find it for the simple reason that I believe cemeteries are often the best place to begin and end stories. I felt this was certainly the case in writing a book about Francisco Castiglia, more popularly known as Frank Costello, the man anointed forever in crime lore as the "Prime Minister of The Underworld."

Costello may not have left a legacy of a crime family bearing his name such as happened with his main nemesis and rival Vito Genovese. But in the annals of organized crime, Costello was in a class by himself. From a dirt-poor background in the southern Italian province of Calabria and only a sixth-grade education in American schools, he rose with a mix of shrewdness, business acumen, and plain luck to amass a fortune that sustained his advance as a power in the mob after emigrating in the early twentieth century as a child with his family to New York. Costello's parents settled in the East Harlem section of Manhattan at a time when it bore the label of Little Italy. It was a community living under the sway of powerful criminal *padrones* and crime bosses as well as in constant fear of the mythic Black Hand, the extortion racket that preyed on the new Italian immigrants. This was the environment in which as a young man Costello learned the ways of the streets of New York.

If truth be told, Costello got his hands dirty with violence as a young man since the gun and the knife were facts of life for a young immigrant man. But bloodshed was not something he became known for. For Frank Costello, his power came from the way he astutely identified ways of making money—be it in Prohibition, slot machines, and other gambling operations—and parlaying his fortune to a position of influence in Democratic party politics through the old and corrupt Tammany Hall organization.

In the 1930s and 1940s, Costello built a reservoir of political influence in New York unlike anything we have ever seen in the history of the Mafia. How else could you think of a man who in 1932, after being part of the cabal that deposed the old Mafia leaders in bloody revolt a year earlier, was sitting among politicians in Chicago and helping the Democratic Party pick its presidential candidate? It seems that he did so through money, which politicians always need, and the value of his reputation as a crime boss, which helped him be—shall we say—persuasive. While later gangsters like John Gotti might be able to emulate the kind of celebrity that Costello enjoyed, they couldn't hold a candle to the power Costello had amassed. Certainly, Gotti and other Mafiosi of his era could kill and grab millions of dollars from their crime family rackets. But Costello didn't have to resort to the gun to get what he wanted.

"He was not 'soft,' by any means," George Wolf, Costello's trusted lawyer and friend for years, would remember after his death. "On many occasions, I found him frightening. But he was 'human,' he was civilized, he spurned the bloody violence in which previous bosses had reveled."

Costello's friends and peers in the Mafia were men like Charles "Lucky" Luciano, Joseph Adonis and Albert Anastasia, leaders who bloodied their hands in the great Mob power struggles of the 1930s and became legends in their own right. But Costello wisely saw the usefulness of corrupting and influencing politicians and police as a way of assuring that what would become La Cosa Nostra could operate in New York with little interference. Costello built alliances with Jewish gangsters like Meyer Lansky and had no trouble working with Irishmen like bootlegger William V. Dwyer and gambler Frank Erickson. For decades, with his political connections, Costello and the mob held sway, at least until reformist politicians like Fiorello La Guardia conducted their own vendettas in an effort to trim Costello's sails.

But to understand the real significance of Frank Costello is to acknowledge that he was a man who was also on a quest to be seen as legitimate, a criminal who could be accepted by society as a man of taste and culture. Costello was like the fictional bootlegger Jay Gatsby, striving to attain entry to the social upper crust and status. To do that, Costello and his wife Loretta bought the house in Sands Point, which in *The Great Gatsby* was located in the more exclusive fictional area of East Egg, the place where Gatsby himself could only aspire to be part of. In the novel, Gatsby's mansion was set in the somewhat socially inferior West Egg section, analogous to the current day Great Neck. So in a sense, Costello got where Gatsby never could and made an effort—sometimes successfully—to hob nob with his wealthy North Shore neighbors like NY *Newsday* publisher Alicia Patterson.

"He came the closest of anybody could ever come to total legitimacy," Mafia journalist and screenwriter Nicholas Pileggi once said about Costello. "When all of these guys are out there shooting each other and acting like idiots, he was at the 1932 Democratic Presidential Convention with the leader of Tammany [nominating] Franklin Delano Roosevelt as President in the Drake Hotel in Chicago."

Still, as hard as he tried, Costello was never able to break through to the legitimate world the way he wanted. He survived mob wars, as well as a bungled attempt by Genovese to assassinate him and a few efforts by the federal government early in life to put him in prison. But then La Guardia and his allies, including the legendary Manhattan District Attorney Frank Hogan, started to nibble away at Costello's power, either using heavy-handed tactics to go after his slot machine empire or by embarrassing politicians, judges, and police officials who were friendly—or financially indebted to him. To La Guardia, Costello was a prime example of the crooks, thugs, bums, and chiselers whom he wanted to chase from New York City. It was a mission of La Guardia, driven by his childhood memories of the way his family had been victimized by criminals, as well as a political rivalry his reform group had with Costello's friends in Tammany Hall.

However, the real major public damage was done to Costello in 1951 when he decided to testify before the U.S. Senate committee investigating organized crime. He thought it would be an opportunity to show the world his legitimate side. But in the end, it was from a public-relations standpoint a tactical and strategic defeat. It was then that the American public saw Costello, mostly through television close ups of his fidgeting hands and the sound of his gravelly voice, as the personification of the mob. He would protest his innocence and claim to be nothing more than a respectable businessman dancing around questions by senators about his unsavory friends. But even children who watched the televised spectacle thought Costello was guilty of something. It turned out he would face another problem when his testimony soon after would lead to a conviction for contempt of Congress.

Costello's conviction for contempt of Congress led to an eighteen-month prison sentence. The publicity and undeniable evidence that organized crime existed in the country forced FBI director J. Edgar Hoover, who had known Costello from his days at the racetrack and socializing at the Stork Club, to initiate something known as the

"Top Hoodlum Program." For years, Hoover wouldn't acknowledge that the Mafia existed. (After his death in 1972, stories arose that Costello and other mobsters passed along racing tips to Hoover that paid off handsomely.) Instead, he labeled people like Costello, not surprisingly, with the designation "Top Hoodlum," and their files were noted accordingly. That was Hoover's way of keeping the gangsters on law enforcement's radar without having to surrender to the notion that there was indeed a phenomenon known as the Mafia. The result was that Costello was eventually tried, convicted, and sent to prison for five years in 1954 for income tax evasion. Old enemies in the government also worked feverishly to get his U.S. citizenship revoked in 1961 and even tried to get him deported, a fate that befell Costello friends Luciano and Adonis.

But Costello still had some charms left in his life. In 1963 the U.S. Supreme Court overturned a decision to deport him. Retired from the Mafia life since the 1957 assassination attempt on him had been bungled by Vincent Gigante, Costello lived out his remaining days growing orchids in Sands Point and spending his time living the life of the country squire he had strived to be. Many of Costello's old friends and associates found themselves in prison or murdered, and his legal issues depleted his wealth so much so that later in life he would have to ask for loans from the few friends who remained. But in the end, he kept his freedom, dying from a sudden bout of heart trouble in 1973 at the age of eighty-two.

It was a chilly day in February 1973 that a small crowd of mourners, which included Costello's wife Loretta, had gathered at St. Michael's to pay their final respects at the mausoleum. Costello's remains were placed in a crypt on the upper level of the classically styled structure, adorned on the front by two Ionian columns. His parents Luigi and Marie also had their own places inside, having been disinterred years ago from a simpler grave elsewhere in St. Michaels. The closing of the bronze doors that day symbolized the end of an era for the Mafia, one that was never to be repeated. Sure, the Five Families of the New York Cosa Nostra would remain a force for decades. But their heyday was approaching its sunset, and time was running out. The FBI, unshackled after Hoover's death in

1972, started to go after the crime families in a more concerted way using the new racketeering laws. Over the coming years, the Mafia in New York was pushed back on its heels, the bosses who remained, presiding over dwindling empires run by second- and third-string acolytes.

Returning to the front of the mausoleum some forty-four years later, I peered through the grimy glass on the doors hoping to feel a sense of the importance of the man whose remains lay within. The interior, lit by sunlight passing through a stained-glass window at the rear, was bathed in a calming yellow light but held no hint of anything special. In addition to his wife and parents, the Costello mausoleum also contains the remains of Loretta's mother and father, her brother Dudley who was a close associate of her husband, as well as two of Frank's older sisters. Each crypt was emblazoned with a small brass plaque: Costello's bearing his ascribed date of birth of January 26, 1891 and the day of his death February 18, 1973. A small broom lay in a corner. The rear window ledge held a vase with some yellow roses of uncertain age and three small books.

Standing in front of the structure, emblazoned with the name "Costello," the moment seemed very undramatic. This was the tomb of a Mafia king. Yet, I felt that there were no secret insights that were going to come rushing at me as I stood there. I didn't even see any damage from the bomb that detonated in 1974, blowing off the mausoleum doors in what police to this day still think was a gesture by dope dealing mobster Carmine Galante as a sign of disrespect. Costello took his knowledge and version of the truth with him when he entered this final resting place. But in reality, that is a perfect metaphor for Frank Costello and the secretive way he projected his power in the underworld. Almost everybody who knew anything about Costello and the way he operated was either inside the crypts or some other graves. The last significant books about him—one by his attorney George Wolf and the other by the late New York newspaperman Leonard Katz—were written around the time of his death in 1973. When they were published, both tomes were state-of-the-art in terms of the information available. (Another book was published by author Henry A. Zeiger in 1974.) The challenge for me was to tell the story beyond the old legends, since many of those who knew Costello were no longer living.

Before he died, Costello himself thought he would finally commit to telling his story to a writer. Beginning in December 1972 he met a number of times with author Peter Maas, who earned fame with crime books like *The Valachi Papers* and *Serpico*. Maas knew from his earlier works the institutional history of the Mafia and saw the unprecedented power of Costello and his uniqueness in American history. Both men met and talked for hours with an eye toward a blockbuster. Clearly, it would have been a ground-breaking book, rivaling even the book about Valachi. But just weeks after Costello began unburdening himself to Maas, he suddenly died after suffering a heart attack. Then in 2001, Maas himself passed away, leaving no trace of any interview notes or recordings of what Costello may have told him—save for a three-page memo I found that sketched out a possible approach to the subject of Costello.

Although death and the passage of time may make things harder for an author seeking to reconstruct a person's life story, in the case of researching and writing *Top Hoodlum* the years actually worked to my benefit. Since the 1990s, the FBI has been releasing its previously secret but historically significant files on famous mobsters as well as a host of other notable Americans, whether they were criminals or not, who had drawn the curiosity of Hoover and his army of agents. Scholars, researchers, and authors can now see reams of materials kept by the agency on the likes of Meyer Lansky, Luciano, and countless other Mafia figures. In the case of Frank Costello, over 3,000 pages of material have been released. The documents sometimes bear heavy redactions, but the pages reveal the inside story of the extent to which the federal government went after Costello with a vengeance. Government agents dug deep in an effort to put him in jail over his income tax problems. In another case, a former Treasury official, who had failed miserably and was humiliated in an attempt to convict Costello in the 1920s for bootlegging, helped the government in the effort to revoke his citizenship.

There were also files about a strange jewel heist in 1935, one never mentioned in the Wolf and Katz's books, involving precious

stones of socialite Margaret Hawksworth Bell. The case was a Run-
yonesque tale involving a shadowy private detective named Noel
Scaffa and some hapless thieves working in Miami. The FBI tried to
implicate Costello in the theft and in fact got him indicted in New
York. But again, as the files showed, Costello eluded the prosecution when it became apparent that the FBI couldn't make the charges
stick. By the early 1960s, a retired Frank Costello was keeping out
of trouble, watching his old mob associates wither away. A police
report in the files noted that Costello wasn't observed in any criminal activity.

Another source of new insight and information about Costello
comes from his relatives. Costello and his wife didn't have any children. But over the years a few of his relations who traced their lineage through the Castiglia family tree became fascinated by his story
and embarked on their own private quest for information. In particular, Noel Castiglia of Maryland, one of Costello's first cousins
twice removed, had met him as a young boy. As an adult, Castiglia
began compiling unique reminiscences from other relatives before
they died about "The Uncle," as Costello was known in family circles. There was one hilarious episode about a Castiglia family parrot
that seems straight out of sitcom and also a more ominous tale about
an elderly uncle who faced off Costello's friends with a rifle. Castiglia also unearthed family photos showing Costello as a young
man, as well as a rare image of Luciano, things he has allowed me to
share for the first time in book form with readers of *Top Hoodlum*.

Active as a gangster *cum* politician from the 1920s until his
forced retirement three decades later, Costello generated a torrent of
newspaper stories, many of which were used to flesh out the por-
trayal of his life in *Top Hoodlum*. In his heyday, Costello was a key
figure in New York night life—he was believed to have been a secret
owner of the Copacabana and other night spots—and provided fod-
der for gossip columnists for years. His gambling parlors ranged
from Saratoga to New York to Miami.

Over at Toots Shor's saloon on West Fifty-first Street, Costello
was part of the crowd of celebrities, movie stars, writers, Nobel
Prize winners, and sports figures who made it into a place where, as

one writer observed, a salesman from Iowa could rub elbows with the likes of Joe DiMaggio and bump into Frank Sinatra while going to the restroom. Costello himself is said to have tipped his glass to Supreme Court Justice Earl Warren, who did the same in return. (Maybe, just maybe, that last gesture passing between the two men meant something since it was the Warren court which, despite ruling against Costello numerous times in other matters, finally decided in his favor in the deportation case.)

Toots Shor and his incomparable establishment reigned when Broadway and its gangsters were the center of the universe. "The Big Street," as writer Damon Runyon called it, was a place where dreams and fortunes were made and lost. Broadway was Runyon's muse and the street's real-life denizens like Costello provided the backbone for his stories. He is said to have modeled his fictional "Dave The Dude," a suave lady killer of a gangster, after Costello. Another character, "The Brain," was inspired by the real-life Jewish gangster Arnold Rothstein, the man credited with bankrolling Costello in his early bootlegging years. Such were the legends inspired by the wise guys and girls of the Big Street era.

Court records are gold mines for writers, but in Costello's case all of them are from legal entanglements that ended decades ago, as far back as the early part of the twentieth century. The signatures on some of the documents are written in cursive script with a fountain pen. They provide an important window to the facts, and, in the case of *Top Hoodlum,* the National Archives provided reams of material useful in rounding out Costello's story. In some cases, the files contain Costello's own statements as well as his signature. Some files outlined the story—remembered only by his surviving relatives and illuminated here for the first time—how Costello and his crew of bootleggers took over parts of Astoria to run their lucrative operations.

At the time he was working with Costello, Maas instinctively knew that there wasn't much to expose about the man. The mobster's troubles and travails had been widely reported over the years, keeping an army of journalists busy. The Senate hearings of 1951 had made Costello's life an open book as well, with hundreds of pages of testimony. But of course there was always room—as Maas also knew—to enlighten the world about Costello. And as I found out from the FBI records, his relatives, and my own digging through the files of history, there *was* always more to uncover. Costello was a gangster, yes, but his life was more nuanced and intricate than the bloody sagas of the more modern—and forgettable—Mafiosi we have come to expect. Maas never got that chance to illuminate his subject the way he wanted. But with *Top Hoodlum*, I hope readers will now have the opportunity to get the fuller story.

CHAPTER ONE
"COME TO AMERICA"

FORTUNE AND HISTORY HAVE NOT BEEN KIND to the Italians of the Mezzogiorno. During much of the nineteenth century, the southern region of the Italian peninsula had been the scene of constant battles between warring factions in the great struggle to unify the various kingdoms into one nation. The south at that time still didn't have a unifying Italian language, with dialects spoken in different regions.

The fighting and the oppressive policies of some leaders and feudal landowners spawned bands of brigands, a veritable army of dispossessed who, disappointed with failed agrarian reforms, took to terrorizing the landowners and creating a state of lawlessness in the region. In turn, the landowners put together their own small armies to resist the brigands. The strife added to the difficulties of the poor trying to eke out a living in areas like Calabria where the land already was difficult to till.

Luigi Castiglia had been part of the army of Giuseppe Garibaldi, one of the generals leading the fight for unification, and had been mustered out of the service with a small pension, reportedly two dollars a month, upon returning to civilian life around 1870. Historical research by Robert Golden indicated that Luigi likely fought with Garibaldi in his later campaign beginning around 1866. Luigi settled in Lauropoli, a hardscrabble Calabrian town about ten miles from the Ionian Sea. He had been preceded by about one hundred years by a Giuseppe Castiglia from Sicily. Records show Luigi Castiglia took a job as game keeper, a position with some responsibility in the local feudal culture.

Historical research, by none other than Frank Costello's close friend and confidante Frank Rizzo, known as *Il Professore*, holds that the town was formed around 1776 by the Marchioness Laura Serra of Naples. Marchioness Laura, sometimes known as the Duchessa, was the Italian version of "to the manor born." She married a prominent landowner, a Marquis, and when he died, she decided to live in the south permanently. With a decree from the King of Naples, she was granted land permitting her to set up a town that she named after herself, calling it "Lauro-poli." The setting was inland from the ancient city of Sybaris, an old Greek outpost close to the Ionian Sea.

The Marchioness invited anyone with a problem with the law to settle in Lauropoli, which—given the way history played out for at least some of the Castiglia family and its progeny—proved to be an interesting bit of foreshadowing. Luigi worked as a game warden for one of the landowners and tried a stint at farming by working a vineyard. The locale had the ruins of an old Grecian temple, and if Luigi cared to, he would have taken his family there on outings.

It seems that the Castiglia family struggled in Lauropoli. Farming was not an easy occupation at that time. Luigi's wife Maria Castiglia worked as well as a "spinner" or weaver of cloth, and since she was more of an entrepreneur than her spouse likely took on work as a seamstress as well. A friend once described her as stout, illiterate, but intelligent—a country woman who had black hair pulled back with hairpins. By early 1891, the couple already had five children—four daughters and a son—when Maria gave birth again to another boy named Francisco, the child who would grow up to become Frank Costello.

Right from the start, there was an issue with Francisco. For years there were questions about when exactly he was born. His birth certificate records a date of "ventidue, di Febbraio" or February 22, in the year 1891. But researchers have uncovered a baptismal certificate date of February 17, 1891, for one "Francisco," the son of "Luigi" and "Maria Saveria Aloise," (which was the maiden name of Frank Costello's mother). What explains the discrepancy? It was common in rural Italy that a birth was recorded on the day officials were notified, and not on the actual birthday, which would have been earlier than the date of baptism. The FBI files don't help clear up the confusion since an agency dossier has noted three different years—1891, 1893, and 1896—for Francisco's birth, along with birthdays of January 23 and January 26. The date that seems settled, based on Social Security Administration records, immigration records, and Costello's own burial place is January 26, 1891.

Of course, by the time he was born, Francisco's accurate date of birth wasn't the Castiglia family's main concern. Luigi's prospects were not getting any better the longer he stayed in Lauropoli. The family was in debt, and even Maria was said to have run up tabs with the local flour mill, which she couldn't pay. So, in 1895, Luigi Castiglia, accompanied by his oldest son Eduardo and at least some of his daughters, Concetta, Sadie, and Saletta, did what many in that part of Italy were doing, crossing the ocean to the United States as part of the early wave of Italian immigrants bent on trying their luck in New York.

Once in New York, Luigi Castiglia found himself in a labor market saturated with workers, mainly immigrants. In the Italian community, men known as *padrones* became crucial links in doling out jobs, arranging travel, and sending remittances bank to Italy, although it is doubtful given his struggles that Luigi sent anything back to Lauropoli. Controlling resources the way they did, the padrones wielded a great deal of power. It is very likely that Luigi got work from the padrones, but he had no great success in making financial headway. He was a laborer. For him the streets weren't paved with gold. Yet, he had nothing to look forward to back home in Italy. He finally wrote Maria. "Sell everything," Luigi told her, "even the bed sheets, if necessary, even if you have to borrow some lire from someone, but come to America."

It was a move of desperation, and one relative remembered that the family vineyard was also sold off. With prospects non-existent in Lauropoli, the only chance for the family was in Manhattan. With young Francisco and daughter May in tow, Maria Castiglia traveled to Naples where she boarded a vessel with third-class tickets bound for New York. The exact date of her arrival with her youngest son hasn't been found on any shipping manifests, but as Francisco Castiglia, later to become known as Frank Costello, would note years later on his application to become an American citizen, they arrived on U.S. soil on April 2, 1895. He would have been four years old.

East Harlem is a section of Manhattan near the East River. The area today encompasses a neighborhood roughly bounded by 107th Street to the south and 125th Street to the north, then stretching a few blocks west to Park Avenue. Back when the Castiglia family first arrived, the tenements attracted so many of the Italian immigrants who arrived in this period that the newspapers labeled it "Little Italy," a designation that would shift decades later to the more well-known area farther south near Chinatown. As often happened, immigrants from particular areas of Italy tended to settle in certain neighborhoods and for those from Lauropoli like the Castiglia family the small block of 108th Street between First and Second Avenues was a magnet.

FBI records indicated that the Castiglia clan first settled in Astoria, Queens, but then took up residence in a tenement building at 222 East 108th Street with other *Lauropolitano*, bouncing around the block and sometimes taking boarders to help pay the rent. Luigi found work as a laborer, breaking stone at the reservoir system in Westchester County. Meanwhile, Maria helped start a small store on the same street selling what newspapers would describe as "Italian products," as well as codfish, ice cream, hot peppers, and all kinds of sundry items. She put in long hours and one surviving photograph showed both Maria and Luigi posing stiffly outside the store. It was never clear how the family got the capital to open the business, although it wouldn't have been unusual for them to have relied on a loan from one of the landlords, who may have also been a *Lauropolitano*. Working as hard as they did, the couple didn't have much time for parental supervision, particularly of their sons Eduardo, who became known as Edward, and Francisco, known on the street as Frank.

There were other members of the Castiglia family who lived on

108th Street and among them were Frank's uncle, also known as Francesco Castiglia, and his son Domenico, both of whom emigrated from Lauropoli. Francesco died in 1902, but his son would later move to Connecticut and establish a farm that would become a family retreat. But before that move, both father and son lived in a building with young Frank and his family—as well as a troublesome parrot, which caused the family some legal problems.

The bird, who had the rather unimaginative name of Polly, did what parrots normally do and imitated the human speech it heard. In the building also lived an opera singer who was in the chorus of a local opera company and would practice during the day, singing the scales as part of a vocal warm-up. The singer could be heard throughout the building and Polly sang the scales along with the singer in a very loud voice, which ended in a screech. The lady singer took offense at what she thought was someone mocking her and knocked on the apartment door. She got no answer and finally in frustration went to the police, who issued a citation.

The Castiglia family showed up in court with the parrot and explained to the judge what had happened. It was a story that amused courtroom spectators, who started to laugh. The judge pounded his gavel and demanded, "Order in the Court, Order in the Court." Polly, again doing what parrots do, imitated the judge with a squawking, "Order in the Court, Order in the Court," causing more laughter. Polly, who lived to the age of about ninety-seven, never forgot the phrase and repeated it whenever she heard singing.

But life on 108th Street was not all humor and conviviality. East Harlem may have been part of New York City and subject to its laws and the power of the police. But in reality, the law on the street that the Castiglia family had to deal with was quite different. The area, as well as other Italian sections of the city, were under the influence— you could say control—of several powerful criminal combinations of Sicilians, Neopolitans, and Calabrese who lived in close quarters for years in uneasy truces. One focal point of crime was about a block east of the Castiglia apartment on 108th Street, a slender alley known in the history of crime in New York City as the "murder stable." It was a passageway that went from 334 East 108th Street south through to 107th Street. It most certainly was a working stable and it was partly owned by a woman named Pasquarella Spinelli, described as "a tall woman with unruly red hair, a square, strong face, and masculine stride." Her clothes were described as unkempt, and it was said that she seldom washed, which must have made life unbearable for those doing business with her in the summer when combined with the reeking odors of horse manure and sweat.

Horses were a significant method of business and personal transportation around town. The city had a small army of sanitation workers to shovel up the piles of manure on the streets. In sweltering summer months, the newspapers featured stories about how overheating steeds would have to be watered down to keep them from dropping dead from exhaustion. Stables were a necessary part of commercial life, and Spinelli did house the working animals in her facility.

But in reality, Spinelli was a horse thief and her stable was something like a modern-day chop shop where thieves wouldn't dismember the hapless animals but instead make deals for the best price to pay before they spirited the animals away. Although, like Costello's mother, Spinelli could neither read nor write, she was a shrewd and violent person, the closest thing to a padrone for someone of her sex. She would keep track of debts people owed her by making lines with a piece of coal on a white board and wasn't above roughing up someone who was late in making payments. In short, she was a *cagna,* or bitch. Still, she always found time to pray and make donations to Our Lady of Mount Carmel Church.

Stories circulated that victims of mob violence were buried under Spinelli's stable ground, and although there is no proof uncovered that any bones were ever found, the urban myth persisted. Over the years at least a dozen men were either killed in or near her horse sheds. Spinelli was labeled by the newspapers as "the wealthiest woman in Little Italy" a widow who some pundits likened to Hettie Green, the "wicked witch of Wall Street" known for her miserliness and success in a man's business.

To make her money, cops believed that Spinelli recruited neighborhood youths to work as toughs and thieves, enforcing the pay-

ment of debts. Police raided her stable but never found any indication that the horses there had been stolen. The Costello boys were
right in her territory and Frank himself spent his time sitting under
the trees outside Spinelli's stable entrance, no doubt watching and
learning the ways of the street and those who tried to rule it. But it
remains unclear if the Costellos did anything more than sit around
the stable. Historian Giuseppe Selvaggi, citing a source he gave the
pseudonym "Zio Trestell" but who claimed to be a close associate of
Frank Costello, reported that Maria Costello didn't allow her young
Frank to hobnob with Spinelli or other street criminals when he first
arrived in New York.

Spinelli's serious rival for power in this part of East Harlem was a
man known as Giosue Gallucci. Dubbed "The King of Little Italy"
and "The Mayor of Little Italy," Gallucci was the closest thing to a
crime boss in the area. He ran an extensive policy operation, also
known as the Italian lottery, in which bettors attempted to pick three
digits to match those that would be randomly drawn the following
day. Galluci was also a money lender and was believed by police to
have a hand in prostitution operations in East Harlem and elsewhere
in Manhattan. His operation was a block north of the Spinelli stable.
A corpulent man with a waxed, handlebar moustache, which seemed
wide enough to almost touch his cheeks, Gallucci sometimes took to
riding horses on the streets. Although he protested that he was only
a successful businessman who owned real estate, a bakery, coffee
houses, and saloons, Don Gallucci was notorious for shaking down
fruit and vegetable peddlers for a dollar a week.

Gallucci, who also bore the sobriquet of "The Boss," also had a
reputation, burnished by reports in the newspapers, that he had significant political clout. *The Herald* in particular said he had long
been the head of several political organizations. This made Gallucci
in the eyes of some the "most powerful Italian politically" in the
city. "His enemies said that his political activities gave him a certain
measure of immunity from police interferences," noted *The Herald*.

At a time when criminals like Spinelli, Gallucci, and other bosses
ran the rackets in East Harlem, dealing with bands of extortionists
known collectively as the Black Hand or *Mano Nero*, Frank Costello

was a mere babe in the woods at the age of fourteen getting up the nerve to pull his very first solo job. This was a period where everyone had to hustle in East Harlem and Frank had to grow up quickly. According to attorney George Wolf, Frank injured his leg while visiting his aunt Concetta's farm in Astoria, then a semi-rural part of Queens. The doctor had asked that he stay at the farm in bed. But Frank knew that his mother was behind in the rent for the apartment and was getting screamed at by the landlady for payment. As related by Wolf in his book *Frank Costello: Prime Minister of the Underworld*, his future client one night boarded the ferry across the East River from Queens, limped to his apartment building in East Harlem and mugged the landlady, grabbing money she kept in her bosom and fled into the night. It was a reckless scheme and could have easily backfired.

"The landlady recognized Frank," said Wolf. "She cried out 'Thief!' and rushed to Frank's mother's door, which was on the first floor. Maria Saveria was stunned. "Your're a liar, my son hasn't been home since Sunday." Sure enough, when police investigated, they in fact found Frank asleep with a bandaged leg at the Astoria farm.

Frank was quite as successful in eluding the law in his next caper three years after mugging the landlady. Records show that on April 25, 1908, Costello had his first arrest for trying to shake down a coal merchant in the Bronx. Charges of robbery and assault were also thrown in. But in a hearing before a judge the case was dismissed, and Frank walked away scot free. Another robbery charge hit Costello in October 1912 when he was accused of trying to rip off money and jewelry from a woman named Philomena Sorgi who was a neighbor on 108th Street. The case bears significance because it appears to be the first time in court and police reports that Frank used the surname "Costello." While the origin of the name has been a subject of speculation, 1910 Census records show that the similar name "Castello" found its way into the enumeration records as an alternate identification for the Castiglia family. This suggests that the family may have adopted a different name and told it to the Census taker, with things changing by the time Frank got arrested for the Sorgi robbery two years later when he used the spelling "Costello."

These arrests of Frank show that he was steadily becoming ensnared as a teenager in the lifestyle of a petty criminal. It was a dead-end lifestyle that held no future. FBI records indicated Costello irregularly attended two public schools in Manhattan and educationally made poor progress. At age fourteen, Costello said he dropped out of the educational system in the sixth grade and later in life was only able to show an educational level through academic tests of third or fourth grade, except for sixth-grade level on the "word meaning" test. Given the environment that surrounded him—parents preoccupied with making a living and an immigrant community where criminals were King and Queen—it is no surprise that Frank got into trouble. It was a surprise, given the mortality rate among young Italian men and women in the criminal subculture, that Frank didn't himself wind up dead or seriously hurt. Aside from the gangs run by Spinelli and Gallucci, there were numerous other criminal combinations which affected Little Italy and they were responsible for a great deal of bloodshed, sometimes for the most insignificant reasons. The so-called "Navy Boys," a group of Neapolitan men, worked primarily out of the Navy Street area of Brooklyn, while other combinations such as the Terranova brothers vied for power in East Harlem. Costello was reputed to have worked as a rent collector for big shot Ciro Terranova. Murders started to pile up, and the newspapers talked of a murder a week in East Harlem among the Italians.

One of the first casualties to rock Frank's world was Spinelli. It was around 6:00 P.M. on the evening of March 20, 1912, that Spinelli entered her stable to talk to the foreman when she was felled by two shots as she walked up a set of stairs: one through her right temple and the other through her neck. She died instantly. Witnesses said two assailants were involved and they reported that Spinelli's partner in the stable, Luigi Lazzazaro, was seen opening a door to let them out.

Speculation immediately arose that the killing was done in retaliation for an act of justifiable homicide committed by the dead woman's daughter Nicolina. The young girl had stabbed to death a suitor she caught trying to break in to her mother's safe. But years later it would turn out that a killer named Ralph Daniello, in a bid to curry favor with the Brooklyn District Attorney's Office, told prosecutors about numerous murders, including that of Spinelli. The prosecution dossier compiled with Daniello's help stated that the old stable woman was murdered on orders of Gallucci, a man described as a person who got a percentage of the sale of stolen horses and artichokes. Gallucci had his eye on taking over Spinelli's stable and so had her killed, according to Daniello.

In the end Gallucci fared no better. He was constantly targeted as a marked man and while he survived assassination attempts the lifespan of his bodyguards was not good. Ten of them were reported to have died during bungled attempts on the life of their boss. Then on the night of May 17, 1915, things went differently. As Gallucci sat in the coffee shop owned by his nineteen-year-old son Luca at 339 East 109th Street, they were fired at by four men who suddenly entered the premises. Gallucci was hit in the neck and stomach while his son was shot twice in the abdomen. Gallucci's men who happened to be in the coffee shop returned fire but apparently to no avail. Gallucci and his son initially survived their wounds but soon succumbed to the injuries.

Gallucci's funeral on May 24 drew a crowd of an estimated ten thousand, about a third of them, police estimated, were people who were his enemies. Cops heard rumors that Gallucci's wife was also targeted for murder as part of some convoluted plot to make sure his $1 million horde of cash from his rackets would revert to New York State since he would have been left with no surviving heirs. Over a hundred detectives were at the Gallucci home for the funeral, lining the stairways and surrounding his coffin, mingling with the crowd and guarding the widow. Fearing a problem with the original ostentatious funeral plan for 150 carriages convinced the family to cut things down to fifty-four. A twenty-three-piece band led the funeral procession, which went off without a hitch. When things were over, Mrs. Gallucci didn't go back home because of all the threats.

There was always someone to jump into a power vacuum in Little Italy, and after Gallucci's death, the Morello family seemed to be in a position to profit. The Morellos, which had numerous alliances through marriage with other gangsters, took over Gallucci's rackets, according to Daniello. This didn't stop the fighting, and for years to come, the existing Italian mobs—the early forerunners of what was to become the modern American Mafia—would devolve into bloodshed.

Frank Costello and his brother Edward survived this fractious time in East Harlem because they didn't really pose a threat to anyone. They were following the paths of losers, destined to become petty criminals. Frank ran crap games on the street in East Harlem. Edward wasn't the brightest even though he was the oldest and should have been more mature. But they had some things going for them. Frank could read the signs of the street well. He was described as being taciturn, a quality that likely kept him out of trouble in an environment where the wrong word could get a person killed. He also cultivated a desire, said historian Selvaggi, to make lots of money as a way of helping his mother and all the poor, miserable people he lived with have a better life. He could see from what happened to Spinelli and Gallucci that friendships were an elusive quality in the gangster life. Even when surrounded by friends, bosses could be killed. The old adage that it paid to keep the friends you trusted close but your enemies even closer became clear to Costello.

Gallucci's life also likely impressed Costello for another reason. The old boss had cultivated political connections. Politics and its bedfellows could provide an additional armor of protection because of the way police and judges could be influenced. All Costello had to do was hear the buzz on the street about Gallucci's friends in high places to know the strength of that kind of protection, beyond what the barrel of a gun might provide, was very important. As will be later shown in *Top Hoodlum,* Costello took the concept of political influence and protection to a level none of the old bosses of East Harlem could have imagined.

Costello's destiny was shaped by the way his street activity brought him into contact with another young, ambitious, but poor Italian immigrant named Charles Luciania, who would become known later as Charles "Lucky" Luciano. What put Luciano apart from the other young men was his ecumenical approach to crime. He became close to two Jews, Ben Siegel and Meyer Lansky, the latter of whom Luciano called "the toughest guy, pound for pound, I ever met in my life." Along with Costello, Luciano, Siegel, and Lansky formed a gang of four who eventually grew to a crew of twenty denizens from the East Side and East Harlem, pulling small bank jobs and stealing from stores and warehouses.

While he was a product of the streets of East Harlem and was involved with Luciano in small thievery, Frank Costello did not succumb to the bloody follies that devoured his paisans. All around him young Italian men were killing and being killed. It was an on-going culling of the herd, which would set the stage for the great Mafia wars soon to come. Costello clearly was using his head, sizing up opportunities and looking for both legitimate and semi-legitimate opportunities. He also fell in love.

CHAPTER TWO
NO MORE GUNS,
THANK YOU

AS SEPARATED AS THEY MIGHT BE BY RELIGION, Italians and Jews had a unusual level of historical tolerance between them. Back in Italy in the early part of the twentieth century a number of Jews rose to prominent positions in the fledgling Italian government. In 1910, Luigi Luzzati became Italy's prime minister and was thus the first Jewish person to head a government. A fellow Jew, Ernest Nathan, served for a number of years beginning in 1907 as the mayor of Rome. At least in the decades before Mussolini came to power and started an official policy of anti-Semitism, Jews and Italians in Italy got along rather well.

Once in the United States, Italians and Jews who migrated to New York lived in separate communities. Depending on when they arrived, Jews concentrated in settlements on the lower East Side of Manhattan, while Italians such as the Castiglia family went to East Harlem while others settled in and around the Five Points and China-town area. Those settlement patterns changed over the years to include the other boroughs. But no matter where they chose to live, the numbers of immigrants were significant, totaling in the hundreds of thousands for both groups by the first decade of the twentieth century.

But this influx spawned a backlash of prejudice that was often voiced by those in government. In 1895, Henry Gannett, chief of the U.S. Geological Survey, remarked in a book how Italians and Jews had flocked in large numbers to American cities, adding, "Hence it appears that the most objectionable elements of the foreign-born population have flocked in the greatest proportion to our large cities, where they are in a position to do the most harm by corruption and violence." Faced with the various Italian gang wars and the rise of Jewish gangsters of the period, New York City police commissioner Theodore A. Bingham later stated in a 1908 article in *The North American Review* that as far as he could see alien Jews committed half of the crimes in the city, with the Italians accounting for 20 percent. Bingham later published a retraction.

No matter what the anti-immigrant sentiment might have been, Frank Costello always liked Jews. He found a strange kinship in the foreign roots of the Italians and Jews he knew. Although he may not have known it, Costello's feeling of connection may have been rooted in things deeper than affection. Modern DNA technology was recently used by Costello's cousin Noel Castiglia of Maryland who discovered through sending a genetic sample to a laboratory that while there was an 83 percent statistical probability that his ethnicity was Italian, there was a 2 percent chance that he had Jewish background as well. Other relatives, Castiglia said, learned through testing that they had probabilities as high as 6 percent Jewish. Calabria had a long history of Jewish settlers, and Marchioness Laura, who founded the town of Lauropoli in the eighteenth century, is believed by some researchers to have herself been Jewish. So there just might have been a trace of Jewish lineage in Frank Costello's genetic makeup.

In early twentieth century New York, if the nativist sentiments regarded both Jews and Italians with suspicion and as criminals, that only seemed to increase the friendship Costello had for those who traced their heritage to the Twelve Tribes of Israel. From Costello's point of view, Jews and Italians had a lot in common as newcomers. So in 1914, when Costello went to a dance in the Bronx and met Loretta "Bobbie" Geigerman, the pretty, dark-haired sister of his friend Dudley Geigerman, the relationship had great potential.

"When I met Bobbie it was like meeting one of my own people," Costello would later tell George Wolf. "She didn't talk Italian but the German dialect of her parents was foreign like mine. Bobbie and me got along great from the first, although neither of our mothers was too happy."

While certainly not unheard-of, intermarriage between Catholic Italians and Jews was an unusual pairing. Intermarriage creates all sorts of issues that suddenly swell to the surface or wait like time-bombs to explode among families later. There are questions about what religion children should be raised in and how to celebrate the holidays. In Costello's case, hc remembered that her parents Jacob and Cecilia, who had raised a total of eight children and lived on upper Park Avenue, thought that Loretta could do better than a dirt-poor Italian man with no prospects from East Harlem. Maria Costello had been hoping for a nice Italian girl for her son, he remembered.

Despite any family trepidation about their union, Frank Costello and Loretta Geigerman got a marriage license on September 22, 1914. A day later the couple was married by Episcopal minister Rev. Thomas McAndless of St. Michael's on West Eighty-eighth Street. It is likely that a Protestant clergyman was picked as a way of finding an officiant who was neither Catholic nor Jewish as a way of avoiding any religious antagonism among the parents. On the marriage certificate, Costello noted that he lived on West 117th Street and, although he never finished grade school, listed his occupation as plumber. Loretta, who on census records had the name "Lauretta," recorded her address as being a few blocks farther west at 1968 Seventh Avenue. He would have been twenty-three years old and Loretta twenty.

Though he claimed to have a legitimate occupation, Costello clearly in the period right after his nuptials was still very much into his criminal ways. We know that because on March 12, 1915, Costello was arrested for carrying a handgun in Manhattan as he left a barber shop. An observant cop noticed the weapon and started chasing Costello, who attempted to flee into an alley. Costello would later complain that the gun wasn't found on him, a fact the judge handling the case agreed was true but quickly noted that was because the cops saw him ditch the weapon before they grabbed him.

Costello already had a brief taste of jail while he waited for his case to be called in court on May 15, 1915, for a guilty plea before General Sessions Judge Edward Swann and was hoping the court would give him a break. Costello's defense attorney admitted to Swann that the young man had not led an exemplary life but that now, as a married man, things could turn out better. He pleaded to the court for a short prison sentence. But Judge Swann didn't like what he saw in Costello's criminal records, even if he was never convicted of anything.

"I have looked him up and find his record is not good," said Swann. "I have it right here from his neighbors that he has the reputation of a gunman . . . and in this case, he certainly was a gunman. He had a very beautiful weapon and he was prepared to do the work of a gunman."

"Will your honor give me another chance?" piped up Costello in desperation.

"You have had chances for the last six years, and those chances have to cease some time," replied Swann, referring to Costello's earlier arrests for strong-armed larceny where he avoided convictions.

Then, Swann sentenced Costello to a year in the penitentiary, noting that he could have given him seven years. Taken away, Costello did eleven months of his sentence in the prison facility on Welfare Island in the East River. They trimmed one month off his sentence for good behavior, and he hit the streets in April 1916.

A lot had happened in Little Italy by the time Costello was released. Perhaps the most significant was the murder of Gallucci and his son two days after Costello was sentenced to prison. For the next year there were a host of other killings tied to the incessant wars between the Italian crime factions in East Harlem. But by being in the relative safety of a cell on Welfare Island, Costello was out of harm's way even if there was any chance of his being drawn into any of the fighting. By being in prison, Costello finally had the time to think about his life and where it was going. Running around the streets with a gun, facing the real prospect of more jail time or even death, was not what he had in mind now.

"That's when I realized I was stupid," Costello told his attorney George Wolf years later. "Carrying a gun was like carrying a label that said: 'I'm dangerous, I'm a criminal, get me off the street.' I made up my mind I would never pack a gun again and I never did."

Well, as will be explained later in this book, while Costello liked to perpetuate the story that he never carried a weapon after that first gun arrest, records uncovered indicate that during the Prohibition years he did walk around with a gun. He even was tempted to use it and came close to doing so at least once.

Once freed, Costello needed to find a steady source of income—legitimate income. That didn't mean he disassociated himself from his friends on the street: his brother Edward, Dudley Geigerman, and his growing number of Jewish friends like Meyer Lansky who had their own ways of making money. He had his Italian gangster associates as well and got arrested in May 1919 with one Vincent Rao on a charge of robbery. The case involved what was described as an alleged pickpocket incident in which Costello, Rao, and another man were observed by a police officer removing $100 from the victim's pants pocket. The case led to a grand larceny charge but was later dismissed at the request of the Queens District Attorney's Office. Clearly, Costello had to break away from these kinds of petty crimes and the rackets of East Harlem. He had to come up with some serious business opportunities. For that, Costello teamed up with a Jewish businessman named Henry Horowitz, who had a novelty company in Manhattan.

Novelties could be many things in the trade but generally referred to Kewpie dolls, razor blades, and similar small items. Costello's contribution to the company, which was formed with an initial investment of $3,000, was to come up with an idea for marketing punchboards, which at the time were popular ways for people to gamble, much like the modern-day lottery. Essentially, punchboards were pieces of cardboard within which were drilled holes containing slips of paper. For a nickel, a customer in a luncheonette, candy store or bar would get a chance to use a stylus to pull a single slip of paper out of one of the holes. A lucky patron might find a slip indicating a prize like a Kewpie doll or something else of nominal value.

The punchboard operation with Horowitz appeared to be Costello's first foray into gambling as a business, although it is entirely possi-

ble he tried his hand at the Italian lottery in East Harlem. The punchboard business was lucrative: newspapers advertised that a punchboard salesman in the 1920s could net $105 from one sale to a
location. Proceeds from the games were split between the owner of
the business that used the punchboard and the many companies that
sold them. The games were quite the rage in some areas but were
frowned upon by local governments, educators, and the police as
being nothing more than illegal lotteries. Newspapers were filled
with stories about how police arrested business owners who they
said ran punchboard games. In some cases, the games were found to
be part of ingenious scams. Cops in Queens discovered that punchboards were used in one store in Astoria that bore the name of a fic-
titious charity claiming to be giving some of the proceeds to help
Jewish orphans. Police also heard complaints from teachers that
their students were spending their money, and learning bad habits,
by playing punchboards in candy stores.

Costello didn't stay in the punchboard business very long with
Horowtiz. Still, George Wolf remembered that the company was
grossing over $100,000 in sales in less than a year. Nevertheless, de-
spite Costello's attention to details of the business, it had to file for
bankruptcy. The company was being stiffed by its vendors, many of
whom were identified in bankruptcy proceedings as being "all East
Side gangsters," noted Wolf.

It is likely that if Costello and his company were dealing with
other gangsters that the bankruptcy was a "bust out," a common tactic in which a broke company hides its assets. While the money is
hidden, the company finds itself deeper in the financial hole when it
can't collect on its own receivables and runs to the protection of the
bankruptcy court. The $100,000 in sales the Horowitz firm grossed
would have been the equivalent of $1.4 million today, accounting
for inflation. But that money was nothing compared to what
Costello would be able to make in his next racket, one that would
make him far richer than the likes of old kings and queens who ruled
108th Street in Little Italy.

CHAPTER THREE
THE BOOM OF
PROHIBITION

ITALIANS, JEWS, AND OTHER NEW IMMIGRANTS who were living in places like New York City in the early twentieth century weren't only looked down upon because of their generally lower economic status and neighborhood crime problems. A significant swath of native-born Americans viewed the immigrants' drinking habits as another problem they brought with them, which threatened the fabric of American society. Germans in particular, with their fondness for beer, became an object of intense criticism of those who were against the evil of alcohol.

Sentiment for Prohibition and the banning of the production, sale, and use of alcoholic beverages had always been significant in the United States and had gathered steam with the rise of temperance movements around the country. With the ascendancy of organizations like the Anti-Saloon League and the Women's Christian Temperance Union, the idea that Prohibition could be enacted nationwide saw wide acceptance. In 1918, the required thirty-six states approved the Eighteenth Amendment to the U.S. Constitution, which in 125 words barred the importation, production, and sale—but not consumption—of alcoholic drinks. A year later, the Volstead Act was passed to implement the Amendment, taking effect on January 17, 1920.

For Frank Costello and his brethren Prohibition, now viewed as one of the biggest failures in a government effort to change public behavior, would turn out to be the defining moment for them in their rise as criminals. Despite its intent of reducing crime and improving the quality of life, Prohibition was poorly enforced because not only did a substantial part of the public want to drink but for years there was no effective way for the federal government to enforce the ban. Saloons and breweries may have been forced to close, but people could still drink because liquor was so plentiful. Estimates of the number of speakeasies in Manhattan, which catered to the drinking life, ran as high as 30,000 and more. Restaurants still served patrons drinks. Even President Warren G. Harding moved his private supply of booze into the White House.

The Mafia saw Prohibition as a business opportunity it couldn't pass up, particularly in New York City. For a start, at the beginning of Prohibition there were millions of bottles of liquor and wine stored in government warehouses. The product was supposed to be under government supervision and released for limited purposes such as "medicinal" use. Sacramental wine was approved for religious services. Mobsters were able to circumvent those government controls by outright theft from the warehouses or use of bribery and fraudulent documents to compromise government officials who had the job of supervising release of the stockpiles.

One very ingenious, but very corrupt, attorney by the name of George Remus of Chicago saw an opportunity to exploit the government alcohol warehouse and did so, at least he claimed, by making substantial payoffs to an intimate friend of former U.S. Attorney General Harry M. Daugherty, the very man sitting atop the law enforcement effort to enforce Prohibition. As Remus would tell Congressional investigators in 1924, in early 1921, he hit upon the idea of buying up ten distilleries in the Midwest and at the same time organized a chain of wholesale drugstores. The businesses were ostensibly able to make withdrawals of liquor for medicinal purposes from the government warehouses, as did the liquor wholesale distilleries. Under what he called a "gentlemen's agreement" with Jess Smith, a friend of Daugherty, Remus said he paid Smith protection money to be assured of getting the permits necessary to withdraw the medicinal liquor from the warehouses. The payment was substantial, over $ 2.8 million, and it secured the release of what Remus estimated was well over 800,000 gallons of whiskey, with some sacramental wines thrown in as well.

The Remus scheme was astonishing and showed how easy the government permit system could be compromised to get around Prohibition. (It perhaps was the inspiration for a drugstore liquor scam alluded to in *The Great Gatsby*.) Remus said he ironed out the corrupt deal with Smith during a meeting at the Hotel Commodore in Manhattan in early 1921 and for a year and a half was making cash payments to keep the booze flowing. The flood of liquor, according to Remus, got into the bootleg trade in New York, Pennsylvania, Illinois, and Ohio and it is a safe bet that some of the stuff got into the hands of Alphonse Capone, Frankie Yale, and Costello. Remus said Smith, who had died by the time of the Congressional hearing, assured him that he didn't have to worry about going to prison for the scheme.

"There never would be any conviction, maybe a prosecution but no ultimate conviction—that no one would have to go to the penitentiary," was how Remus remembered Smith explaining things.

Remus did wind up in the penitentiary for violating the Prohibition law. Smith had died well before the scandal became known. There was never any evidence that Daugherty was aware of what was going on, or that Smith tried to influence his official actions. While Remus was convicted of bootlegging offenses, he kept recanting and then denying his recantation of his claim that he paid off Smith, so in the end it is hard to say where the truth lay on his bribery claims.

But there were certainly payoffs flying around the Atlanta federal prison where Remus and Emanuel Kessler, one of Costello's bootleg partners in New York, were incarcerated. In April 1924, the warden of the prison was convicted of conspiring with none other than the penitentiary chaplain to take payoffs from the so-called "Savannah crowd" of inmates, which included Kessler and Remus. The payments were to assure that the inmates got certain privileges and "soft jobs" like working in the prison library while incarcerated.

No matter how much liquor passed through wholesale and drug-store operations like that operated by Remus, public demand for alcohol would soon supplant the warehouse stores that were being tapped. People wanted their drink, and this is where Costello and others saw their opportunities and took full advantage of the situation. As recalled by Luciano in his biography *The Last Testament of Lucky Luciano*, he and Costello's crew got involved in bootlegging after one of their group, Joe Doto, met Philadelphia smuggler Waxey Gordon and did a deal to take $10,000 in whiskey. There was one problem: Doto, known also as Joe Adonis, didn't have the money and looked to Costello, Luciano, and others for some $35,000 in funding. The group cemented the deal with Gordon in Philadelphia and never looked back.

Bootlegging became an industry for the nascent Mafiosi who had only known more modest rackets and had the prospect of making them richer than they could have imagined. The hardcore killers like Alphonse Capone of Chicago and Frankie Yale of Brooklyn, Jewish gangsters like Gordon and Dutch Schultz, became major bootleg entrepreneurs. But others became involved as well, with various criminal groups becoming experts at importing and transporting rum, whiskey, wine, champagne, and beer to a seemingly insatiable marketplace.

However, Frank Costello navigated the bootlegging business in a way that even his rivals had to admire. He cheated when he had to but his strength was that he knew how to vertically organize his smuggling business and did so by thinking big and outside the box. The novelty business, which generated so much cash for Costello with the punchboards wouldn't be enough to sustain his bootlegging operation. For funding, he is said to have turned to Arnold Rothstein, the master gambler widely credited with fixing the 1919 World Series, although he would later claim that he knew of the plan but took no part in it. Rothstein was the scion of a wealthy Jewish family—his father Abraham was an old racketeer—and is credited by some with being the real brains behind the way the Mafia consolidated its operations and took advantage of Prohibition.

"Rothstein knew all there was to know about business practices, ethical and unethical. It was he who financed Frank when he got started, and showed him the way to success in business: how to organize, how to cut costs—and how to cut your rival's throat if necessary," said Wolf.

Liquor companies in Britain, Canada, France, and other countries didn't want to stay out of the lucrative U.S. market and welcomed the chance to sell to Americans. Backed by Rothstein's money, Costello soon saw a way of setting up a pipeline to get their product to market. For that, he looked northward to two small sand spit islands off Canada, the French possessions of St. Pierre and Miquelon. Since they were French territories, the islands were outside the jurisdiction of Canada, which at the time was under British control and nominally cooperative with U.S. efforts to stop the smuggling of alcohol across the Canadian border. The French islands had different rules and for an enterprising smuggler like Costello that fit his plan perfectly.

By December 1921, there were reports in the American newspapers about "parties of well-dressed, black-cigar smoking gentlemen" who went to the two French islands to purchase and arrange for the delivery of "whiskey and the like" to U.S. bootlegging rings. The financial enticements for local sailors and boat owners to run the gauntlet of government vessels was said to be attractive, so much so that there were "certain sailors who used to be impecunious, but have become free spenders and flashy dressers." While some small craft had been caught, many more got their cargoes to buyers all the way from Canada to Florida.

Costello was said to have been one of those out of towners who visited St. Pierre and Miquelon. He made one trip in a tramp steamer in 1921, dressed in a bulky sweater and other seafaring clothes, reportedly to see the mayor of St. Pierre. By this time, he had already talked about getting into business with Kessler. It was then that Costello made a deal to import liquor for two dollars a case, stuff he could eventually sell for a markup of a hundred times more in the U.S., said Wolf. St. Pierre and its sister island of Miquelon, because they were French, became in a unique position to become major transshipping points for liquor, including rum, to the U.S. Even some nearby provinces of Canada which were also laboring under their own Prohibition constraints became a market. Newfoundlanders were so hard up and eager to buy liquor on the islands that they bartered firewood, partridge, moose meat, lamb, mussels, or clams for the high-alcohol-content and coveted black rum produced in the other French island of Martinique in the Caribbean, wrote maritime historian J.P. Andrieux in *Over the Side,* a history of Canadian smuggling during Prohibition.

While Canadian tourists to the islands could easily fill up on liquor during port visits to St. Pierre, the process for Costello and his cohorts to get liquor back to the U.S. required a lot more planning ingenuity and money. In this, Costello seemed to excel as a businessman. He had a bit of help from the ineffective way the U.S. government was enforcing Prohibition.

When Prohibition took effect in 1920, the federal government spread enforcement of the Volstead Act among a number of agencies. Notable were the IRS Bureau of Prohibition, the U.S. Department of Justice Bureau of Prohibition, and the U.S. Coast Guard. While that array of agencies may have sounded impressive, they were ill-equipped to fight the vast army of bootleggers who were ready, willing, and able to smuggle in liquor for an urban public that held the law in disdain. The Italian, Irish, and Jewish mobsters in Chicago and Detroit were able to evade the ill-equipped federal government to set up smuggling routes through Canada via the Great Lakes.

Then there was Rum Row, a stretch of the East Coast that Costello and others working with him exploited so well. Ships laden with tens of thousands of bottles of liquor of all sorts would arrive at points outside the three-mile limit for U.S. territorial waters and thus protected from seizure by the Coast Guard. The booze the vessels contained was produced in places like England and the Caribbean, transshipped to the French islands adjacent to Canada and then sent by vessel to wait off places like Montauk Point, New York, or Atlantic City, New Jersey.

To get the Rum Row product to market, Costello's smuggling operation took vertical integration of bootlegging to an unheard-of level. After securing orders for liquor in St. Pierre and Miquelon, where up to 13 million bottles would be sold, Costello went about assembling a flotilla of vessels that could outrun the poorly equipped Coast Guard, meet the transport vessels sitting in territorial waters, and bring the merchandise on shore.

"His fleet of ships included everything from tramp steamers to former luxury yachts as well as flotillas of Jersey skiffs to make the run to the beaches," recalled Wolf, referring to the small, fast flat-bottomed boats that can be powered by motor and could be inconspicuous.

To communicate with the larger smuggling ships, Costello commissioned the creation of some ship-to-shore radio stations situated in obscure locations on Long Island. He also had what amounted to a small air force, seaplanes that could fly over Rum Row and detect Coast Guard activity. Those were all pretty ingenious uses of what was then new technology.

But once the liquor was on shore, Costello and his associates, who now included his older brother Edward, had to get it to customers in New York City and points as far south as Philadelphia. To do that, Costello used convoys of trucks, which in the cut-throat world of bootlegging were susceptible to hijacking. Liquor loads were lost all the time in the business, and the roads from eastern Long Island to Manhattan were winding, dark, and prone to ambushes by competing gangsters. Costello lost his share of business to poaching by fellow gangsters, and to stop the hemorrhage he hired men like Meyer Lansky and Bugsy Siegel, two New York Jews he liked and trusted from the Lower East Side, to provide gunmen to protect the loads. Of course, the relationship he had with Lansky and Siegel would continue well beyond Prohibition as will be noted in detail later.

By 1922, despite hijacking losses, it seemed that Costello's bootlegging operation was thriving. He was making millions of dollars because the simple economics of the business allowed a substantial markup for liquor in the Prohibition era. Whiskey brought in from Canada could be cut with grain alcohol, given some color, and sold at an incredible markup. He paid back Rothstein's initial invest-ment—even loaning the gambler funds—and although he had the money now, Costello was careful in how he spent it. He helped his mother move out of East Harlem to a modest two-story home in Astoria on Halsey Street. Maria Saverio Aloise Costello's husband Luigi or Louis had died on December 12, 1921, from bronchitis, a disease easily treated today but not so back then. He had also suffered from chronic heart failure. But Costello stayed close to his mother, who suffered from diabetes, and remained the doting younger child. For himself and Loretta, Costello moved to a pleas-ant home in Bayside, a residential part of Queens not far by car from his mother.

Bootlegging soon also became a spur for the economy of some Long Island towns, notably seafaring places like Greenport, Sterling Cove, Gardiner's Bay, and other locales situated around inlets and small bays westward of Rum Row. The Jersey skiffs and other fast-moving boats could bring the liquor ashore for transfer to Costello's trucks. Robert Carse, author of *Rum Row: The Liquor Fleet That Kept America Wet and Fueled the Roaring Twenties,* described how a place like Greenport thrived in the bootlegging days with the crush of smuggling business Costello and the other bootleg entrepreneurs brought.

"Unemployment was practically nonexistent. Men strong enough to carry a case of liquor were hired and paid an average of twenty dollars a night from the contact boats to the waiting trucks," said Carse. "The boatyards were busy at work on craft for which no con-tract had been drawn but none were needed: everything the rum run-ners ordered was on a cash-on-advance basis. Gasoline was sold in five-hundred-gallon quantities."

Despite Prohibition, there was such a market for liquor in Man-hattan that the Italian mobs set up a curbside exchange near the in-tersection of Elizabeth and Kenmare Streets, which so happened to be around the corner from police headquarters. The brokers didn't handle liquor themselves or pass any money, so it was difficult for agents to make arrests. Rather, the brokers there quoted prices to buyers by the case: $110 for Scotch whiskey imported from England, $90 for Canadian rye, $45 for Italian vermouth. Territories were also carved out by those selling the product.

"The exchange became a melting pot for the gangs involved in the bootleg trade," said Leonard Katz in his biography of Costello titled *Uncle Frank*. "Italian, Jewish and Irish mobsters mingled together and did business with each other for the first time."

One up-and-coming gangster in the bootlegging operations was Frankie Yale of Brooklyn. Yale ran the Harvard Inn in Coney Island and was a rival bootlegger to Costello and close for a time with Capone. In fact, Yale had hired Capone as a waiter for his club in Coney Island. It was at the Harvard Inn that Capone got slashed in the face after he made a crude remark about the backside of Yale's sister. Yale had been a frequent object of assassination attempts and managed to survive. But in 1928, after Capone learned that Yale was hijacking loads of liquor meant for Chicago, he had Yale machine-gunned to death as he drove on a Brooklyn street.

Although Prohibition was the law of the land, it was held in much disfavor by the public and the politicians. By 1924, there was a growing clamor for changes, at least to moderate the Volstead Act so that people had some options for drinking. Appearing before Congress, labor leader Samuel Gompers, head of the American Federation of Labor, joined with scores of other officials and lobbyists to push for changes. Gompers urged Congress to approve beer that was 2.75 percent alcohol by volume, a boost from the "near beer" then allowed. Workers wanted beer, were entitled to it, and felt they needed "the stimulation that is contained in a good glass of wholesome malt." Besides, said Gompers, beer was nutritious and could be part of a meal. Gompers and his allies also thought it was a good thing to legalize light wine and cider.

The other problem with Prohibition, according to Gompers and other "wet" forces, was that it wasn't having the intended impact on crime and lawlessness. In cities around the country speakeasies were all around. The Volstead Act, as the New York City and Chicago experiences had shown, was impossible to enforce. The bootleggers were just too resourceful, too well financed, and garnering too much support from the public. Bring on legal beer and the workingman would take to it with ease, leading to more observance of the law generally and reduce the activity of bootleggers who trafficked in harder liquor—or so the argument went.

But the federal government was not going to give up easily on Prohibition no matter how public opinion was shifting against it. Stung by the ineffectiveness of the Coast Guard to stop bootleggers off Rum Row, Washington finally woke up and authorized the use of surplus Navy destroyers and the purchase of other vessels after World War One to supplement the existing, outgunned fleet, which had been run circles around by Costello and the other smugglers. The destroyers, known as "four-pipers" because of their smoke stacks, sometimes had large search lights, which could throw a bright light across the water. Still, the bootleggers persisted in their cat-and-mouse games with the Coast Guard and used decoy vessels or moved farther out to sea to try and frustrate the federal vessels. The destroyers, although large and well-armed, couldn't hide their presence very well.

"They burned coal in an age of oil and spread wide banners of smoke astern . . . and at night belched sparks that a sharp-eyed observer on Rum Row could see for miles," said Carse.

By 1922, the notorious curbside liquor exchange and the brokers on Kenmare Street had moved uptown to be on West Fortieth Street, near Broadway. The location was not far from Costello's offices at 405 Lexington Avenue, a site now occupied by the Chrysler Building. Katz claimed that Costello "was a daily visitor to the exchange." But being a careful operator, it was unlikely that Costello frequented the curbside operators since their exchange was under constant surveillance by the Prohibition police and the NYPD, the latter having a number of homicides to investigate that stemmed from the fighting among the Italian mob brokers. Costello did most things out of Lexington Avenue: communicating with his overseas contacts, making deals and receiving his intelligence reports from his well-placed sources in the police department and the federal government.

It was Costello's network of official spies that gave him a leg up on other bootleggers. This became particularly useful when the Coast Guard, beefed up with surplus Navy destroyers and faster boats and cutters in 1924, decided to become more aggressive. Costello was tipped to those changes when one of his men, Mike Terranova whose job was described by Wolf as plying Coast Guardsmen with beer to sniff out their plans, was handed an official memo describing the plans to send out patrols of longer duration and to the inlets scattered around Long Island and Connecticut.

Costello greased the wheels for such intelligence by throwing around hundred-dollar bills to be paid to the "Coasties," as the sailors were known. Costello needed timely intelligence and also had to compromise enough of the Coast Guard fleet so that the officials' boats, particularly those smaller craft patrolling the inlets, would look the other way when bootlegged cargo was ready to come ashore. Because of the increased Coast Guard presence and U.S. government policy, which extended the old three-mile territorial waters to twelve miles, the freighters bearing liquor from the French and British colonies had to be met farther out at sea and off-loaded quickly.

Sometimes the freighters would get lost, and to find them Costello had seaplanes at his disposal. When one schooner from Canada got lost on the way to Rum Row, Costello had his operative, a Long Island man named William Newman, go to Curtiss Field near Mineola and fly out to find the errant vessel. Once it was spotted, Newman landed with the seaplane and got aboard to help guide it. The seaplane companies didn't care what Newman's business was when they went aloft. Besides, their pilots got cases of liquor as tips for their service.

"Our planes are like taxicabs in that it is none of the driver's business what his passenger is about," one seaplane company manager later told reporters. "The hiring of the seaplane in that case was merely a matter of business."

As smart as Costello was with aircraft and clandestine radio stations in his bootlegging, he used a decidedly low-tech way of assuring that his cargoes weren't ripped off. When the contact vessel such as a Jersey skiff came to the schooner to pick up the liquor load, the skiff captain presented a dollar bill to the crew of the larger ship. If the serial number on the bill matched that on a list Newman had been given from Costello's office, then the cargo could be off-loaded safely. It was a simple way of keeping the transaction safe and secure.

CHAPTER FOUR
WHISKEY ROYALTY

THE TITLE "KING OF THE BOOTLEGGERS" was an honorific that was claimed by a number of people in the Prohibition Era. Those who laid claim to the title were constantly being arrested and then replaced in the anointed position by a seemingly never-ending parade of others. It is a testament to his low profile, craftiness, careful dealings, and payoffs that Frank Costello wasn't given the "King" sobriquet, even when his activities became more widely known among the police. But those who were part of bootlegging royalty were the very people Costello dealt with and partnered with in significant ways, particularly in the early days when Prohibition was just getting underway and federal officials were stumbling around trying to deal with the bootleggers. He just turned out to have better luck than most.

George Remus, the Chicago lawyer who was first anointed "King of the Bootleggers" around 1921, was the one who came up with ingenious schemes of buying liquor wholesalers and drugstore businesses as a way of exploiting the medicinal use exemption on the sale of booze. As described earlier, Remus claimed to have paid handsome bribes to a confidante of the U.S. Attorney General Harry Daugherty to get illegal permits which allowed liquor, ostensibly for medicinal use, to come out of the special government warehouses. Gangsters in New York and elsewhere had taken to breaking in to the warehouses but Remus's scheme refined the theft, and some say he was the inspiration for Jay Gatsby's character in *The Great Gatsby*.

Remus got caught fairly early in Prohibition, and with his constant recantation of his claims of payoffs in high places and his murder of his wife Imogene, there were questions about his sanity. He spent time in prison for violating the Volstead Act as well as the murder of his wife. He died in 1952.

Remus said that the liquor he finagled out of the warehouses wound up in New York City. He never mentioned Costello by name as a business contact. But one man Remus did say he did business with, Emanuel "Manny" Kessler, had significant ties to Costello in getting liquor to market. The relationship between Kessler and Costello—examined for the first time here in depth—was responsible for the handling of large quantities of booze that kept Broadway speakeasies well stocked. Kessler's operation involved millions of dollars' worth of product and the corruption of public officials at all levels: federal, state, and the NYPD.

"For enforcement during Prohibition in New York, there was a federal agency that, in all but a couple of cases, operated on the principles of a collection firm: if you paid, they went away," said the late Jimmy Breslin, in his biography of Damon Runyon.

Clearly, Kessler had learned a trick or two from Remus. Described as a real estate agent and wine salesman, Kessler knew that the stock of liquor in the government bonded warehouses was a potential gold mine. To get his hands on the product, Kessler paid off government Prohibition agents who helped him get forged permits for removal of whiskey and gin. Once the booze was out of the warehouses, it was shipped to a number of holding areas around New York City where it could then be sold off.

Conventional wisdom holds that Frank Costello received his early start in bootlegging with money from Arnold Rothstein, and to some extent Rothstein did provide him with cash. But years later in court testimony Kessler said that in 1920 Costello told him that if he bought some trucks for Kessler and his brother Edward that they would haul the booze for him coming in from Long Island.

"I advanced him the money or I bought the trucks," said Kessler. "I think I advanced him the money and they bought the trucks."

The system they used was fairly straightforward, remembered

Kessler. The Costellos would truck the liquor to their house at 114 Halsey Street in Astoria, which had an adjacent garage. After the booze was stored in the garage, Kessler had smaller trucks go out to Queens to bring the product to his other warehouses around town. Court records would later show that Kessler gave Edward Costello a $5,800 check for the purchase of two trucks. As it turned out, Kessler was actually financing Frank Costello's scheme for trucking the liquor which landed on Long Island from Rum Row.

Kessler was moving a great deal of liquor. His bank accounts showed that he moved at least $4 million worth in the course of a few months. By telephone, Kessler talked frequently with Frank Costello at his office on Lexington Avenue about the large-scale movement by truck—about 3,000 cases a week. Being so busy, Kessler attracted the attention of federal officials who developed evidence that he played a major role in 1921 in the fraudulent removal of whiskey from a government warehouse in Brooklyn to other locations until he could unload the product. Charged with Kessler in January 1921 was a former Prohibition inspector who had resigned his job to work for the bootlegger. Also charged were four state inspectors whose job was to enforce New York state prohibition laws. Those arrests of officials was just the tip of the iceberg in terms of the morass of corruption in the years of Prohibition.

Kessler made bail in the case, and despite the arrest didn't stop his bootlegging activities. In September 1922 he was arrested, along with his partner Morris Sweetwood on charges they again used forged and fraudulent permits to remove during the previous May and June over $1 million in whiskey and champagne from the Republic Storage facility in Manhattan. From evidence and documents found during the arrests, federal agents in November 1922 showed up at the home of Edward Costello, identified in news reports by the surname "Costella" and found in his possession twenty-seven cases of stolen Auld Scottie whiskey taken from the Republic Storage warehouse. The liquor was found in a garage around the corner from Costello's house on Halsey Street in Astoria after he gave agents permission to search the location. The cases were found in a walled-up compartment in the garage.

Halsey street (later renamed Third Street) is also where Frank Costello was listed as having a home at No. 124, a frame dwelling where his father also was said to have lived before he died in 1921. The area was in one of those out-of-the-way pockets of New York City. The neighborhood was a mix of stone masonry businesses and residential buildings and in the era before construction of the Triborough Bridge wasn't the easiest place to visit except by boat or a circuitous route by auto. Known as Astoria, the community surrounding Halsey Street abutted the East River and had numerous piers and docks, making it an easy place to bring in bootlegging speedboats or larger vessels. Costello family stories held that a secret passageway existed between Edward's house and the East River.

Halsey Street saw a lot of bootlegging activity for the Costello clan. The volume of alcoholic beverages they handled for Kessler was large, about 3,000 cases a week from boats that came in every night. For that, Kessler paid the Costello brothers $3,000 a week for shipping, plus a dollar for each case for storage for a weekly total of $6,000.

"Either cash or check, or in merchandise once in a while," was how Kessler remembered making the payments.

At one point, Kessler built a storage vault underneath a garage adjacent to the Costello home on Halsey Street to hide the liquor. The entrance to the underground space was concealed by a large floor slab, which when moved led down into the vault.

Secrecy with the Costello family was important in the bootlegging operation. While Frank and Edward were in on the smuggling in a big way, it appeared that other relatives, including Frank's own mother, well knew what was going on and were part of the conspiracy. This was made apparent when Albert Feldman, one of Kessler's customers, visited the home at 114 Harley Street to inspect a shipment in the garage at the back of the dwelling. Arriving at the house, Feldman said he met two women who played dumb when he asked to see Edward.

"They pretended that they didn't know who he was and that he did not live there. They asked me to identify myself," Feldman would later remember. "When I told them who I was, there was a young man who came down from upstairs that I had known, having seen him around, and he knew me, and he called me by my first name.

"He told the women in Italian language that I was O.K., then right after that, he took me out through the back of that house and in through a small door of a brick building and he showed me the pile of liquor that had been piled up in the garage and told me 'That's the 1,000 cases of Scotch that came in from Long Island,'" remembered Feldman.

Costello's mother Maria was also shown to be in the know about the bootlegging when she told her son to give a seemingly naïve new immigrant from Lauropoli named Frank Rizzo a job in his booze operation. The whole incident was recounted in Wolf's book, which quotes Costello reminiscing how Rizzo was foisted upon him by Maria to work as a bookkeeper.

"A bookkeeper! They're a dime a dozen," Costello complained.

"Now listen to me," Maria said sternly to her son. "This boy [was] the youngest teacher in college. He's a genius. He keep the books for you."

Despite his misgiving, Costello kept Rizzo on, paying him $500 a week to make a notation whenever a case of liquor arrived. It was a sum that was astronomical for the young man from the Calabrian countryside, whose boss demanded that he buy a new suit. Over time, Costello and Rizzo, dubbed "the Professor," became close friends and confidants.

The Halsey Street neighborhood wasn't the only Queens place where Frank and Edward Costello stashed their smuggled liquor. One of the strangest—and all but forgotten—episodes the Costello clan was involved in during Prohibition involved an old mansion in Astoria once owned by the famous Blackwell family, which traced its heritage to England. The family at one point owned the sliver of land in the East River between the borough of Queens and Manhattan.

The Blackwell family also bought property just across the inlet in Astoria and built a number of homes, including a colonial style mansion on Fulton Avenue that became a landmark for the village. It had long driveways, lush lawns, gardens, and a greenhouse. The location was known as "The Hill" because of its somewhat elevated land and was deemed a fashionable residential area. The property was just a few blocks from the Costello homes on Halsey Street and was reputed to be the oldest mansion on Long Island—which Astoria is technically part of.

At some point in 1922 right after he got involved in bootlegging, Frank Costello made arrangements to start using the Blackwell Mansion, as the house was called, to store liquor in large quantities. In later years, Kessler remembered that he had the Costellos store up 3,000 cases of liquor, including 2,500 gallons of grain alcohol and 1,000 cases of whiskey he had shipped in at the mansion. The house had been outfitted by Costello with false walls to conceal the contraband. A number of Costello relatives used the Blackwell Mansion as a residence, apparently to guard over the cache of liquor. The location was right next to the home of a deputy police commissioner and the historic Dutch Reformed Church. What better neighborhood to operate from.

But apparently Costello's business at the mansion wasn't unobtrusive enough. Neighbors complained to police about the incessant truck traffic and liquor activity at the mansion. In bucolic Queens of that time, the shady business was too much for authorities to ignore. So, on the evening of November 11, 1922, members of the district attorney's staff and NYPD detectives raided the mansion at 157-159 Fulton Avenue. They were tasked with enforcing the state's version of the Prohibition law, but in this case, they didn't work with federal authorities on the scene.

The police operation was something right out of an old gangster movie. According to newspaper accounts of the day, cops waited for three hours before anything suspicious happened. Then, about 8:00 P.M. two large trucks were driven through the large gates of the mansion's side entrance, a location shielded by trees. The vehicles bore the markings of "Farm and Florist Supplies," "Pork Products," and "Window Shades." It seemed like eleven men were on the property and around the trucks. A signal was given and an assistant district attorney, cops, and detectives rushed the building. Pandemonium then ensued.

As described in the *New York Evening Telegram*: "A lookout blew a whistle and the eleven men, panic stricken, rushed into the building and attempted to bar the way of the police. The door was knocked off its hinges and with revolvers drawn the detectives ordered all the men to raise their hands. There were eight gathered in the room and a search disclosed the other three in the cellar, one of whom was inside an old furnace."

"Fist fights and scrimmages marked the invasion of the premises," reported the *New York Tribune* in its version of the story. "Other short, sharp scrimmages happened in and about the old house when the eleven alleged liquor runners ran headlong into the advancing police column."

Things didn't end when the police breached the mansion doors. Twice officers from a nearby station house had to be brought in as reinforcements as other men tried to recapture the liquor seized in the raid. There was plenty of contraband. At first cops only found a small number of bottles. But by tapping on the mansion walls they discovered recently constructed false walls that hid hundreds of cases of booze, some bottles still with their packing straw. The haul included what was described as "the finest scotch whiskey" and Spanish sherry. There was also whiskey that had been diluted in unlabeled bottles, a common tactic of bootleggers to get more out of the product. In all, cops estimated that the prevailing "bootlegger" prices of the seized product had a value of over $100,000, a stash that was better than many Manhattan millionaires had.

Investigation revealed that the Blackwell Mansion liquor had arrived a week earlier by boat at the small Long Island town of Bayville, on the north shore about 42 miles as the crow flies from Astoria. The product had been trucked to Astoria, a standard practice by the Costello crew. There was so much contraband that the police used the two trucks seized at the mansion to transport the liquor to a local station house. Kessler would later admit that the booze seized at the mansion was his—at least in part.

But where were Frank and Edward Costello? Federal investigators years later would say definitively, as did Kessler, that the Blackwell Mansion operation was part of the Costello smuggling venture.

However, of the eleven men arrested that night the Costello brothers were not among them. Nevertheless, the group of men arrested included four brothers of the Aloise family, the family of Costello's mother Maria. Those arrested included Frank, age fifty-seven, and what *The New York Times* said where his four sons: Edward, twenty-eight, Michael, sixteen and Jack, twenty-four, and Joseph. *The New York Evening Telegram* identified one of the man simply as Jack, twenty-four-years-old, as actually being a cousin of the others. The Aloise connection indicated Frank Costello's ties to the bootlegging set up. He always relied on family for help in what he did and in fact used a Jack Aloise—which one isn't clear—as his driver in later years. Some of the Aloise family members gave the Blackwell Mansion as their address to police.

The case took a strange twist when one of the Aloise men, identified in newspaper accounts and court records as John Aloise, claimed that he owned the mansion and that all the liquor seized was his personal property, having purchased it prior to Prohibition and that he was keeping it for his friends. A local Queens judge was incredulous with Aloise's explanation, saying that he found it hard to believe that a laborer like Aloise had the means to buy and stockpile so much liquor. The jurist wryly noted that Aloise must have a large circle of friends to need so much alcohol and trucks to move it. The court, noting that the Blackwell Mansion was nothing more than a "whiskey warehouse in which people lived," refused to return the booze to Aloise. There was some speculation that the court might order the local sheriff to take the alcohol and distribute it to a local hospital—for medicinal purposes of course.

But an appellate court overruled the trial judge and said Aloise could have the stock back only to have the Court of Appeals agree with the trial judge, depriving Aloise of the stockpile. Aloise had his attorney try and present new evidence that he had the wherewithal to buy such a large quantity of alcohol, but no records could be found saying whether he succeeded.

With many in the city suspicious that bootleggers had corrupted cops and federal Prohibition agents, one result of the Blackwell Mansion raid was a libel lawsuit brought by NYPD Commissioner

Richard Enright against a city magistrate and a state assemblyman after they indicated that some of the liquor seized had been diverted to police precincts. Enright, who was dogged by police ineffectiveness in the area of Prohibition enforcement, lost the lawsuit. The litigation was an odd postscript to the Blackwell raid and ultimately contributed to Enright, considered a good commissioner, resigning from his job in 1925. The mansion itself had its own peculiar fate. In 1926, it was sold to a builder who razed the structure and cleared the property to put up nearly two dozen homes. There were other Blackwell mansions in the area and many also suffered the same fate.

Clearly, Frank and Edward Costello's involvement with the Blackwell operation and Kessler showed the extent to which he and his brother were cooperating with the big-name bootleggers. Kessler was no small-time player in the booze market. As federal agents poured over his checkbook and bank accounts, they found leads into corruption of police and others tasked with stopping bootlegging. In one case, the agents noted a $100,000 loan to a coat manufacturer whose chief executive had until retiring been a government Prohibition enforcement official. Checks were also found to police officials.

"Because of the large sums which are mentioned in the drafts [checks] the authorities seem convinced that they are on the scent of a liquor ring powerful enough to buy any amount of protection," blared the *New York Tribune* in one story. Just how large was soon uncovered when a Manhattan federal grand jury indicted thirty-three people, including six suspended Prohibition agents, as well as Kessler and his associates. However, neither Edward Costello nor his brother Frank were named as defendants. The main charge centered around the use of forged customs permits and other documents to purloin thousands of cases of whiskey and hundreds of cases of champagne from the Republic Storage warehouse months earlier. The case showed the extent of Kessler's dealing and the money he was earning when he made withdrawals from twenty-seven bank accounts of over $4 million, using various fake names.

When it came time for Kessler to go to trial a year later in November 1923, prosecutors called Edward Costello—but not Frank

Costello—as a witness. The newspapers called Edward an "Astorian," meaning he lived in that section of Queens. Prosecutors were intent on showing that a $20,000 bond issued in the mythical name of "Frank J. Sullivan" was to mask the purchase of some of the stolen liquor. For dramatic effect, the government brought six cases of the Auld Scottie whiskey to court and stacked it near the jury box. Edward explained that a $5,800 check given him two years earlier by Kessler was to allow him to buy two trucks to add to his fleet of equipment he kept at Halsey Street. Checks that Edward said he gave to Kessler since that time were for payments on the trucks, although he explained that the money went to another man—not Kessler. Whatever the story, investigators knew that the Costello brothers were in league with Kessler.

Bootleggers knew they were playing in a league filled with dishonorable business partners. It went with the territory. Liquor loads were "lost" and stolen all the time. There was no honor among the smuggling class and Frank Costello may have been one of the biggest culprits. Kessler himself recalled how in late 1922 or early 1923 some 500 cases of Scotch valued at $55,000 supposedly seized in the Blackwell raid had suddenly appeared on the market and were being sold in New York. The issue of the lost Scotch sparked an argument between Kessler and Costello in the lobby of the fashionable Ansonia Hotel, where Kessler was living with his wife.

Kessler said he and Costello had to settle their dispute. But Albert Feldman, a bootlegging associate of Kessler, put a more dramatic spin on things when he told federal investigators that both men got into a *violent* argument at the Ansonia.

"Kessler had accused Frank Costello of having disposed of a quantity of liquor belonging to Kessler," remembered Feldman. "He [Costello] denied it, that he had only delivered the liquor according to the orders that he had from Kessler's office."

Kessler insisted that he was going to hold Costello responsible for the missing liquor and upon hearing that Costello got angry.

Feldman continued the story: "So Frank Costello got pretty excited and he pulled out a small, pearly handled gun, supposedly to shoot him . . . He pulled the gun out of his pocket and everybody in the group grabbed him and held him before he even had a chance to point at Kessler. They grabbed him with the gun and yanked him away, and of course the whole argument then broke up."

The legend of Frank Costello over the years was that after he spent a year in prison in 1915 for gun possession that he vowed never to be caught with a firearm again. That was why he was considered a statesman of the mob, one who preferred conciliation over violence. But if Kessler's story about the gun is true, Costello not only packed a weapon but wasn't above recklessly pulling it out in public, and risking another arrest.

Edward Costello insisted that his dealings with Kessler had been legitimate. In describing himself, Edward noted that he had arrived in New York some thirty years earlier, which would have been around 1893, close to the time his father Luigi first arrived in the city from Lauropoli with him and his sisters. In another family wrinkle, Edward said that he and his father, who by the time he testified had been dead for well over a year, had been in business for years in Queens, likely referring to the old trucking business. But it was just a year earlier Edward said he had decided to leave trucking and focus his attention on real estate. When his testimony ended, and perhaps to burnish his reputation, Edward told the court that he would be donating the fee he earned as witness to a local Knights of Columbus center in Astoria.

After nearly a month on trial, Kessler and ten others were found guilty of the bootlegging conspiracy. Among the others convicted was Morris Sweetwood and Kessler's bookkeeper known as "Joe The Book." Three of the Prohibition agents were acquitted. Kessler, who had been living in a hotel apartment and was said to be worth between $5 million and $10 million, had his bail revoked and was taken into custody. The same day news broke about the conviction, federal officials trumpeted the seizure of five loads of beer from Canada, which investigators believed was sent as part of a plan to flood New York City with enough of the beverage in time for Christmas. Kessler was sentenced to two years in prison and was sent off to the penitentiary in Atlanta where he was pampered with the equally unfortunate George Remus.

Despite his near violent disagreement with Frank Costello about the 1922 Blackwell Mansion raid and the loss of his whiskey, Kessler made a deal with Frank Costello just before he was sent off to prison. It would, according to Kessler, turn out to be another chance for his bootlegging associate to cheat him.

As Kessler would tell federal agents just before he was to go off to prison in Atlanta in 1923, Costello asked him for some money to continue with his own bootlegging. Kessler didn't have the cash but instead provided Costello with up to 200 cases of liquor, which in the Prohibition market was as good as gold. The prison-bound bootlegger had done similar deals with others in the bootlegging market. Kessler expected to be paid back when he got out of prison in two years. He would be in for a big surprise.

"Never paid me," Kessler testified years later about what Costello did to pay him back for the loaned liquor. "Everybody else I left money with—and it amounted to a lot of money—I gave one man $50,000; another man $40,000, everybody paid back," said Kessler. "I asked him for it and he laughed it off and I forgot about it."

The Kessler case showed not only how much money was being made—and lost—in the bootleg trade but how closely smugglers worked together. The lesson wasn't lost on Frank Costello and his brother and showed the value of making the right connections. True, if he wasn't cheating his friends, Costello had been losing some loads to hijackers and Italian gangsters like Capone and Yale who themselves were involved in deadly feuds. But for Costello, making the right alliances was an important way of assuring his survival and prosperity in an illicit market that was rife with trouble and bloodshed.

William Vincent Dwyer, known as "Big Bill," was one of those larger-than-life characters on the New York scene in the 1920s. He was born and bred in the Hell's Kitchen area of Manhattan, which really served as a recruiting station for the gangs of New York. While working as a stevedore on the West Side docks, Dwyer saw early the potential of using warehouses to hide smuggled liquor. He brought in loads from Canada and Europe on a fleet of nearly two dozen vessels and employed hundreds and was soon anointed the new "King of the Bootleggers." But, Dwyer didn't just earn his reputation as a bootlegger. He was a sportsman of sorts, plowing his bootlegging profits toward the purchase of sports teams, notably some hockey franchises from Canada and later a football team he renamed the Brooklyn Dodgers, which played at Ebbets Field in Brooklyn, the same venue for the baseball team. Dwyer also took over an old greyhound racing track and turned it into a regular horse raceway and bought a few more tracks around the country and in Canada.

Dwyer worked out of an office at 1540 Broadway, the old Loew's State Theater Building, a few blocks west of Costello's operation on Lexington Avenue. With their competitors being knocked off by Prohibition agents, at some point Dwyer and Costello decided to work together, perhaps as early as 1921. The combination took things to a grand level. Both men controlled vessels and trucks to ship the liquor, while Dwyer had numerous warehouses in the city to store the merchandise. Costello also had his secret facilities such as the garages in Astoria and the Blackwell Mansion as well as hiding places on the North Shore of Long Island. Sometimes, Costello used vessels painted and marked to look like those of the Coast Guard. Both men also paid off Coast Guard officials, cops, and others to make sure their product got through from Rum Row. While Kessler's earlier operation was significant, the Dwyer-Costello alliance was believed to have dwarfed it, pulling in tens of millions of dollars a year.

Costello and Dwyer were in league for at least three years, possibly four. They appeared to control much of the market in bootlegged liquor and were making astronomical profits. Dwyer's outsized personality and sporting interests kept him in the public eye. Costello stayed out of the limelight. Sure, he hit the nightclubs on Broadway and appeared to be just another businessman. But Costello didn't relish publicity. He liked staying off the radar. Yet either way, Dwyer and Costello wouldn't stay out of trouble and it came for them in the form of an angry Long Island housewife.

CHAPTER FIVE
A WOMAN SCORNED

COMPARED TO THE FASHIONABLE STANDARDS of the Roaring Twenties, Mrs. Annie L. Case Fuhrmann was rather plain and frankly not much to look at, at least based on the newspaper pictures of her that survive. A flapper she was not. A stout, bespectacled lady with a square face and hair pulled back from her forehead, Mrs. Fuhrmann looked like a schoolmarm and a stern one at that. Still, the Greenport, Long Island, woman was married, and her husband Hans worked as a sailor and crewman on vessels that worked out of their hometown. Hans Fuhrmann was a lanky man with curly, sandy-colored hair with a handsome face. He bore a tattoo on his left hand. The couple had married in the summer of 1924.

Things seemed fine in the Fuhrmann household. But then Hans Fuhrmann would disappear for long periods. During his absences, Annie Fuhrmann found that she had no money to run their household. When Hans did finally show up he was usually dead drunk on the near-toxic liquor concoction widely available and of no use to anybody, including his wife. Intoxicated, Hans didn't even recognize Annie and would beat her up with anything he could grab, including milk bottles, bloodying her face, and breaking her glasses.

The reason why Hans Fuhrmann would disappear was that he could make a lot of money crewing any one of the Rum Row smuggling vessels as a ship's master plying the waters off Long Island. It was good money, and just about every other able-bodied sailor in the area was doing the same thing. As soon as local saloons were closed, others popped up. Prohibition had given Long Island a gold rush economy. The local cops knew that and when Annie Fuhrmann called them after she sustained a beating the officers told her to shut up.

" 'He is a good fellow, too,' " Annie remembered one of the local cops telling her after she had been smacked around by Hans. " 'All the bootleggers are good fellows. You think I am going to arrest him and hurt my own graft. Not on your life. You better go back to bed and forget this.' "

In the days before a woman had a number of social service agencies to turn to in cases of abuse, Annie Fuhrmann's options were limited. The cops were no help and since none of the money Hans earned found its way to Annie Fuhrmann's purse, she decided she had had enough. One day in mid-May, 1925, she traveled into Brooklyn and walked into the offices of the *Brooklyn Eagle,* the borough's big daily newspaper. She figured that the only way to get her husband out of the bootleg trade was to reveal what he was doing and hope that her information would wake up federal investigators so they would arrest the "higher-ups" responsible for the smuggling of alcohol. To show how serious she was, Annie Fuhrmann gave the newspaper the names, addresses, and telephone numbers of the many bootleggers she claimed to have personally met. She also talked about smuggling plans the men talked about in her presence.

"He is always in debt," Annie Fuhrmann told the newspaper about her spouse. "He gets drunk and loses his money at poker. I have had to pawn our furniture to keep alive."

There were times when Annie Fuhrmann admitted sailing with her husband when he delivered as much as 2,300 cases of whiskey to City Island in the Bronx and farther north to Port Chester. She claimed that most of the big bootleggers had come to her house at some point to do business with Hans.

"I know them all," Annie Fuhrmann said. "I have handled their money to pay the men. I have heard them talk of their plans. I have heard them talk of fixing this man and that. I know just how they operate."

The Brooklyn Eagle got a sensational scoop from Annie Fuhrmann and her struggles against the grip rum had on her husband. But no doubt conscious of the libel laws at the time, the newspaper only presented the initials of the names of the men Fuhrmann claimed were involved. However, the newspaper did forward the complete information, full names included, to the U.S. Attorney for Brooklyn and a woman by the name of Mabel Willebrandt, who was the highest ranked lady in the Department of Justice and was in charge of liquor prosecutions. Willebrandt said the information from Fuhrmann was of "distinct value" and passed it to other officials in charge of smuggling investigations in New York City and Long island.

In its blockbuster articles, *The Brooklyn Eagle* reported that Annie Fuhrmann said the main bootlegging headquarters was in a hotel "not far from Times Square." She could have been referring to Costello, Dwyer, or some other syndicates in the area.

A couple of months passed and Hans Fuhrmann still had not shown up back home. There didn't seem to be any movement on the investigations, at least none that Mrs. Fuhrmann was aware of. Traveling back to Brooklyn, she again pleaded with prosecutors to help find her spouse. Although she didn't know it, Hans Fuhrmann had actually been arrested on the freighter *Nantisco,* which had been seized off of Astoria with a cargo of lumber and 3,000 cases of liquor from Nova Scotia. However, Hans Fuhrmann had been using an alias: "Oscar Nelson of Greenport, L.I."

Told of the name, Annie Fuhrmann asked investigators to describe the man and they told her as much as they could, including the fact he had a tattoo on his left hand.

"That's it!" Annie Fuhrmann blurted. "That's just what he looked like."

Hans Fuhrmann, had been released after being grabbed in the *Nantisco* seizure. But for reasons only he knew, he didn't return home to his wife. Still, he had an upcoming court date and Annie Fuhrmann vowed to be there when he showed up.

"I'll be here then too," she told federal agents. "I know that when he is sober and away from the big liquor smugglers, he's willing enough to give up that sort of life and go straight. That is what I want him to do—go straight."

Some federal investigators and prosecutors were at first coy about the value of the intelligence information that Annie Fuhrmann provided. But it became clear that the leads were turning out to be useful. She also seemed to convince her husband to become a paid government cooperating witness, something Annie Fuhrmann had already become. As the Fuhrmanns talked, investigators began to focus on William Dwyer, Frank Costello, and a host of other suspects such as Irving Wexler, known also as Waxey Gordon and a cabal of other Jewish gangsters who had been immune from prosecution but who were major Manhattan bootleggers.

Bootlegging had always been a violent trade. Hijackings, gun battles, and even skirmishes at sea between the Coast Guard and smugglers took lives. The loss of life among the smugglers at the hands of government agents was one thing that further turned off the public to Prohibition. State police in New York, with sticky fingers for payoffs, sometimes got involved in ripping off bootleg convoys and in one case a corrupt cop was wounded in a shootout near Montauk. But the profit motive of bootleggers drove them to take risky and foolhardy action to bring liquor through Rum Row. In one case, Dwyer's men used an unseaworthy vessel known as the *William J. Maloney* to pick up liquor, only to have it sink with the loss of its twelve crew members.

The sinking of the *William J. Maloney*, the explosive claims by Annie Fuhrmann, and the general lawlessness in New York City, where there were an estimated tens of thousands of speakeasies being supplied by numerous bootleggers, finally became too much for the federal government. By the fall of 1925, the top federal Prohibition official in Washington, D.C., a former military man named General Lincoln C. Andrews came to Manhattan and shook up the local Prohibition enforcement operation. On September 24, 1925, he arrived in New York and replaced the federal administrator for the Prohibition district. He and Manhattan U.S. Attorney Emory Buckner then met to go over what to do about the international activities of the city bootleggers who they expected to be bringing in large hauls of liquor.

The situation in the city was pressing because just days before Andrews arrived, investigators appeared to profit from Hans and Annie Fuhrmann's information by conducting raids in a suite of offices near Times Square in the Longacre and Knickerbocker Buildings based on information that in part came from the Fuhrmann family. By then, both Annie and Hans had decided to become government agents of a sort. The seizure by federal agents of the vessel *Nantisco,* upon which Hans Fuhrmann had been the master, was the first large ocean-going ship they had taken. As it turned out, the *Nantisco* first traveled to Nova Scotia, took on a load of timber and then met up with a Rum Row ship and took on 500 cases of Scotch. As brazen as the *Nantisco* was in its voyage, it was seized as soon as it entered New York harbor and docked in Astoria, the area where Frank and Edward Costello's garages were located.

As word of the raid circulated, it became known that the Fuhrmanns had indeed furnished valuable information for the investigation. Since Hans Furhmann had actually crewed the smuggling ships he gave investigators critical leads about the actual operations of the bootleggers. When officials raided the Longacre and Knickerbocker buildings, Hans Furhmann was present with investigators and helped identify some of the suspects. Some agents feared that the publicity the Fuhrmanns had received put their lives at risk.

The main organizer of the *Nantisco* ring was Irving Wexler, whose sobriquet "Waxey Gordon" was said to have come from his days as a pickpocket when he waxed his fingers to help separate wallets from the pockets of their owners. Wexler had a contact in Nova Scotia to help pull off the liquor deal. Early in his bootleg career Wexler had teamed up with Max Greenberg, and the duo brought in whiskey from Canada across Lake Michigan to Detroit. When Wexler and Greenberg wanted to expand they went to Arnold Rothstein, who had been Costello's early investor, for cash. According to Rich Cohen in *Tough Jews,* his history of Jewish gangsters, Rothstein agreed to fund Wexler but only if he switched his operation and started taking his liquor cargo from Europe via Rum Row. During raids in Manhattan, the federal agents found documents that showed how the European bootlegging trade worked, as well as the customers and the warehouses used to store the product. The agents also seized over two dozen bottles of Scotch.

Wexler wasn't arrested initially because he was out of the country with his family on a vacation. He would later surrender. His other conspirators, including Greenberg, represented a substantial Jewish group of bootleggers and made clear to prosecutor Buckner that he was wasting his time going after small operators when so many ships were targeting New York. Buckner asked for—and got—the help of squads of agents and police officers to carry out a big offensive. That didn't bode well for Frank and Edward Costello, as well as their partner in crime William V. Dwyer.

CHAPTER SIX
"THE GREATEST ROUNDUP"

EVEN BEFORE THE MASSIVE CHRYSLER BUILDING opened in 1931 to take the title for a short time as the world's tallest building, the middle of any weekday morning at Lexington Avenue and Forty-second Street in Manhattan was a busy place. The five-story building at number 405 Lexington Avenue was just around the corner from bustling Grand Central Terminal and a host of office buildings. Park Avenue was one block down the street. On the particular morning of December 3, 1925, around 11:00 A.M., the streets turned out to be busier than usual—much to the distress of Frank and Edward Costello, and a great many of their friends.

In coordinated action, federal Prohibition agents hit Frank Costello's office at 405 Lexington and those of William V. Dwyer at the East River Savings Bank building at Forty-second Street and Broadway with warrants for their arrest. Scores of other men were sought. Other offices were being sought in places like Montauk Point and Hempstead on Long Island, as well as Astoria, Bayside, Jamaica and Belle Harbor in Queens. Agents even went to New London, Connecticut, where the Coast Guard had offices. The warrants didn't give much detail but in the case of Costello they essentially accused him of violating the Volstead Act.

In the weeks before the raids, a curious mailman whose route covered 405 Lexington came across a man in the building working rather secretively. The man had visited the rental office and said there was some trouble with nearby telephone service and had traced the wires to 405 Lexington. The office manager led the man, who was actually an NYPD officer, to the basement junction box for the telephone service. Secretly, the detective placed a tap on the telephones going into Costello's suite of offices and returned the next day to admonish the postal worker to keep things secret.

"These wires are being tapped," said the detective to the postman. "If there is any leak, you are the only outsider who knows anything about it."

The tapping was being done so that investigators could have a better sense of when people were in the Costello office and move in for an arrest. They hoped to grab Costello with his gang and take away all kinds of records. The mailman naturally felt put on the spot by the detective but kept the secret until the day of the raid.

As it turned out, Frank Costello wasn't at 405 Lexington Avenue when the agents arrived there. He happened to be that morning in Hempstead at the home of C. Hunter Carpenter to visit a parcel of real estate in the town of Babylon on the south shore of Long Island. Costello at this point in his life was holding himself out to be in the real estate business and listed a business address for himself in Jamaica, Queens. Costello was interested in buying some property, and both Carpenter and another man named Percival Corson were interested in acting as brokers for the deal. Given Costello's activities, he likely wanted the property to hold bootlegged liquor. It was 10:00 A.M. and Costello, Carpenter, and Corson where getting ready to drive away when they had two visitors who suddenly drove up in a roadster.

"As we were about to start from Mr. Carpenter's back yard, an automobile entered Mr. Carpenter's private driveway and two men, who said they were government agents, and who were armed, told us that a Mr. Foster wanted to see us at his office over in Manhattan at two o'clock that afternoon," Costello remembered later in an affidavit he filed.

Carpenter remembered both of the agents, identified as C.V. Schneider and Mr. Green, actually drawing their pistols as they approached the car. The agents said they had warrants for the arrest of the three but wouldn't serve them if they agreed to accompany them peacefully back to Manhattan. Costello and his colleagues told the two agents that they were planning to go to Babylon to look at real estate. Since there was still four hours before the time Foster wanted to see them, Costello and his group thought they could easily go on the short business trip and get into Manhattan in time. While it might seem unusual during an arrest situation, the two agents agreed and accompanied Costello and his associates in Corson's car to Babylon. The group then went back to Carpenter's place and prepared to split up: Costello and Corson got into one car with one of the agents; Carpenter and the other agent, C.V. Schneider, got into a different vehicle. Then things got peculiar.

Schneider suddenly remembered that he needed to try and collect evidence, so he left the car and went back toward Carpenter's house, telling him that he needed to use the telephone. Carpenter said he watched Schneider and saw that instead of using the telephone he began rummaging through the real estate broker's desk, taking papers, check books, ledgers, and all sorts of documents that he found. Carpenter bolted from the car and went back into the house, telling Schneider he had no right to seize his documents. Besides, none of the materials related to bootlegging. Schneider ignored Carpenter and told him that since he had a warrant for his arrest he could do what he wanted. If he had a problem, Carpenter should tell it to the judge, said the agent.

By the time Costello and his two friends got back to Manhattan, the roundup had grabbed a number of the other suspects, most notably Dwyer. Costello and his brother had generally been under the public radar in terms of bootlegging, having avoided arrest until now. The big fish, at least as far as the newspapers were concerned was Dwyer, who was identified as the "widely known race track owner." The bust was said to involve what was touted as "the greatest roundup in the history of Prohibition" and based on the allegations the case was unprecedented. Estimates of the business the Costello-Dwyer ring did ran anywhere from $40 million to $60 million yearly, sums that would amount to $557 million to $835 million today accounting for inflation.

Dwyer, the big fish, was charged with running an international "rum ring controlling many millions in money, ships and liquor." General Andrews himself is said to have directed the roundup. There had been many bootlegging busts over the years, each one always touted as bigger than the last. But now Dwyer—and Costello—were alleged to be masterminds behind a wholly unprecedented liquor ring, one in which they were said to have had an intelligence service, thanks to Costello, that rivaled anything the federal government had arrayed against them. For the last two years, a federal prosecutor said during the initial court appearance of the defendants, the conspiracy was responsible for bringing into New York harbor a greater part of the bootlegged liquor hitting the marketplace.

What made things worse for the government was that the Dwyer-Costello combination had no trouble bribing members of the Coast Guard with "money, wine, women and song." The night before the big raids in Manhattan, federal agents arrested four members of Coast Guard vessel No. 126 when the vessel docked for the night. That particular vessel sometimes went out to Rum Row, and took cases of liquor ashore as well as helped lost smuggling boats find their way so that the booze could be off-loaded and stashed, officials charged.

The U.S. District Court in lower Manhattan was where the Costello brothers, Dwyer, and the other defendants were brought for an initial appearance before a federal judge. The main issue in these first appearances, aside from the entering of not-guilty pleas, was what to do about bail for each of the nineteen people who were arrested, a group that would grow with more arrests to over fifty people. Dwyer was the first of the group to appear before Judge Henry Goddard and his entry into the courtroom was memorable for the confidence he showed. "He had a broad smile," *The New York Times* reported. "He wore several large diamonds, including a swastika ring set with gems."

The prosecutor was an assistant U.S. attorney named Henry Stichman, who told Goddard that Dwyer, both Costellos, and one

William Gallagher specifically brought in some five months earlier a load of just over 4,000 cases of liquor hidden under the coal of the steamship *Augusta*. Smugglers often hid contraband under all sorts of cargo, so this was no surprise.

"This man," Stichman said pointing to Dwyer, "is the leading figure against whom the energies of the Prohibition Department in this case has been directed. By him, various Coast Guard officials have been bribed, the bribery having been done through Dwyer's agents in the *Augusta* case, so that the vessel was enabled to proceed up the Hudson River to Yonkers."

The prosecutor described how the bribery insured for over two years that the Coast Guard would protect the smugglers. The payoffs of some of the lowly paid Coast Guard men, which included wining and dining, took place sometimes at Dwyer's restaurant, the Sea Grill on Forty-fifth Street. The more Stichman talked in court, the more apparent it became how sophisticated the Costello-Dwyer ring was. One of their vessels, a power boat named *Klip,* had armor plating and was so fast that it was able to elude Coast Guard vessels, dodging around river craft while agents fired shots, narrowly missing members of the public. The smugglers had piers on the West Side of Manhattan by Christopher Street, and just north of the Fulton Fish Market by the Brooklyn Bridge. At least twenty-four vessels, including a half-dozen schooners and eighteen speedboats were used to move the liquor.

Turning his attention to the Costello brothers, Stichman told Goddard that Frank was the other big principal in the conspiracy and that, along with Edward, worked on the "purchasing end" of things. Edward Costello, the prosecutor alleged, had brought in liquor from the French colonies of St. Pierre and Miquelon, as well as other points in Canada, to the vessels on Rum Row. Frank Costello, the prosecutor also charged, was the man who paid off the Coast Guard members at the instigation of Dwyer. To buttress the case against Costello on the bribery charge, a total of five members of Coast Guard were arrested. Another defendant turned out to be Jerome Geigerman, one of Costello's brothers-in-law whose listed occupation was that of chauffeur, although it wasn't clear who he drove.

Back in the 1920s, bail was usually set to assure that a defendant would show up in court. In the case of Dwyer, the prosecutor seemed to want to set an example and asked the judge to set a bond of $75,000, a rather exorbitant sum. "Pure romance," responded Dwyer's attorney Louis Halle. Dwyer had a wife and five kids in school and college, plus a house in the Belle Harbor, Queens, said Halle. The defense attorney low-balled the amount and asked Goddard to set bail at a mere $500. That was all that was needed, Halle insisted, to assure that Dwyer would stay around to answer the government's ridiculous charges. Goddard, the judge, thought differently and required Dwyer to post a $40,000 bond.

Showing how important they were in the alleged conspiracy, Frank and Edward Costello were required to post a $20,000 bond each, as were real estate brokers C. Hunter Carpenter and Philip Coffey. Jerome Geigerman had to put up a $2,500 bond while the Coast Guardsmen accused of taking payoffs had to post bonds ranging from $5,000 to $10,000, high amounts for men who didn't earn much with their modest government salaries ranging from $36 to $100 a month.

Manhattan U.S. Attorney Emory R. Buckner noted that not all Coast Guard members surrendered to the temptations allegedly offered by Dwyer and Costello. Some resisted or else took token payments and turned over the money to their supervisors, thus helping to build the criminal case. But in all the publicity surrounding the Dwyer-Costello arrests, one name that didn't initially surface was that of Fuhrmann. Annie and Hans Fuhrmann, the beleaguered couple from Long Island, had for several months been giving federal officials information and intelligence that led to the break-up in September of the Waxey Gordon bootlegging ring. With the bigger indictment of the Costello-Dwyer combination, the value of the Fuhrmann information had definitely increased.

But the results of the investigation apparently were too much for Hans Fuhrmann to bear. On the night of January 28, 1926, just days after the big indictment, the body of Hans Fuhrmann was found in the Hotel Arito, at Sixth Avenue and Forty-fourth Street. A policeman said he was found by a hotel maid lying in bed. In Fuhrmann's left hand was a .38 caliber automatic pistol. He had a gunshot wound to the left temple.

Annie Fuhrmann was convinced her husband had been murdered by mobsters to prevent his testifying at any trials. She pointed to the fact that the previous September another informant had been found murdered in a limousine in Manhattan. Before he died, Hans seemed like he was in a better place, making legitimate money and out from under the yoke of the bootleggers. She also speculated that if it wasn't the mob then the fault for Hans's slaying lay with the federal Prohibition agents themselves. Her husband had told her that many of the agents themselves were taking bribes, and she explained that a notebook her spouse had kept recorded which government officers did and didn't accept payoffs.

"His life as a bootlegger was bad but this was worse," Annie Fuhrmann said. "They should have watched him . . . they shouldn't have given him a gun. Now that he is gone how are they going to convict the men who were indicted?"

The Manhattan U.S. Attorney was forced to acknowledge that Fuhrmann had been an important witness against the Wexler and Dwyer groups. But both police and the coroner felt certain that the ex-bootlegger had taken his own life. He left no note. With or without Fuhrmann, the prosecutors were going to push along with their criminal cases.

The arrest of Frank and Edward Costello and the others in the Dwyer case signaled a shift in focus for the federal Prohibition Department. There had always been thousands of petty offenders who violated the Volstead Act, small fish who complained about the way the bigger fish could escape arrest and prosecution. But now the government was willing to gather intelligence, follow leads overseas, and cultivate informants to build cases against the ringleaders. For Frank Costello and William Dwyer, they faced a sea change that could swamp them in a way the worst nor'easter on Rum Row couldn't.

It didn't take long for things to get worse for Costello and Dwyer. On January 26, 1926, just over a month before they were initially arrested and two days before Hans Fuhrmann killed himself, federal officials unsealed indictments in the case that indicated how serious the government was in going after both men and their cronies. A total of sixty-two men were charged, including Dwyer, Frank and Edward Costello, the Coast Guard crew members and the others initially arrested the previous December. But there were additional defendants charged, including Frank Costello's close friend and driver Jack Aloise, more Coast Guardsmen, as well as some former Prohibition agents who had retired and allegedly joined the conspiracy. Also charged was a businessman out of St. Pierre, the French colony off Canada, who came to Manhattan frequently and sold liquor directly to the Costello-Dwyer group, as well as a pilot who had flown out of Curtiss Field to help smuggling ships find their way at sea.

Although no charges of violence were included, the indictments accused Dwyer and Brooklyn businessman and bootlegger James McCambridge of responsibility for a dozen deaths through a mishap at sea. Investigators determined that in November 1924 Dwyer and McCambridge sent the vessel *William J. Maloney* out to sea on a rum-running mission, knowing that the craft was unseaworthy. The vessel sank on November 16 with the loss of twelve men who left behind a number of widows and a total of twenty-two children without their fathers. Both men were charged under a little-used maritime law and the families of the lost men eagerly gave evidence to help get Dwyer and McCambridge indicted.

"Dwyer's passion for expansion has been most helpful to us," chief prosecutor Buckner said sarcastically as he announced the new charges. "His elaborate organization included so many subordinates that when the house began to fall many took refuge in the cyclone cellar of [my] office, gave their testimony and received immunity."

Dwyer and Costello's operation had been so large, the prosecutor said, that their underlings rushed to cooperate with investigators to save themselves. This fit perfectly into the government's plan to move up the food chain and go after the bigger fish. Dwyer, whose flamboyant lifestyle and stature as a sports impresario with his hockey

and football teams always grabbed headlines, was the main focus of
the government's wrath. But it was Frank Costello who had been the
real architect of the smuggling operations, the man whose sense of
organization and contacts had made things work. The problem was
that his genius peaked at a time when the Prohibition police, shamed
enough by their failures to stem the tide of alcohol, finally started to
take action.

CHAPTER SEVEN
"KING OF THE BOOTLEGGERS"

WITH OVER SIXTY PEOPLE CHARGED in the Costello-Dwyer case, there was no way the government was going to try all of the defendants together. So in July 1926, the trial of William V. Dwyer, whom investigators believed was the main "king of the bootleggers," began in Manhattan federal district court. Jury selection took three days and wasn't easy because a number of potential jurors frankly told the trial judge Julian W. Mack that they were prejudiced against the Prohibition laws, reflecting a widespread attitude in the public. Eventually a panel of twelve men was selected and included a salesman, coffee merchant, insurance broker, and a jeweler.

Both Frank and Edward Costello were not included in the Dwyer trial. Their charges were scheduled for a later date. But the Dwyer case was really a dress rehearsal for what would happen when it was their turn. The prosecutor, Stichman, outlined the case for the jury and said Dwyer was the head of the ring, a man who took tribute from other bootleggers for a set price for each case of liquor they brought ashore from Rum Row under Dwyer's protection. The ring had a clear division of labor, with different men like Jack Kirsch procuring the booze overseas, unloading vessels which made it into New York harbor, building and repairing speed boats and recruiting crews to man the vessels, noted Stichman. The prosecutor also added that two Coast Guard officers helped Dwyer land 500 cases of liquor on their own Coast Guard vessels.

Just before Stichman called his first witness, Jack Kirsch, the man who was Dwyer's contact and who located foreign sources of liquor, decided to plead guilty to the three counts in the indictment. The move caused a protest from Dwyer's lawyers and the other defense counsel but there really was nothing they could do to stop Kirsch from entering a plea. Judge Mack didn't make any announcement about why Kirsch decided to admit his guilt but in any case, it wasn't a good omen for Dwyer.

The first witness for the government was Charles Augustus Smith, a mariner, who testified how in March 1923 he met Dwyer in the Loew's State Theater Building at Broadway and Forty-fifth Street in Manhattan. After the interview, Smith said that Dwyer put him in charge of the boat *Dorin*, which contained liquor. About a month later, Smith said Dwyer made him navigator of another vessel, the *William A. Morse*, and told him to go to St.Pierre and Miquelon, the two French islands where earlier Costello traveled to do business for liquor and set up his supplier connections. Dwyer told the crew to pick up as much liquor as they could on the islands, but the *William A. Morse* had to detour to Halifax after it got stuck in some ice, said Smith.

As he continued his testimony, Smith made matters worse for Dwyer, showing how much pull the rum baron had with law enforcement—and how adverse police were to enforcing the Prohibition law. He told jurors how members of the NYPD had been present when two hundred cargoes of liquor had been brought in from Rum Row for Dwyer during a two-year period from February 1923 to March 1925. Sometimes the cargoes were unloaded at a Bellevue Hospital pier on the East River, again in the presence of uniformed patrolmen of the NYPD, as well as cops from Weehawken in New Jersey during unloadings on the Hudson River, said Smith. In all, Smith reported that Dwyer had paid him a total of $40,000 for his work smuggling in mostly whiskey but some champagne and sauterne. He had only had five loads seized by the Coast Guard.

More damaging testimony was given by a former Coast Guardsman named Paul Crim, who quit after only about six months in the service to become Dwyer's chauffeur. Crim told the jury how just a month after he joined the service he met Dwyer in Manhattan. Crim agreed to have the vessel he served on act as a convoy vessel for Dwyer's Rum Row boats to provide protection. Initially paid $100 by Dwyer, Crim said that when he asked for more money he was told that he would have to smuggle liquor to earn the cash. It was in December 1924 that the Coast Guard vessel, known by the acronym "C.G. 203," traveled to Rum Row and picked up a load of 700 cases of Scotch from a schooner anchored thirty-five miles southeast of Ambrose Light, said Crim. The crew of C.G. 203 then circled the schooner to throw off a nearby Coast Guard cutter and delivered the cargo to piers at Christopher Street on the west side and also on the other side of Manhattan by North River. For their services, the Coast Guard crew got two cases of champagne; Crim said he got $700 from Dwyer.

While Augustus Smith in his testimony had indicated that Dwyer and his associates had the help of NYPD cops, Crim showed that the bootleg king had hooks even into the office of chief Manhattan federal prosecutor Buckner. Crim said that after he left his job with Dwyer he had no contact with him until he suddenly called him at home in early January 1926 to say that sealed indictments had been filed against the ring. Dwyer said he knew that, stated Crim, because he had received information from "someone in Buckner's office." Crim should hide, said Dwyer, who helped him stay in a Manhattan hotel. A few days later Dwyer and his lawyer, a slick operator named Louis Halle, advised Crim to go to Montreal, where Dwyer was a part owner of the Mount Royal race track. But federal agents soon tracked him down and showed him a letter from his wife back in New York, all of which Crim said convinced him to return home.

The way Dwyer and his lawyer tried to get Crim out of town was a strong indication of the smuggling king's consciousness of guilt. The trial wasn't going well for Dwyer and his nine other co-defendants. Of course, Frank Costello wasn't facing the music in court, at least not for a few months anyway. But as testimony in Dwyer's trial continued to unfold, things were happening that would later have an impact on Costello's fate, as well as that of his brother Edward and their cohorts. It all revolved about a strange, unorthodox federal official named Bruce Bielaski, a former spy who in the years before Prohibition stirred up his share of commotion in an international incident with Mexico.

Bielaski was born in Maryland ten years before Frank Costello. His father was a Methodist minister of Lithuanian descent while his mother was Polish. After earning a law degree, Bielaski became a bit of a rising star in the Department of Justice, straightening out the court system in the territory of Oklahoma before it became a state. Back in Washington, Bielaski in April 1912 was appointed head of what was then known as the Bureau of Investigation, the forerunner of the FBI. It was as head of the bureau that Bielaski made allegations that German businessmen, during the period before the U.S. entered World War One, had attempted to buy newspapers in the States in an effort to get Germany's position before the American public. He left government service in 1919 to practice law.

It was in 1922, while on a trip to Mexico, that Bielaski was kidnapped in the town of Cuernavaca and held for 10,000 pesos ransom. Bielaski managed to escape from the cave he was held in and walked to the town of Tetecala where an American newspaper reporter brought him back along with the ransom, which had been assembled by a friend. While the Mexican press accused Bielaski of staging his own kidnapping, nothing ever happened to him.

But the lure of government service for Bielaski was strong, and by 1925, Gen. Andrews, the man in charge of the federal effort to enforce Prohibition enticed him to return to government employment as an agent. But it wasn't just as any ordinary agent. His job was to find out, among other things, who had been bribed by the bootlegging ring, and to do that Bielaski decided to go undercover and bring some of the corrupt Coast Guardsmen into the government's fold as witnesses. This was the era before undercover operations were common and the tactics used by Bielaski were ahead of the times. Defense attorneys called him and his associates "superspies" who were part of some invisible government. During the Dwyer trial it was shown that some of the cooperating witnesses had been given money by Bielaski while they waited to testify against

Dwyer. Under cross-examination the witnesses denied that they were part of a government plot to frame Dwyer or that they agreed to work for Bielaski as part of a bargain to "save your own carcass from a dungeon." Crim did concede that Bielaski held something over him while he testified: he had never been arraigned on the smuggling charges he faced in the case.

Dwyer's case went to the jury on July 26, 1927, and from the way Judge Julian Mack instructed the jurors on the law you wouldn't be far off the mark to think that he was trying to prejudice the panel against the defendants. Even the reporters covering the case back then thought there was bias.

"There is no contradiction by other witnesses of the things stated by the government witnesses" said Mack. Unless the testimony was untrue "it is your duty to accept it," he explained. In other words, the government witnesses had carried the weight of the day, unless it could be shown they were lying. He even seemed to tell the jurors that if Dwyer or his co-defendants wanted to take the stand to explain away things they could have—but didn't.

Mack also told the jury that it didn't matter one bit what they individually thought about the Prohibition laws or if they drank in speakeasies or in private. He said the panel was "duty bound, as jurors, to apply the laws as I give it to you, the evidence, utterly without regard to your personal observance, or non-observance of that law."

If the jurors also had any feelings about General Andrews or his aide, Bielaski, they should put them aside, although Mack said that if they misused government funds then that could affect Bielaski's credibility. Mack did make one important statement favoring the defense and that was that government witness Augustus Smith was found to have lied in parts of his testimony, something he said worked to the benefit of two of the defendants—but not Dwyer. Although he didn't know it at the time, Mack planted a seed in Costello's mind as he watched the trial about how he should handle his own defense. If Bielaksi and his tactics were viewed as problematic by potential jurors, then maybe the case could be won, Costello thought.

The jury got the case just before noon on July 26. It was at 11:00

P.M., after just over six hours of full deliberations that the panel came back with a decision. It was a split verdict: six of the defendants were acquitted; Dwyer was convicted of one count of conspiracy. One of those acquitted was Edward Gallagher, a former Coast Guard captain who was alleged to have protected the rum boats and used a Coast Guard cutter to bring in 1,400 cases of liquor.

Dwyer took his verdict calmly and even shook hands with Manhattan U.S. Attorney Buckner who then asked the defendant if he had received a "square deal."

"Positively," Dwyer answered, with a smile.

The judge didn't hide his own feelings either, saying that in all his years on the bench he had never seen such a clear-cut case of guilt.

"The facts cry out to heaven for wholesale violation of the law in every way," said Mack. "There is no shadow of doubt of the existence of the conspiracy alleged."

Mack decided to sentence Dwyer and Corson immediately. He wouldn't even let the defendants have the weekend to spend with their families. For being found guilty of the one count, Dwyer got two years in prison, a relative bargain. Outside the courtroom, Dwyer's attorney called the verdict "asinine" and vowed to appeal and asked that his client be given bail as soon as possible.

Even if he didn't get to go home, Dwyer spent the night after he was convicted in the McAlpin Hotel in the custody of two U.S. marshals. The next morning, he was picked up in style at the hotel with a limousine furnished by a friend and rode with the marshals downtown to the Tombs, the prison on Chambers Street. Ever the friend of the press, Dwyer said he had the limousine circle the block around the Tombs so that no reporter would miss his arrival.

Yet, the question remained about who was the big leader of the conspiracy. Was it Dwyer, as Buckner insisted? Or was it Frank Costello, the man for so long in the shadows who had the real connections, money, and power in the underworld? Round two might give the world the answer.

CHAPTER EIGHT
"PERSONALLY, I GOT DRUNK"

THE ORIGINAL THEORY OF THE PROSECUTION in the Costello-Dwyer conspiracy was that the defendants represented a combination of two groups working together closely. Dwyer led the one cabal while Costello and his brother Edward, along with the Kelly brothers (also named Ed and Frank) were in charge of a group of liquor purchasers. It was Frank Kelly who had chartered a ship that he moored off Long Island and first met Frank Costello in 1925 during a meeting in Montauk. When Kelly, Costello, and another man named Philip Coffey worked on a shipment of liquor from Kelly's schooner, payments for the service were arranged at Costello's Lexington Avenue offices. Costello was the consummate payoff artist, also helping to bribe government agents and officials, as well as police officers.

"Frank knew that many of the facts and witnesses the government would present against Dwyer actually had to do with him," his attorney George Wolf recalled later.

While Dwyer and Corson were convicted, the government saw from the acquittals of the other six defendants that their case had some big problems. So, with another big trial looming, against Costello, the Manhattan U.S. Attorney's office decided to simplify things. On December 3, 1926, prosecutors filed a request that charges against many of the other defendants indicted in 1925 be dropped. Top prosecutor Buckner wrote, "I do not believe that there is sufficient evidence to secure a conviction" against twenty-three men, including Costello's brother-in-law Jerome Geigerman and C. Paul Chartier, the Canadian man who was Costello's contact for liquor. Buckner didn't spell out the reasons why the charges should be dumped but it is likely that he sensed the anti-government feelings fomented by Bielaski's undercover tactics which welled up in the Dwyer trial and decided to cut his losses.

The trial of Frank and Edward Costello and sixteen others went off on January 3, 1927, before Judge Francis A. Winslow, a jurist who would have his own share of controversies. From the very start, it was clear that Costello was going to bring up the issue of Bruce Bielaski and his undercover tactics. Costello's attorney asked each prospective juror if they knew Bielaski or if they had any connections to the Anti-Saloon League or other groups promoting what he called "a national drought." That was an obvious tactic to weed out jurors who would be biased against bootlegging or hated the notion of consumption of alcohol.

Edward Costello, older than Frank by about ten years, was not the more sophisticated of the brothers. While Frank liked to be the businessman and hang around nightclubs and speakeasies, Edward was more blue-collar. He had started a trucking company in Astoria with his father and promptly got into trouble during Prohibition. At a private garage on Shore Boulevard in Astoria, Edward kept barrels of alcohol that had come from Dwyer's operation. It wasn't the most serious of cases but in October 1926, just before going on trial with his brother, Edward had to go before a judge to explain how he wound up with the three barrels. Edward at first said that the alcohol was really ginger and peppermint, which his son had contracted to haul. Okay, said the judge, bring your son to court so we can hear it from him. Hearing that, Edward decided then to plead guilty and paid a $50 fine.

Prosecutors were certain that Edward Costello's guilty plea in the barrel case was so incriminating that he would be convicted in the larger conspiracy trial with his brother and the Kelly brothers. The sneaky undercover agent working for Bielaski would be able to trace the load to Dwyer's "rum-ring stock," as the government called it. It also wasn't the first time Edward had been compromised. About four years earlier he admitted that he did some deals with Manny Kessler, the older bootlegging king.

If the Costello brothers were the main target in the government's case, it didn't seem like it from the first bits of testimony from government witnesses. It would take two days for the government to present evidence against the Costellos. But in the meantime, the public got an interesting look at how the brothers operated through their co-conspirators. The first witness, William R. Newman of Freeport, Long Island, related how he was recruited by Ed Kelly in 1924 to be his agent responsible for liquor cargo on several ships operating between Canada and Long Island.

Known as a "supercargo" or agent of the owner of the cargo, Newman testified about his various adventures—as well as misadventures—plying the ocean between Canada and the U.S. In one trip, the schooner *Vincent White* got lost on its way to the Rum Row staging area. This was when, according to Newman, he was taken to Curtiss Field, near Mineola, and then flown out in a seaplane, eventually finding the ship and going aboard with a list of dollar bills from the "home office," meaning Frank Costello's suite on Lexington Avenue. This was when the smaller pickup boats coming by would show a dollar bill and if it matched the serial numbers on the list then the liquor could be off-loaded to go ashore, said Newman.

As knowledgeable and convincing a witness as Newman may have been in the beginning, he also spelled trouble for the prosecution. From his spies in the courtroom during the Dwyer case, Costello knew about the undercover operation of Bielaski and the distaste his operation caused with the public. Newman admitted he had been working for Bielaski and did so for mercenary reasons. Newman said he felt cheated by the Kelly brothers over wages and decided then and there to earn money by working undercover for Bielaski.

"How much money did you get from Bielaski for being a spy?" Costello's attorney Nathan Burkan asked Newman.

"I received $250 a month," was Newman's reply, explaining that the number dropped to $125 when Washington cut Bielaski's appropriations.

Showing how vindictive he could be, Newman admitted that after his argument with the Kellys over wages he wrote a letter to General Lincoln C. Andrews, the Treasury Department's chief of Prohibition Enforcement. In a major show of *chutzpah,* Newman said he told Andrews of his predicament and asked for a job working for the government. He was then passed on to Bielaski who hired him.

Newman was a hired hand of the Costello ring. Another witness, William R. Hughes, had been a machinist on Coast Guard vessel 126. The government boat was like a taxi service for the bootleggers, said Hughes. No. 126 ran liquor ashore from Rum Row, including from the *Vincent White* and helped out skippers who were off-course or lost in fog. The Coast Guardsmen took money and whiskey for their services and often got stone-cold drunk while on duty. When the former captain of vessel 126, a fellow named Nicholas Brown, was asked on the witness stand what he remembered about a case of whisky given to his crew from a smuggling ship, he was at a loss.

"I don't know what happened to the rest of the men; personally, I got drunk," said Brown.

Costello knew that the Bielaski connection to the witnesses was a key to the defense. Hughes then added to the furor when he admitted that he pled guilty to his personal corruption in the case and had also gone over to work for the Prohibition forces, although not for Bielaski personally. But one witness who really caused an uproar was Nicholas Brown, the often-drunk captain of CG 126. Brown was arrested with the Costellos a year earlier, released on bond, and then suddenly taken back into custody by the Coast Guard. He then got a taste of brutal maritime justice.

Brown recalled being home when suddenly Bielaski's agents seized him and took him aboard the Coast Guard vessel *Seneca.* Once on board, Brown said he and three other former Coast Guardsmen were placed in irons and confined to the vessel's brig as it went out to sea for a week. The *Seneca* was a real rat trap for the confined men.

"The place was like a mad house," said Brown. "I was almost out

of my head. We were shackled with double irons and kept in con-
finement for the whole week. The hatches were battened down and
the air was foul. They fed us rotten meat and gave us rotten water."

The conditions Brown described were basically torture, which is
how the New York tabloids described it. He couldn't talk to the
other men and when Bielaski sent a radio message to the *Seneca*
asking if Brown wanted to confess, he said he did.

The *Seneca* pulled into the Battery in lower Manhattan, where
Bielaski had offices. Bielaski asked Brown if he wanted to plead
guilty and of course he said he would. Suddenly, things got better
for the sailor.

"You got different treatment after you left Bielaski's place?"
Burkan asked him.

"Sure, I went home to Boston after that," Brown answered.

The tabloids had a field day with the story, blaring that Brown
had been "tortured" by Bielaski and his men. Clearly, Brown had
been coerced into cooperating by the rough treatment he had received in the brig of the *Seneca*. This testimony played right into the
defense strategy of trying to undermine the government's case by
showing inhumane tactics in the effort to convict Costello and the
others.

Aside from being corrupt and drunk most days while aboard ship,
Brown seemed to be the conduit for payoffs between Costello's men
and some higher-ups in the Coast Guard. He testified that he received just over $1,000 from Phil Coffey, who was allegedly one of
Costello's paymasters, to bribe Samuel Briggs, one of the executive
officers of the Coast Guard working out of the New London, Connecticut, office. Called to testify, Briggs admitted that he took the
money but turned it over to his superior officer and Bielaski. There
had also even been a more explosive allegation of bribery when
Brown claimed in his testimony that General Andrews, the assistant
secretary of the Treasury, was in on the scheme, taking $2,000 a
week from liquor cargo carried on the schooner *Athena*. Contacted
by journalists after the allegation was made, Andrews scoffed at the
notion and said the only contact with the gang was to put them all in
jail.

Through the first few days of testimony, there was clear evidence that the Costello gang had been paying off the Coast Guard to protect its rum running. Coast Guard vessels protected the smuggling ships, tipped off the smugglers about the routes of government patrols, and acted as nautical convoys that landed the booze all over Long Island. The Coast Guard may have had a flotilla of destroyers to beef up its efforts against the bootleggers but the service seemed to be riddled with corruption at the lower levels, which protected the gangs. But the main piece of evidence that had been missing in the trial was a tangible connection to Frank and Edward Costello. That all changed on January 11 when rum runner Frederick Pitts took the witness stand.

A marine engineer, Pitts admitted that he threatened to turn in Frank Costello if he didn't get over $2,000 in back pay. Pitts said that Costello had twice employed him to run the engines on one of the smuggling ships, the *California.* The pay was to be $75 a week with an additional $100 for each trip Pitts made out to Rum Row. But payment became an issue and Pitts said he gave Costello a week to pay him $2,000 he was owed or that he would turn him in to authorities. The threat against Costello wasn't the smartest thing Pitts could have done, given Frank's connections to the Italian underworld. But Pitts justified his action by explaining that he was on the brink of going to jail because he had deserted his wife. Pitts had also been arrested earlier in the bootlegging case so he faced prison if the federal government prosecuted him. Costello apparently called Pitts's bluff, and the engineer, in desperation, said he decided to become an informer for Bielaksi for the princely sum of $5 a day.

But Pitts also admitted he was playing both ends against each other. He said that he offered not to testify against Costello if he was paid $4,000—double what he said was owed to him in back wages.

"So," Burkan asked on cross-examination, "you offered to sell out Bielaski for $4,800?"

"Well, if you want to put it that way, it's true," said Pitts.

Nevertheless, the evidence presented by the government showed how extensive the criminal operation had been and how brazenly

Costello and the others had used payoffs to assure that millions of dollars in bootlegged liquor reached American shores.

"Frank was a worried man," George Wolf remembered later about the impact of all the testimony. "The prosecution had uncovered *everything*. All he had going for him was the weakness he had discovered in the government's case. On cross-examination, each of the government witnesses was asked whether he was now—or had been—paid as an undercover agent by the Treasury Department's Bielaski. All but one were forced to admit it was so."

If Frank Costello was worried, the same couldn't be said about his brother Edward. It was clear from Edward's past dealings that he had trucked liquor and alcohol for various bootlegging operations. He had been involved. The question was how much new evidence came up at the trial to show Edward was guilty of being part of his brother's conspiracy. The answer was not very much. Judge Winslow decided that the government had not proven Edward was involved and dropped him from the case. Out of the eighteen defendants who started the trial, four including Edward had been dropped, two others had the indictment dismissed, and another became so ill that Winslow ordered a mistrial. In total, seven defendants walked away. Things weren't looking good for the government.

It was clear that the tactics of Bielaski had been a big problem for the government in Costello's trial, and his defense attorneys exploited that when it came time for final summations. Defense attorney Nathan Burkan hit on Bielaski's secret operation, calling it an insidious tactic that went against the grain of fair play and was un-American. The witnesses in the case were "rats . . . pirates, hijackers, crooks and bribe-takers," Burkan told the jurors. Bielaski himself was a "mysterious and invisibile power," the lawyer insisted. Of course, years later the kinds of tactics Bielaski used—paid informants, plea bargaining, even coercion to get cooperation from witnesses—became an acceptable part of law enforcement operations. But this was the Roaring Twenties and the sensibilities of the public, and many in politics, went against this kind of secret stuff.

The jury verdict was another stunner. The panel acquitted eight of the defendants who were viewed as minor players. The jury then couldn't agree unanimously on Frank Costello, the Kelly brothers and three others, all considered to be principals in the bootlegging operation. Costello and the other main defendants received a mistrial, and angry prosecutors said they would be retried.

But based on what one juror told Burkan, the government really had to think twice about taking another shot at Costello and the others. The juror told the lawyer he would "hold out to doomsday rather than convict anyone on the testimony of such witnesses." Years later, Costello would tell his close friend George Wolf that the jury was split 11 to 1 for conviction but that he "owned" the one holdout. But Costello was clearly lying about his reach and corrupt influence. Jurors were polled after the trial by Judge Winslow and they said they never considered convicting any of those who were acquitted. As to Costello and the others, the first ballot had shown a vote of 9 to 6 for conviction and the final poll was evenly split at 6 to 6. Any verdict had to be unanimous, and Costello had dodged a bullet by a wide margin. Winslow reduced his bail to $10,000 from $20,000 while the Kellys' was cut to $5,000 from $10,000. A retrial never happened, and at some point the bails were cleared.

After the verdict, the press beat up the government. *The Daily News* said the case had been a "Black Eye" for the government and "another black eye for Volsteadism generally," referring to the Volstead Act. Bielaski got a "sock in the eye," the paper said in its editorial.

Even *The New York Times* reported that the Costello case was causing murmurings in the Department of Justice about Bielaski's undercover tactics. Out of ninety-four men indicted as major bootleggers in recent cases, there had only been two convictions— Dwyer and Corson. While prosecutors wouldn't comment, the *Times* reported that the outcome was seen as a "severe blow to the Government's methods of prosecuting liquor conspiracy cases."

Costello was able to repair to his old haunts like the 21 Club to celebrate what really was a victory. He faced a possible retrial but as would be discovered decades later, the government's file in his case somehow got lost and he would never have to go to court for boot-legging again. But Bielaski would soon face more problems of his own making. It had come out during the Costello and Dwyer trials that Bielaski's office had actually set up an undercover speakeasy in Manhattan known as the Bridge Whist Club. While such clandestine operations would become standard operations decades later with police, in this era the public and politicians were aghast. One New York member of Congress, Fiorello La Guardia, was one of the most vocal critics of Bielaski and demanded that federal prosecutors investigate the club and find out how much government money had been spent.

During a court hearing over a dispute about the lease at the Bridge Whist Club, which was located at 14 East Forty-fourth Street, Bielaski testified that the renting of the location was approved at the highest levels of the Treasury Department and that he hired an old colleague to run the place as a speakeasy. In the days before sophisticated electronic surveillance, Bielaski used Dictaphones planted in the club to record conversations, without the speakers knowing. In one case, noted Bielaski, the device picked up a man trying to bribe a government agent. The club, he insisted, was vital to the government's effort to go after the bootleggers. The drinks sold there had some of the best liquor and the Bridge Whist gained a reputation of having great drinks for fifty cents, undercutting some of the other speakeasies.

"When I began my work here," Bielaski said, "Prohibition had been a law for five years. During that entire period no real effort had been made by any Attorney General to bring to the bar the large operators. The rum-runners and bootleggers had grown so bold and confident that they had been giving out interviews which were published in the newspapers, and were also writing articles for magazines concerning their operations."

The club, Bielaski insisted, helped uncover evidence about most of the big liquor syndicates. But he admitted that he would never again use such a business in an investigation. La Guardia was unforgiving in his criticism and pointed to the nearly $45,000 spent by the government in the speakeasy operation, including vests for the waiters and alpaca coats for the bartenders purchased from Brooks Brothers, as well as $95 spent for engraving club membership cards. It was all a misuse of government funds, La Guardia complained, insisting that the $4,000 paid to Bielaski was improper.

Given how La Guardia would years later as mayor of New York City go after Frank Costello's various mob operations, his flailing of Bielaski and the government for the Prohibition prosecutions is laced with irony. Costello was able to avoid conviction, in part because of the public loathing of the government tactics in his case. But Bielaksi and prosecutor Buckner were the ones who had their wings clipped. In March 1927, orders came down from Washington that Buckner's Prohibition enforcement unit was being disbanded. Assistant U.S. attorneys, clerks, office boys, stenographers, and Prohibition agents were all sacked or reassigned. When the low-level women stenographers and typists heard the news they were in tears. The order was a galling humiliation for Buckner and Bielaski. Although he couldn't have planned things that way, Costello had bested his foes.

With the Prohibition unit closing, Bielaski headed for the door. By March 26, 1927, the word was out that he was quitting to go back to his private law practice. He told *The Sun* newspaper, "I am getting tired of it." But Bielaski's tactics were based on the fact that many of the big bootleggers, Costello included, got to be very tight-fisted with money. As Bielaski would later tell reporters, once the bootleggers got arrested and had to hire lawyers they became stingy and didn't pay their employees. This caused a great deal of resentment among the lowly workers who he said were broke and with empty stomachs. At least some of the men became vulnerable to recruitment by Bielaski. As would be shown decades later in some major Mafia trials, gangsters who cheated their underlings risked having them turn on them and become cooperating witnesses. It seems Bielaski was just ahead of his time.

After beating back the government in court, Costello could relax a bit when he found the time. Sure, he hit the speakeasies and nightclubs in Manhattan. But being a southern Italian and coming from an extended family that had many members in New York City, Costello had another outlet for socializing. His first cousin Domenico Castiglia, the one of Polly the parrot fame, purchased land in Westport, Connecticut, and built an imposing stone house with thick walls on a large slice of land not far from Long Island Sound. The house on Lyons Plains Road had a quarter-mile-long circular driveway and concrete deck. Domenico's business in New York City had been a partnership with a friend, Jack Delarmy, in which they produced ostrich plumes, a fashionable item of the day. Delarmy actually had first acquired a house in Westport and it was through that connection that Domenico decided to build.

Being a member of the Castiglia clan, Frank and Loretta Costello would visit the stone house property often, making the trip in a caravan of vehicles. Frank Aloise, a cousin, would drive the Costellos. After Domenico left the ostrich-plume partnership, he tried his hand at farming on the property and when that didn't prove very profitable started bussing in boarders from the city to make extra money when the egg production fell short. Noel Castiglia, Domenico's grandson, remembered Costello, his wife, and his business associates coming to the farm often, although never by bus.

"There was a fresh water river and a swimming hole on the property and Compo Beach, located on Long Island Sound, was only a few miles away," recalled Noel. "The food at the replica of an Italian country cottage was always fresh and local."

Among those visiting was Charles Luciano, Costello's immediate boss in the Italian mob. With many visitors already at the stone house, Luciano would stay at the nearby home of the Cognato family. A surviving group photograph from the period showed Luciano, dressed in a suit and tie, smiling and sitting on the front steps of the house, surrounded by young Cognato children. The photo had to have been taken prior to Luciano being sent to prison in 1936.

Yet, Luciano's presence made at least some in the Cognato family uncomfortable at times. In one anecdote recounted to the author by Tom Cognato, whose parents owned the house, Luciano noticed one of the Cognato girls sitting with a doll on the lawn. The girl was Lillian, who would eventually grow up to become Cognato's mother. Luciano approached her and asked if that was the only doll Lillian had and she told him it was. Luciano, so the story goes, whipped out a $20 bill and told Lillian to have her mother buy her a new doll. However, Lillian's mother was well aware of how Luciano made his money and told her to give it back. No doubt miffed at the slight, but unwilling to do anything more, Luciano took the money back, lit a match and burned the bill.

"If Lillian can't have, nobody gets it," Luciano said as he burned the cash, according to Cognato.

The money episode aside, Costello, Luciano, and the other visitors found the farm a welcome respite from the troubles and constant dangers of life in Manhattan. At least in Costello's case he visited from the 1920s to the mid-1930s, said Noel Castiglia, who also remembered the wine there to be home made and copious. The gatherings would be punctuated by rounds of the games bocce, badminton, and horseshoes. There was also music. Another pastime for the adults, including Costello and Luciano, was the drinking game fittingly known as "Boss and Under Boss" or in Italian as "Passatella." Basically, the game called for drinkers, who would designate a "boss" and "underboss" who controlled when other participants, known as equals, could drink shots of liquor or gulp wine. Basically, the game led to group inebriation and sometimes fights, although it is doubtful anybody took a swing at Luciano or Costello.

The results of Costello's trial were a strong indication of just how much public sentiment was against Prohibition and how flagrant was the disregard of the law. Proponents of a dry country may have insisted that the nation's productivity and state of law and order had improved with the ban on liquor. But the situation in New York City and elsewhere showed how crime and corruption had increased in certain areas with bootlegging. The proliferation of speakeasies, said by some estimates to number over 20,000 to 30,000 in the city, showed that the law was being disobeyed quite openly. At the Waldorf-Astoria, where Costello lunched and held court, diners at a banquet heard a vice president of the New York Central Railroad—in the presence of the former mayor and police commissioner—blast Prohibition as "the most indefensible law ever written on our state books. It has resulted in a carnival of murder, a carnival of crime." With that Costello and his cronies had to gleefully agree.

CHAPTER NINE
THE GREAT BLOODLETTING

WITH COSTELLO DODGING THE BULLET and his government tormentors humiliated, bootlegging merrily continued in New York City. That didn't mean that the federal government gave up totally. New York State under a local law tried to enforce the dry concept and cops still went about shutting and padlocking speakeasies. But Prohibition had made Costello and many other gangsters wealthy beyond their dreams. Italian, Jewish, and Irish mobsters still raked in the money. They just needed to be more careful.

Costello made millions with his liquor operation, although one would be hard pressed to find a piece of paper that listed his assets. Costello didn't keep bank accounts or checking accounts; his wife Loretta did for a while in this period. He dealt in cash and other physical assets. He held nothing in his name, barely. One indication of how much money he had in this period can be seen indirectly through William Dwyer, his partner in crime. Having beaten Dwyer in court, the federal government went after him for back taxes, which revenue agents said he owed from the tens of millions of dollars he made in bootlegging. After years of court battles, the government finally won a judgment for $3.7 million in back taxes and penalties against Dwyer, who despite his sports teams and racetrack holdings would eventually die a poor man. The government said the money was owed for illicit income he received going back to 1922, just before he is believed to have teamed up with Costello.

Dwyer should have taken a lesson from Costello about banks. Dwyer's problem in the tax case was that he kept a lot of his cash in banks but brazenly reported to the IRS a pittance in income. There was a total of $6.5 million found by the IRS in Dwyer's bank accounts, an amount that today would be worth $90.5 million accounting for inflation. In 1923 alone, the year Dwyer is believed to have begun doing business with Costello, he reported a gross income of $6,824 but at the same time banked about $2 million or $28.5 million in today's money. In 1924, Dwyer showed income of $11,000 while banking $1.5 million or over $21 million in 2017 money. One can only guess how much Costello was pulling in during those years, but it had to be as much or greater.

With so much money being made in bootlegging, the mob was awash in cash—and that made for trouble. The Italian gangsters were in a state of continual strife. By 1927, one of the bosses vying for control was Joseph Masseria in New York. Masseria had risen to a position of power among the Italians, and with the rise of Prohibition started to partake of the money that could be made. His loyal lieutenants included Lucky Luciano, with whom Costello worked closely. The old Morello gang was still active but considerably weakened and subservient to Masseria. Another boss, Salvatore D'Aquila, split off from the Morellos and had started his own sphere of influence.

Death was a constant among the Italian mobsters. Masseria dodged some assassination plots believed to have been instigated by a rival bootlegger Umberto Valenti. When the time came, Luciano is said to have shot Valenti dead outside an Italian Restaurant on the Lower East Side. Then in October 1928, D'Aquila, who police described as a Bronx businessman with a record as a swindler, was gunned down in Manhattan as he was visiting his cardiologist. His wife and four daughters watched as he was shot dead. With D'Aquila's death, Masseria was the top Italian boss in Manhattan. Among his chief lieutenants was Luciano, assisted by Costello, and William Moretti, who happened to be Costello's cousin. Rounding out the cadre was another Italian immigrant named Joseph Adonis, whose real name was Joseph Doto, and Vito Genovese, another Sicilian transplant.

Over in Brooklyn, bootlegging was also the racket of choice, and nobody did it better than Frankie Yale and Salvatore Maranzano, a relative new comer from Sicily. With his good looks and fearsome temper, Yale was a young force to be reckoned with. Known also by his Italian surname of "Ioele," Yale had his hand in a number of mob enterprises. He organized the ice merchants—this was in the days before refrigeration—into a cartel and kept unions out of the laundry business. He also developed a brand of cigars known as "Frankie Yales" and suggested in his persuasive way that stores sell them. Yale also owned a funeral parlor; given the death rate among bootleggers that wasn't a bad investment either.

Yale started a saloon and restaurant in Coney Island, close to the surf and sand, where he employed a jolly young waiter and gangster known as Alphonse Capone, on a referral from a courtly old gangster named Johnny Torrio. The Harvard Inn had nothing to do with the university but everything to do with gangster nightlife at the time. There were plenty of fights and shootings in the vicinity of the club.

Eventually, Capone went to Chicago where he squeezed out his mentor Torrio—who narrowly escaped an assassination attempt—and became the top bootlegger in the region. Yale and Capone had worked together well in the liquor racket. Yale imported the whiskey and shipped it to Capone's numerous speakeasies in Chicago, where he had additional smuggling operations bringing booze down from Canada. When it became necessary, Yale and Capone finished off an Irish gang led by Richard "Peg Leg" Lonergan with an ambush in a Brooklyn social club Christmas Night in 1925. But among gangsters, things never stayed peaceful, particularly with Capone who began to have suspicions about his old friend Yale.

It was July 1, 1928, a Sunday morning, when Frankie Yale was driving a new Lincoln car with running boards in the Fort Hamilton section of Brooklyn when he sensed something was wrong. There was another vehicle to his rear with four men inside. Having already survived other hit attempts against him, Yale made a quick turn and drove down Forty-fourth Street. Yale was speeding and so was the pursuing vehicle. A shotgun blast from the other car tore into Yale, killing him. His vehicle, still in motion, traveled a short distance and then came to rest in the front yard of Number 932 where a bar mitzvah party was going on. The large vehicle took out some shrubs in the yard and crumbled some masonry by the front steps.

The next morning, New York newspapers showed the crime-scene photographs of Yale's body outside the vehicle, a cop standing guard. There had been other mob killings over the years but none as sensational of late than that of the murder of Yale. His funeral was grand, and he was buried in a $15,000 silver-colored casket and the funeral procession was watched by an estimated 100,000 spectators. Two women showed up at the grave in Holy Cross Cemetery claiming to be Yale's wife. One was his official spouse Mary with whom he had two children, and the other was an attractive brunette identified in the newspapers as Luceida Gullioti. Both women would fight over Yale's property. But police were more concerned about finding out who had killed him.

The immediate suspicion fell on Capone. The Chicago crime boss had suspected Yale was stealing loads of whiskey, and Capone was the likely suspect. In fact, since Capone had taken over the rackets in the Windy City from Torrio he was suspected of orchestrating a number of murders of his rivals. There was the killing of Irish gangster Dean O'Banion and the brutal beating to death of three Sicilians at the Hawthorne Inn located in the town of Cicero. Then there was the infamous slayings of a group of mob associates in a garage on St. Valentine's Day. Killings followed in Capone's wake wherever he went, which prompted J. Edgar Hoover, the head of the FBI, to label him public enemy No. 1. Back in New York, the Italian gangsters believed the bloodshed in Chicago had the potential to destabilize things and turn the public against all the bootleggers. That could really ruin business. The New York mob tried to talk sense into Capone. Costello always believed that there was enough bootlegging to go around for everybody.

"We sent some of our boys out to talk to Al in a nice way," Costello told Wolf. "He chased them. So we waited."

By mid-1929, Luciano, who was chief lieutenant for Masseria, put together a group of gangster-bootleggers who historian Nelson Johnson in his book *Boardwalk Empire* called the "Seven Group." There were a few Jews—Lansky, Siegel, Longie Zwillman, and Harry "Nig" Rosen. And Italians—Willie Moretti, Joe Adonis, and of course Luciano. Added to the mix was Nucky Johnson, the boss of Atlantic City, New Jersey. Strictly speaking, there were more than seven names, but that didn't really matter. As author Johnson would, note the alliance controlled a great deal of the bootlegging, "buying, selling, distilling, shipping and protecting twenty-two different mobs from Maine to Florida and west to the Mississippi River."

Luciano, who saw the benefits of organization and cooperation among the various bootleggers, decided to pull together a convention of all the different mobs to talk about business, which at that point was still a money-maker no matter what the government did. But the violence and killing had to be stopped. The Seven Group, plus others, agreed to come to Atlantic City, Nucky Johnson's fiefdom, and try to hash things out.

The meeting of May 13-16, 1929, goes down in Mafia lore as one of the first big national conclaves of gangsters. Johnson was the host and originally wanted everyone to stay at the exclusive Breakers Hotel. But the Breakers catered to upper-crust white Anglo-Saxons, not the likes of Capone and Jews like Rosen, said historian Johnson. The Breakers wouldn't take the guests and Luciano recalled later that his friend Nucky had to do some fast stepping to avoid a disaster.

"Nucky and Al had it out right there in the open," Luciano recalled in his autobiography. "I think you could've heard them in Philadelphia, and there wasn't a decent word passed between 'em. Johnson had a rep for four-letter words that wasn't even invented, and Capone is screamin' at him that he had made bad arrangements."

Finally, all the mobsters took off for the President Hotel which was more accommodating. With everyone settled, Nucky Johnson hosted a party which lasted a day. Then, when they had the time the delegates walked out to the beach where, as was reported, "they took off their shoes and socks, rolled their pant legs to their knees, and strolled along the water's edge discussing their business in complete privacy."

The big meeting took place in a large room. The New York group was led by Luciano, Costello and Torrio, At the other end of the large conference table was the Chicago delegation lorded over by Capone, his trusted enforcer Frank Nitti and a bodyguard named Frank Rio. Torrio ran the meeting and said all of the strife had to stop. Costello was introduced and according to Wolf's account took over the meeting.

"The reason we got to organize is that we got to put ourselves on a business basis," said Costello. "That is what we are in, a business. We got to stop the kind of things that's going on in Chicago right now.

"You guys are shooting at each in the street and innocent people are getting killed and they're starting to squawk," Costello continued. "If they squawk loud enough the feds get off their tails and start cracking down. And you know what that means. We got a thing where millions of dollars can be made just in getting people what they want. When I was on trial three years ago on the whiskey deal, all the people were behind me. And I was able to stay in business."

As he told it to Wolf years later, Costello said he insisted to his gangster pals that if they make people afraid of them then the government would start cracking down. It was a very brassy move by Costello, considering Capone's volatility and that the boss of Chicago must have felt singled out. But Costello had a plan, which he wanted Capone to consider in order to stop the bloodshed.

Torrio then, nudged by Costello at their end of the table, got up and told Capone the plan: He had to go to jail. Capone was perplexed, said Wolf.

"To jail. We have to smooth this thing over right now," said Torrio, according to Wolf. "You have to go back to Chicago after that Valentine Day shoot-out and O'Banion's boys will be at war, the heat will go higher. We think you need a vacation, Al."

Capone thought Torrio was joking. But Costello emphasized that nobody was kidding around.

"This ain't a joke, Al," said Costello, as Wolf recalled. "We got too much invested for you to ruin the gravy train. Make it easy on yourself. Think of a way. But we need you off at 'college' until things cool down."

Capone was angry. But he knew that the entire group was arrayed against him. He left the meeting. Later, he told police that he just effected a truce agreement which, as one newspaper account portrayed it was to "restore peace and cooperation in the ranks of Chicago's beer syndicates." He and Bugs Moran, the Northside Chicago gang leader who lost seven men in the St. Valentine's Day Massacre, had signed "on the dotted line" to make peace.

But just hours after the conference ended, Capone managed to do what Torrio and Costello asked him to do—he got arrested. The bust was for carrying a concealed deadly weapon as Capone was entering a theatre in Philadelphia early in the evening of May 16. Capone made no secret of his presence in the city and as he and Frank Cline exited the cinema, they were approached by police detectives. Things couldn't have gone down easier.

"Here's my gun," Capone said as he handed off a blunt-nosed .38 caliber pistol. Cline did the same, and both men were taken to appear before a magistrate, who set bail at $35,000. The next morning, May 17, Capone and Cline appeared in court and given time to confer with their lawyers. At noon, instead of going to trial, Capone and Cline pled guilty to the weapons charges.

Before hearing his sentence, Capone bantered with newspapermen and spectators in the courtroom, pointing out that the big diamond ring he was wearing was 11.5 carats and worth about $50,000. The boss of Chicago crime seemed to be in a good mood.

Earlier, Capone had spoken with a police official and told him about his career in the rackets and how disillusioned he had become of the gangster life. Capone even said he was "retired" and living off his money.

"I went into the racket in Chicago four and a half years ago. During the last two years I've been trying to get out," said Capone. "But once you are in the racket you're always in it, it seems. The parasites trail you, begging you for favors and for money."

"I have a wife and an 11-year-old boy I idolize, and a beautiful home at Palm Island, Florida," Capone continued. "If I could go there and forget it all, I would be the happiest man in the world. I want peace and I am willing to live and let live. I'm tired of gang murders and gang shootings."

In fact, Capone confirmed for the police that the reason he was in Atlantic City was to forge a peace pact between himself and a warring faction led by Moran, although he apparently didn't name all the other gangsters like Costello and Torrio who forced him to bury the hatchet. Capone contended he had come out all right in the bloodshed but that the constant fighting was "an awful life to live."

"You fear death every moment and worse than death, you fear the rats of the game, who would run around and tell the police if you didn't constantly satisfy them with money and favors," added Capone.

Capone and Cline were each sentenced to one year in prison, the maximum term. Capone's lawyer said after sentencing that any report that his client had invited arrest to protect himself was false. Nevertheless, back in Chicago the word on the street was that the gangster world was thanking Philadelphia and was relieved that Capone and Moran had come to an agreement. There were also rumors that Johnny Torrio, the elderly man who Capone had once chased from Chicago, would assume leadership of some of the city's mob.

The deal Costello had helped to broker would stabilize things in Chicago for a while, at least for as long as Capone was in jail. Back in New York, the situation was still volatile. Masseria, the man to whom Costello owed some allegiance but who wasn't invited to the Atlantic City meeting, was feeling threatened in his position and was preparing to lash out against his growing list of enemies.

Masseria had a significant group of Italian men under his command: Luciano, Costello, Moretti, Genovese and Adonis. Also nominally in alliance with Masseria was Capone, although through May

1930 he was cooling his heels and doing gardening in a Pennsylvania jail for the weapons charge. The bootlegging money was what drove the group, and there was still plenty of it coming into the coffers.

Masseria's men were largely immigrants from the area around Naples and parts of the southern Italian mainland. Another faction, composed mainly of Sicilians was led by Salvatore Maranzano and included men such as Thomas Lucchese, Joseph Bonanno, Joseph Profaci, Joseph Valachi and others, many of whom hailed from the area around Castellammare del Golfo, a key port city in Sicily. Maranzano himself looked like a banker, unlike the stout Masseria who looked more like a laborer. From his Brooklyn base, Maranzano and his men ran their own bootlegging operation.

Frank Costello and Johnny Torrio may have done a real service by getting the Capone situation all straightened out. But back in New York, by 1930 the Neapolitans under Masseria and the Castellammarese with Maranzano were approaching the boiling point. Masseria struck first against one of his own when he ordered the slaying on February 26, 1930, of Gaetano "Tommy" Reina, an ice distributor in the Bronx. Like Frankie Yale, Reina had run an ice-distributing cartel. A cartel is a form of restraint of trade that carved up the territory for ice distribution and kept prices high. Masseria apparently wanted Reina to give up some of his profits. Reina resisted and was assassinated.

The murder of Reina, according to fabled Mafia informant Joseph Valachi, who was married to the slain man's daughter, caused some of his men to shift allegiance to Maranzano, who was plotting major moves against Masseria. It was a time when the factions "went to the mattress," hiding out in secret locations, armed and wary about where they went. The killings continued.

As he later confided to Wolf, Costello thought the war started by Masseria was pointless. The dangers forced him to stay away from his office in Manhattan, which was still running his bootlegging operations. Luciano was kind of a favorite son of Masseria, and since Costello was close to Luciano he had a kind of favored status as well. But in the volatile world of the mob you could be a favorite one moment and then on the outs the next. Masseria was on a course of war, and the situation was very unstable. As Valachi remembered and told Peter Maas in *The Valachi Papers,* the fighting was taking its toll on Masseria.

"The tide of battle swelled in Maranzano's favor. There had been so many defections to him, like that of Carlo Gambino, that his forces actually outnumbered the enemy," said Maas. "Moreover, for those who still sided with Masseria there was an increasing economic problem because of the struggle. Their well-fixed rackets were rapidly becoming a shambles."

Valachi may have overstated the financial impact on Masseria allies like Costello and Luciano from the fighting. But both Masseria allies saw that the situation was becoming more untenable. In a meeting on Broome Street in lower Manhattan, Costello told Wolf that he, Luciano, and Genovese decided that Masseria must be killed. Luciano came up with a plan.

Coney Island was a premier restaurant and fun location in the city, and on April 15, 1931, both Masseria and Luciano traveled there for lunch. Luciano suggested the Nuova Villa Tammora, a family-run place run by Gerardo Scarpato at 2715 West Fifteenth Street, a few blocks north of Surf Avenue. A total of four people were at Masseria's table at one point, and Scarpato's mother-in-law went out to get some fish to bring back for the luncheon.

The meal lasted until about 3:30 P.M. and by that time most of the other customers had left. Luciano suggested a game of cards to Masseria, and they started playing. At some point Luciano excused himself to go to the bathroom. When he left the room, two or three men—accounts vary as to how many—suddenly entered the Nuova Villa Tammora and started shooting at Masseria. About two dozen shots were fired, and five found their mark in Masseria's plump body. He had no chance and was dead at the scene.

Luciano exited the bathroom and called police and when the cops arrived they found Masseria sprawled on the floor. A news photograph showed a playing card in his dead hand but there was speculation that the shot was staged. In any case, Luciano bemoaned his boss's death to the officers, saying he couldn't figure out who would do such a thing. The gunmen had got away unscathed in a waiting car and were never caught. Various accounts later alleged the gunmen to be Joseph Stracci and Frank Livorsi, with Ciro Terranova, the old "Artichoke King" from the Morello gang, as the driver of the getaway car. Frank Costello may have known about what was going to happen but he was nowhere in the vicinity.

The immediate result of the killing of Masseria was that Maranzano was emboldened to be the top boss among the Italian gangsters in the city. Still, he had to be assured that others like Luciano and his money-making allies like Costello backed him. To cement his position, Maranzano called a number of meetings of gangsters, including one in Chicago. But the big one was in the Bronx, at a social hall on Washington Avenue in which many sent money to Maranzano as tribute. Valachi said that $9,000 came from Capone and $6,000 from Luciano, for a total of $115,000. There was never any mention of cash from Costello, but it is likely that he followed Luciano's lead and gave something.

The mob structure that emerged from the meeting was the Five Family organization, which has survived to this day in New York City. Costello's friend Luciano was given control of Masseria's old family. The other bosses were old Maranzano supporters: Tom Gagliano, Joseph Profaci, Joseph Bonanno, and Vincent Mangano. As far as Valachi could remember, there were only three underbosses who stood out: Luciano had Vito Genovese, Mangano had Albert Anastasia, and Thomas Lucchese was the right hand of Gagliano.

But while Maranzano said that things were going to be organized and that he was going to be the supreme boss "Boss of All Bosses" among the Italians, there was already trouble brewing. In a move spawned by Maranzano's paranoia, he wanted to kill many of the old Masseria allies: Costello, Luciano, Capone, Genovese, and Dutch Schultz. It was supposed to be a long list and apparently it wasn't a very well-kept secret.

Costello never liked Maranzano. He saw through his well-dressed façade and told Wolf that "a greaseball is a greaseball." Maranzano seemed to have a Julius Caesar complex and his plan to kill off Costello, Luciano, and the others was enough justification for them to take action to defend themselves. Since Luciano and Costello had close ties through bootlegging with the Jewish groups of Meyer Lansky and Longey Zwillman, they were able to draft them into helping with a preemptive strike against Maranzano.

On September 10, 1931, at about 2:00 P.M. a group of four men assembled by Lansky and dressed as cops entered the offices of Maranzano on the ninth floor of 230 Park Avenue. Maranzano heard the commotion and when he came out to investigate he saw the menacing armed team, which included Lansky men Red Levine and Bo Weinberg. Maranzano retreated to his office where he was stabbed and then shot four times in the head and chest. The gunmen fled and as they did so passed coming up the stairs a group led by Vincent Coll, a hired killer who was supposed to ambush Luciano and Genovese at a bogus meeting Maranzano called so that he could ambush the pair. Told to "beat it, the cops are on their way," Coll did what he was told and fled.

There were never any arrests made in the slaying of Maranzano. Luciano then emerged as the major Mafia leader in New York, having engineered two stunning coup d'etats by killing off two bosses. He kept the basic five-family structure and added positions of *consiglieri*, advisors to give sage advice to the bosses, and made sure the bosses or their designees would meet in a commission to settle disputes among the families and develop policies. Organized and with the bad blood from the Castellammarese war in the past, Luciano and the other bosses could concentrate on making money.

Costello was the man who could show everyone how to make money and to do it peacefully. His *modus operandi* was to work out disputes and come to accommodations, a method Luciano preferred. Costello was the diplomat, a mob minister without portfolio who didn't head any crime family but could get things done. He was the political animal who strived to build consensus so that everyone could make money. It would be an approach Costello would take time and time again as he cemented business deals—legal or illegal—all around the country. As his friend and attorney George Wolf would later say: "It was during this period that Frank earned the title 'Prime Minister of the Underworld,' a role which he liked and for which he was ideally suited. Let others become the boss of bosses. Frank would show the boys how to make money and how to stay out of jail, the two most important factors of underworld life, next to sheer survival."

CHAPTER TEN
"THE MOST MENACING EVIL"

AS THE 1930S GOT UNDERWAY, Frank Costello had been very lucky. He had dodged the bullet in the federal bootlegging case. Since he wasn't a shooter or a guy who needed to resort to violence, he survived the Castellammarese War by having the good fortune of having his friend Luciano come out on top. Costello was making money with bootlegging and started to plow his profits into legitimate businesses. There was a realty company in the Bronx, which built homes, and the Frank Costello Auto Company, also in the Bronx. Teaming up with old partner Harry Horowitz, the pair started a company that marketed chocolate-covered ice cream pops. Costello also put his money with other partners in a night club known as Club Rendezvous.

It made perfect sense for Costello to diversify because as the decade progressed it was becoming increasingly clear that Prohibition, the unwitting cash cow of the Mafia and organized crime generally, wasn't going to be around forever. Sentiment was growing that the dry laws should be abolished, and if that happened booze would again be legal and the mob would have to look for another way of making money.

With thousands of speakeasies in a place like New York City, clandestine breweries were springing up and rum runners were having a field day around the country. The public knew that Prohibition was a bust. But politicians need a commission or study group to show them the obvious, and in 1929 President Herbert Hoover established the Wickersham Commission to determine how Prohibition was impacting the country, particularly the criminal justice system. Chaired by former U.S. Attorney General George W. Wickersham, the eleven-person panel studied the situation for two years. In 1931, the panel issued a report the findings of which were certainly anticipated by Costello and the rest of the Mafia bootleggers, who could have saved the commission a lot of the time it spent trying to uncover the obvious.

The report concluded that the public, including some politicians and labor leaders, viewed Prohibition with disdain. Enforcement of the Volstead Act was next to impossible, with widespread corruption in law enforcement at every level. The commissioner still concluded that Prohibition should continue. But one member of the panel, Monte Lehman, decided in his own written opinion that the situation was hopeless: do away with the Eighteenth Amendment he said.

With the election of President Franklin Delano Roosevelt in 1932—something Costello helped bring about and will be dealt with a little later in this book—the anti-Prohibition sentiment gained traction. Soon after his election, Roosevelt revised the Volstead Act to allow the production of beer with 4 percent alcohol by volume, as well as certain wines. Prohibition was hemorrhaging to death from the proverbial thousand cuts. Then on December 5, 1933, with Utah ratifying the Twenty-first Amendment, which repealed the Eighteenth Amendment, Prohibition ended on the federal level.

The end of the national experiment in temperance was a time of great rejoicing in New York City. But among the gangsters like Costello, it was also a time where they knew they had to start looking at other ways of making money. Bootlegging had made them rich beyond their earliest dreams. Costello would likely have been mired in a life of street extortion, theft, and scams had he not started moving liquor. But to sustain that income flow, he and people like Luciano, Genovese, veteran gangster Owney Madden, Schultz, and Lansky needed to look to other rackets—or go straight, which Costello was trying to do with other businesses.

For Costello, the new frontier was a variation on the old punchboard business he had worked on with Horowitz in the early 1920s. By 1930, the new device Costello turned to was the slot machine, the proverbial one-armed bandit where a patron inserted a coin, or a metal slug bought from a vendor, and tried his or her luck. Unlike what the public would see later in Las Vegas and other gambling meccas where somebody could win money, the patron would either be unlucky and throw away money or receive a token prize of nominal worth. Costello's idea was to have the machines dispense candy mints or slugs that could be redeemed for money from the store owner where the machine was situated.

Costello made deals with a company in Chicago, the Mills Novelty Company, to make the machines for his New York-based Tru-Mint Company. Costello was able to make money because he was able to place the machines in candy stores, speakeasies, restaurants, and other establishments, which paid him part of the proceeds. The retail owner would also get a cut, as would the salesman of the machine who worked for Tru-Mint. Since the machines delivered a mint into the hands of the patron, Costello could plausibly argue that it really was just a candy vending operation, with somebody occasionally getting small change back. Costello is reported to have even provided small ladders so children could reach the machines and play.

Costello had an estimated 5,000 machines in the city alone. But even his friend George Wolf said it was unclear how much Costello made off the operation. With the salesman and store owners getting a cut, Costello had to share the wealth. There was also political protection needed to assure the machines weren't vandalized or removed by competitors, Wolf recalled. Police also noted that owners of the machines would provide money to establishments leasing the machines to cover any legal costs and fines.

Costello had developed the political hooks to protect his businesses through his ties to Tammany Hall, the Democratic Party organization that by this time had control over much of the action in the city. Costello's power with Tammany Hall was enormous and will be discussed a little later in greater detail this book. But as omnipresent as Tammany had been in so many levels of city government, the sea was starting to change and getting caught in the shifting tide were Costello's slot machines.

Fiorello H. La Guardia had been the consummate politician and civil servant. Born of an Italian father and Jewish mother, La Guardia served as a young man as a mid-level diplomat in Europe for the State Department before returning stateside in the period before World War One. After finishing law school, La Guardia entered politics and as a Republican served through the 1920s as an energetic and feisty congressman, mostly representing East Harlem. It was while he was in the House of Representatives that he made a failed run to become New York City mayor in 1929, losing terribly to incumbent Mayor Jimmy Walker. La Guardia had tried to make a political issue out of some land deals done with the city by Arnold Rothstein, Costello's old financier, but the issue gained no significant traction.

Walker would get mired in scandal and was forced out of office. La Guardia made a run for the job in 1932, putting together a coalition of Republicans and Independents, Socialists, Jewish and Italian voters, the latter group having been traditionally allied with Tammany. Despite the presence of another powerful candidate favored by President Roosevelt, La Guardia won the three-way election by a margin of just over 250,000 votes. La Guardia was a progressive who favored labor but didn't always like what the government did, as was seen when he castigated Bruce Bielaski and his undercover Prohibition enforcement action during the Dwyer-Costello bootlegging trials. But that didn't mean that Costello or the other Mafiosi were going to have an easy time of things under the "Little Flower," as La Guardia was known. No, the new mayor was going to be a thorn in the side of Costello and a lot of his friends for a long time.

La Guardia hated the gangster element. He thought the petty thugs of East Harlem and later the more entrenched Mafiosi were a stain against the Italian people. He also thought gambling was a vice that ruined families and sent children down the wrong road. As mayor, La Guardia didn't have a great deal of police power, particularly in a city where Tammany and corrupt politicians were still deeply entrenched. The boss of Tammany was James J. "Jimmy" Hines, who was a friend of Costello and other gangsters, notably Dutch

Schultz. Politician historians also point out that two of the city's most important prosecutors, Manhattan District Attorney William C. Dodge and Brooklyn District Attorney William Geoghan had been elected with the approval of Hines.

But La Guardia did control the police department and found a soul mate of sorts with William Valentine, who was appointed NYPD commissioner in 1934. Valentine had risen through the ranks and had earned a reputation as being an "incorruptible" cop who wanted to root out corruption, which he attempted to do as commissioner. As the Costello, Dwyer and other bootlegging trials had shown, corruption had reached many levels of the NYPD, and Valentine made it a mission to combat this. He also was well aware of La Guardia's mission against gambling, and even before he took over as commissioner, in the rank of chief of detectives, Valentine took action under the command of then-commissioner and his immediate predecessor John Francis O'Ryan and La Guardia.

However, there was a fly in the ointment so far as La Guardia going after the Costello slot machines, or anybody's machines for that matter. In 1933, before La Guardia took office, the Mills Novelty Company, the Chicago-based supplier of the machines, got an injunction from a federal judge in Manhattan that restrained police from seizing the slot machines unless they were actually being used for gambling purposes. The key distinction for the court was that NYPD officials and city lawyers had conceded that the machines were not gambling devices "per se" and that police admitted that they were making illegal seizures. The state law would have to change in order for the cases to stick.

An appeals court upheld the ruling and a clearly frustrated La Guardia vowed to fight all the way to the U.S. Supreme Court. La Guardia also carried out his own publicity stunt in February 1934 at a Brooklyn police station when, using the rarely used mayoral power to act as a committing magistrate, ordered a Brooklyn man who had been freed on charges of possessing an illegal slot machine rearrested. He tried to get the store owner to tell him who provided him with bail earlier.

"I don't know—the machine people I guess," answered the per-

plexed store owner. He had been accused when an undercover officer put ten nickels in the machine and got ten slugs in return. The
cop then used them to get a package of cigarettes and thirty-five
cents in cash. It was a questionable case and seemed on shaky legal
grounds, given the federal court rulings.

"I supposed the machine people will bail you again," said La
Guardia. "If they are going through with this case I will welcome the
opportunity of having them here."

The whole proceeding seemed like a stunt to give La Guardia a
platform to criticize the federal court rulings and insist that the law
prohibited the devices, as well threaten Costello and the other slot
machine operators.

"I want to serve notice now on the owners, operators, racketeers,
criminals, the riff-raff and the pimps who own them, they will find
no comfort now," said La Guardia, who called the machines "me-
chanical larceny."

Other stunts done by La Guardia included his token smashing of
seized slot machines—his blows of a sledgehammer barely dented
them—before they were taken out to sea on a barge and dumped. To
La Guardia, Costello's machines were part of a fast-growing racket
generating huge profits, although it was unclear how large. What
really troubled La Guardia about what he called "the most menacing evil" was that children were losing their money and tempted to
steal from relatives to feed the one-armed beast. The city subway
system was also losing money because the slugs, some 720,000 in
one year, would fit into subway turnstiles, as well as telephone coin
slots which took in 250,000 of the tokens.

La Guardia stuck to his guns and city lawyers finally won in a
critical legal victory when the U.S. Supreme Court in 1934 said the
case against the city on the slot machine injunction should be dismissed. La Guardia was ecstatic with the brief order from the court.
Coupled with the fact that bills in the Albany legislature outlawed
slot machines, the Mayor went after the operators with new found
zeal.

During a series of raids in May 1934, the NYPD hit Costello's

Tru-Mint Company, also known as the Tru-Mint Mills Novelty Company at 1860 Broadway, and took away over 500 slot machines, as well as records showing the company's operations. The records led cops to three other Manhattan locations where hundreds more machines were found. Some of the devices contained slugs but many were apparently in—pardon the pun—mint condition and had not yet been used. In all, newspapers reported a total of 1,825 machines had been confiscated. Some of the machines had been stored in a space rented by Edward Costello.

"There has been a stream of gold flowing into the pockets of racketeers which will now be stopped," said Commissioner O'Ryan.

The raids also rousted hundreds of bookmakers, slot machine operators, and others involved in gambling. Fixated as he was on gambling and slot machines, La Guardia would later claim victory and boast that the racket had been eliminated from the city. However, slot machines were only one aspect of gambling in New York, and bookmakers were all over the city, including one Stephanie St. Claire, an indomitable black woman who controlled a sizeable numbers operation in Harlem and kept Dutch Schultz, the Bronx beer baron, at bay when he tried to squeeze her out of her territory. For Costello, when one door was slammed shut another opened for him in a place where La Guardia couldn't interfere and probably never thought would become a gangster refuge.

Huey Long was one of those flamboyant, boisterous politicians who while he was on the scene had a career that was simply unforgettable and earned a special niche in American history. Born in August 1893 in a dirt-poor part of Louisiana, Long distinguished himself as young man as a debater and won a university scholarship, only to have to give up the opportunity because he was too poor to cover the other necessary expenses. Long bounced around for a few years as a traveling salesman, attended a seminary, and went to law school where after only a year he convinced officials that he should be able to start his own practice. After setting up shop in Shreveport, Long started a law practice representing mostly poor plaintiffs. He also earned a reputation of taking on big corporations doing business in the state like Standard Oil and became an advocate for the common people against public utilities.

In 1928, Long was elected governor of Louisiana and pushed programs that were progressive for the day: a free textbook program for school children and adult literacy courses. Such programs were popular in a state like Louisiana, which was generally poor and dominated by some wealthy businesses that for decades had their way in the state. When in 1929 Long proposed a five-cents-a-barrel tax on oil produced in the state to fund his social programs, a move erupted to impeach him. The impeachment effort failed and only emboldened Long's drive to advance his progressive and populist agenda.

In 1932, Long ran for one of Louisiana's U.S. Senate seats and won. Once in Congress, Long, like Frank Costello would in his own way, worked to get Roosevelt elected president. Historians credit Long with helping Roosevelt retain in his camp some wavering state delegations during the Democratic Party convention, which ultimately gave Roosevelt the candidacy. As a populist, Long backed Roosevelt's New Deal but often ended up criticizing the President when he didn't seem to be doing things fast enough or appeared to sell out to business interests. He was never shy about speaking his mind and cut his own wild path through Washington.

"Long strode into the national arena in the role of the hillbilly hero and played it with gusto," wrote historian David Kennedy. "He wore white silk suits and pink silk ties, womanized openly, swilled whiskey in the finest bars, swaggered his way around Washington, and breathed defiance into the teeth of his critics."

Being a boozer, Long got into his share of trouble and he did it in a big way in the small, upper-crust community of Sands Point on the North Shore of Long Island. It was during a charity ball and dinner at the Sands Point Bath and Country Club in August 1933 amid the long gowned and staid women that Long made his own special spectacle of himself. As Long biographer Richard D. White Jr. reported, the Senator "got rip-roaring drunk, flirting with women and insulting other guests," including calling a black musician a "coon" and a "shine." To top things, when Long went to the bathroom he wasn't good with his aim as he stood at the urinal and apparently peed on the shoes of a man standing at the next commode. The offended gentleman apparently slugged Long, who eventually left the bathroom with a swollen and bleeding left eye, said White.

In an account he gave to Associated Press of the incident and published in *The New York Times,* Long said the incident was a "ganging" by up to four strangers who he said struck him from behind and then continued to strike him with "a knife or something sharp." Huey also took his lumps in the Louisiana newspapers for the Sands Point incident and it would dog him when he tried to give speeches. He got so angry with reporters that he told his bodyguards to "bust 'em up" when they tried to take pictures. The boorish conduct soured many Louisianans toward Long—not so Frank Costello.

As the story goes, Costello, facing La Guardia's unrelenting campaign against slot machines, which survived the purge and were mothballed and producing no income, saw an opportunity in Louisiana. Costello apparently had met Long in a nightclub and talked about bringing the slots to Louisiana. What happened next depends on who is doing the talking. As Costello would remember it in 1940 (five years after Long was assassinated in 1935), he and the Senator met in 1935 and agreed that Costello could bring one thousand slot machines into New Orleans, provided he paid Long's political organization a yearly fee of $30. Testifying in 1951 before a Senate investigating committee, Costello told essentially the same story, claiming that the money he paid out was supposed to go to a charity in Louisiana.

Others question whether Long would have met Costello without having an intermediary set up the deal. It was also open to question whether Long, who was in the U.S. Senate at the time and not in local Louisiana government, had the connections to assure the deal worked the way Costello said it did. Author Dr. T. Harry Williams, who penned the 1969, Pulitzer Prize-winning biography of Long titled *Huey Long,* thought Costello was actually shielding someone else.

"His overeagerness to connect his entrance into the New Orleans slot-machine business with Huey suggests that he was trying to

shield somebody who had permitted him to come into the city later,"
opined Williams. "But there was an even bigger hole in Costello's
statement. Slot-machine operators never went into a city without
concluding a 'protection' agreement with the municipal government; they agreed to pay a specified sum of money in return for a
promise that the police would not raid the places where the machines were installed and seize them. In 1935, Huey could not provide this protection in New Orleans, for the city government was
controlled by his bitter enemy Semmes Walmsley, who would have
rushed to confiscate any machines operating under Long sponsor-
ship."

But whomever he cut the deal with, Costello's slot machines *did*
enter New Orleans openly and for a time flourished. It was in 1935
that both Costello and his friend Philip Kastel, who had run a slot
machine operation in Manhattan before La Guardia went after the
businesses, traveled to New Orleans to check out the market for
slots. Kastel and Costello had shared offices at Tru-Mint and had
worked together for years. Once in New Orleans, Costello wasn't
impressed. He had apparently told Kastel that he had spoken to
Huey Long who told him of the license or tax on each machine,
which was to go to a special fund. Records later submitted to a federal tax court showed that Costello was turned off by the prospect of
such an arrangement, didn't want to participate but encouraged Kastel to go ahead if he wanted.

Kastel, born on Manhattan's Lower East Side, had a reputation in
New York of being a con man who reportedly ran some stock market bucket shops with Arnold Rothstein back in the 1920s and did
his own bit of swindling. He dodged an extortion rap back in 1918
when the charges were dismissed. But he got involved in one of the
Roaring Twenties' big stock swindles involving the brokerage firm
of Dillon & Co, located at 32 Broadway at the tip of Manhattan. As
would be revealed in the firm's bankruptcy case, the firm used as its
namesake one Daniel Dillon, a writer of market newsletters and a
former war correspondent, who signed a contract with Kastel and
two other investors who provided the initial working capital. For
lending his name and respectability, Dillon was to get a salary of

$200 a week and five percent of the profits. Kastel was to take 65 percent of the profits and the other two investors, who happened to be swindlers, were to split the remainder of the earnings.

As things turned out, according to a report filed by a bankruptcy trustee, Dillon & Co. was something of a Ponzi scheme. When the company failed in September 1921, it had assets of $3,000 and debts to customers of $575,000. Just prior to the filing of the bankruptcy, Kastel called a meeting in his private office and got a drunk Dillon to sign over cash, securities, and notes. Then Kastel disappeared after having received more than $150,000 of the firm's money. The trustee found that most of the money received from customers had been "squandered in the profligacy of upper Broadway, in cabarets, restaurants, road houses and on race track touts, moving picture actresses, and gambling." In short, the kind of world Costello, Luciano and even Damon Runyon were very familiar with.

Neither Dillon nor Kastel or anybody else in the firm was a member of the New York Stock Exchange. Dillon & Co was unable to earn any money as a legitimate stock brokerage and attempted to use other firms that were members to make transactions. Of the over $575,000 collected from customers, which included gullible families with children living outside of the New York City metropolitan area, less than $219,000 was actually used to buy stocks, said the trustee. The money not used for securities went all over and was used for housekeepers, fur coats, monogrammed cigarettes, as well as alimony. Some cash was even traced to Saratoga, New York, for betting on horses.

Kastel's reputation for the nightlife, funded by his unwitting stock customers, earned him the sobriquet "Dandy Phil." According to Leonard Katz, in his 1974 book about Costello titled *Uncle Frank,* Kastel loved putting up a good front.

"He was quiet, soft spoken, suave, debonair, and wore expensive clothes that he chose with taste and care," noted Katz. "He looked like he had just completed a deal to buy the Bank of England. During the twenties, especially, he was a sight to see along Broadway, a little man dressed to the hilt with a gold mounted walking stick and pearl gray spats."

As natty as he was, Kastel was also a bonafide crook and his escapade with Dillon & Co, sounded similar to a stock scam that Fitzgerald included a veiled reference to in *The Great Gatsby*. For his involvement, Kastel went to trial three times on federal mail-fraud charges and prosecuted by no less than Manhattan U.S. Attorney Buckner. After two hung juries, in April 1926 Kastel was convicted on one of six fraud counts and sentenced to three years in the Atlanta penitentiary.

Released from Atlanta and back in business with Costello with the slot machines in Manhattan, Kastel decided to enter the business in New Orleans and talked about it further with Costello and businessman C. R. Brainerd. In the fall of 1935, Kastel formed a partnership with Brainerd and two of Costello's brothers-in-law, Dudley and Harold Geigerman, who had worked in the slot-machine business in Manhattan. The deal was all done on a handshake. The partnership, known as Bayou Novelty Company originally called for Kastel and Brainerd to get 30 percent shares, with the Geigermans each getting 20 percent interest. After Brainerd died in 1937, Kastel's share increased to 40 percent of the business. Costello may not have wanted to go into Bayou Novelty officially, but he still managed to get a piece of the action, and Kastel agreed to split whatever money he got with him. In fact, Costello loaned Kastel, when he was short of cash, some $15,000 to originally invest in the business. However—and this would be crucial in later legal troubles—Costello stayed away from the daily operation of the company, receiving what one court found was only his cut of the profits directly from Kastel.

Bayou worked out of 2601 Chartres Street, near the French Quarter, and was in operation until the spring of 1938. It had a repair shop for the machines which had been purchased from Mills Novelty in Chicago and a storage area on the premises. Teams of sixteen collectors or agents went around town three times a week to gather the proceeds from the machines of which Bayou retained 50 percent. The stores where the machines had been placed got 40 percent of the take and the collectors the remaining 10 percent. Business was good and in 1936 showed net earnings of over $514,000. The business had at least 1,000 machines and didn't get robbed or have any obvious problems with the police or any other officials.

Bayou's affairs represented the one instance in which Costello, even though he was formally not part of the company, was said to have resorted to violence. George Wolf made no mention of it in his book, but Leonard Katz did in his. Quoting an unnamed "friend" of Costello, Katz related how one of the key people in the New Orleans operation was stealing money from the company. Frank was informed and upon arriving in New Orleans called a meeting of the company. While speaking from a podium, Costello asked the thieving man to approach and then suddenly Costello pulled out a monkey wrench and struck the man, according to what Katz said his informant told him. The assault was meant to be a lesson for anyone who was thinking of doing the same thing in the future, said Katz.

But thievery wasn't the big problem that confronted Costello and Kastel. On September 8, 1935, shortly after a bill Long proposed to remove Judge Benjamin Pavy passed the legislature, the jurist's son approached Long in the state capital and fired at him four times with a handgun. Long's bodyguards killed his assailant. But two days later Long died of his wounds. If Long had been the guardian angel of Costello's slot machine empire in Louisiana—and there are those who think he really wasn't—things were now in a bit of disarray since the boys from New York had lost their political protection at what seemed like the wrong time.

It was about a year after Long's assassination that the new mayor of New Orleans, Robert S. Maestri made a move, announcing that slot machines would not be permitted to operate in the city. He ordered the cops to confiscate machines and word spread among bars and other establishments that the "syndicate" which owned the Chief machines, which was Bayou, had ordered everyone to sit tight. According to Wolf, Maestri took a vacation to Hot Springs, Arkansas, a place where Costello's old friend Owney Madden controlled gambling, and when he returned to New Orleans, Costello's slot machines didn't have a problem. This was so despite significant public opposition to the presence of the machines.

While their Bayou Novelty slot machine business was prospering, Costello and Kastel couldn't rightly do business in New Orleans without cutting in Carlos Marcello, the mob boss of Louisiana and its key city of sin, New Orleans. Born of Sicilian parents and brought to the U.S. in 1911 from Tunisia, where he was born, Marcello rose from the life of a petty criminal to the main Mafia boss in the state. Costello knew of his clout and paid him the appropriate tribute. This was done in 1945 when Kastel and Costello took over the Beverly Club in Jefferson Parish. Once an old plantation converted into a roadhouse, the Beverly billed itself as an exclusive dinner and supper club, which in the days before Las Vegas pulled in entertainers like Carmen Miranda, Rudy Vallee, and Joe E. Lewis. Kastel had a significant 47 percent interest, Costello 20 percent and Marcello 12 percent. The Beverly had slot machines and despite the dicey legal nature of gambling in Louisiana, they made the club a money-making attraction.

Costello also retained some interest and significant ties to New Orleans proper. One of the them was the friendship he had with James "Diamond Jim" Moran Brocato. To say Brocato was flamboyant doesn't do him justice. A former boxer—he used the name "Moran" so his mother wouldn't learn of his pugilistic career as a young man—Brocato became a legendary character in the French Quarter from the 1930s until his death in 1958. He was a restauranteur of note, who, his family recalled, clawed his way up from poverty by working as a bootblack and then a barber, in whose chair one day came Huey Long. A man can get to like his barber and in the case of Long their relationship grew as the politician stopped by for a shave and haircut. Brocato, so the story goes, saved Long from embarrassment by having the then-U.S. Senator sleep off a drunken bender at the Roosevelt Hotel while Prohibition agents raided his Ming Toy speakeasy. Brocato got arrested in the raid, didn't give up Long, and did six months for violating the Volstead Act.

Brocato became such a wealthy man that he bought up diamonds as easily as if they were crayfish. He was known around town for his diamond-studded ties, diamond-studded cane, diamond-studded watch, diamond-studded cufflinks, diamond-filled dental bridge, diamond-studded—-well, you get the picture. Movie stars like Marilyn Monroe, Barbara Stanwyck, and Robert Taylor flocked to his popular La Louisiane restaurant in the Quarter. Sports stars like Joe DiMaggio and Rocky Marciano were also regulars. The food was so good because it was all homemade.

"The fabulous food was cooked at the Moran home by Diamond Jim's devoted wife, Mary, and delivered every lunchtime and dinner time to the restaurant; the place was packed every night. Jimmy held court, and every now and again, some lucky lady would cut into a meatball and find a one-carat diamond inside," George Gurtner wrote years later in *New Orleans* magazine.

Brocato was the kind of outsized, connected personality Costello gravitated toward during the years of his New Orleans slot machine business. Costello also liked him because he was a loyal, standup guy as the incident at the Ming Toy showed. When Costello learned of an early plan to assassinate Long at the Roosevelt Hotel, he tipped off Brocato, who told Long of the danger he faced. Long's bodyguards raided the location where the plotters were supposed to be, found some guns, and apparently broke up the plot. Long was reportedly so grateful to Brocato that he said, "Tell your friend in New York thanks, and tell him I owe him one." Was that the reason for Long's slot machine offer to Costello? That is something we will never know.

Several times a year Brocato would entertain Costello, Luciano, Lansky, and others on Lake Pontchartrain where he had a family camp. Brocato got his own cut from the slot machine action in his places and it helped make him a rich man. Costello always seemed to feel comfortable around him, cared for, protected.

CHAPTER ELEVEN
"YOU'RE A HELL
OF AN ITALIAN"

THINGS MAY HAVE BEEN GOING WELL in New Orleans for Costello. The slot machine money was flowing, and police and public officials there, while spouting off about the evils of gambling, seemed to have turned a blind eye and were happy to take whatever cut they were getting. The food at La Louisiane was like the best home-cooked Italian meals he could get back in New York. Costello and Loretta felt comfortable and secure among the likes of Diamond Jim Brocato, who he sometimes took Holy Communion with at St. Mary Italian Church on Chartres Street in the French Quarter.

But things were not so good back in the Big Apple. La Guardia and his police commissioner were going after the rackets with zeal. As far as La Guardia was concerned, he wanted to drive the racketeers out of town and marshaled as many city agencies as he could to do his bidding. The ice and artichoke cartels, employment agency scams, all became fair game. Lucky Luciano was Costello's boss and was the public face of the crime family so it was natural that the authorities had him in their sights. After 1933, Luciano was earning illicit profits from other kinds of gambling and, some say, heroin. The sex trade was also a big earner for the Mafia and turned out to be big trouble for Luciano and would impact Costello in ways he wasn't expecting. The Mafia was in for some big changes.

There were some similarities between Luciano and Costello. Both had immigrant parents and had grown up in immigrant ghettos: the

East Side for Luciano or East Harlem for Costello. But their career paths in the Mafia had been different. Costello was the businessman who—mostly—eschewed violence. He wanted to be legitimate and kept a low profile when he could. Luciano had the brashness of a mob boss. He wasn't afraid of a fight, and his criminal record showed arrests for felonious assault, disorderly conduct, narcotics violations, and weapons possession, most of which were discharged. Costello liked having an office, a home in a quiet area of Queens, and a record of being a businessman. A probation official at one point said Luciano's idea of life, was to spend his money on beautiful women and silk underwear.

Both Luciano and Costello were key parts of the old Masseria organization, at least as long as the old boss was alive. With Masseria dead, Luciano proved to be the more adventuresome, reckless and hungering for action. It was no surprise that Luciano had the nerve to kill not one but two bosses—Masseria and Maranzano. Costello was the man who was happy to play second fiddle. That didn't mean that Costello didn't influence his boss. Costello's sense of style rubbed off on Luciano who developed a penchant for the cutaway overcoat, so much so that one newspaper columnist likened him to the mythical Dracula.

Luciano, with Costello as an influence, aimed his sights higher in terms of his lifestyle. Having lived in a suite at the Barbizon-Plaza, Luciano moved into the Waldorf-Astoria under the name "Charles Ross." The hotel was a favorite of Costello, a place where he loved being seen and hobnobbing with people he wanted to impress. If Luciano wanted to spend the money he made from the rackets then living in the Waldorf was one sure way of burning through cash. He entertained out-of-town gangsters with lush parties with showgirls and sometimes prostitutes whom he secured from the madam Polly Adler. Luciano didn't seem to need call girls for himself. He usually had a girlfriend but never wanted to settle down and get married, unlike Costello and some of the others. In his biography of Luciano titled *Luciano: The Man Who Modernized the American Mafia*, author Tony Sciacca related the reason why Luciano was shy of going to the altar.

"I will never get married . . . because then I would want to have kids. And I'd never have a son of mine goin' through life with the burden of the name Luciano, the gangster," Luciano told friends, according to Sciacca.

Luciano, Costello, and the other racketeers had cultivated their political connection through the power of Tammany Hall, the bastion of crooked city politicians. Various investigative commissions such as the Seabury Commission had pinpointed political corruption as being behind so much of the power of the racketeers. But getting something done had been a challenge in New York. With the arrival of La Guardia, and Governor Herbert Lehman taking the reins in Albany, things were starting to change. But the path to reform would be slow and circuitous.

The Manhattan District Attorney in this period was William C. Dodge, an ally of Tammany Hall. Dodge made cases but only seemed to do so to get quick headlines and, his critics said, give the illusion of being tough on crime. He went after Polly Adler, Luciano's favorite madam and arrested her for prostitution and charges she possessed a lewd film, which back then was an offense. Adler was ultimately convicted and sentenced to jail. But critics of Dodge said he wasn't prepared to push forward where the Adler investigation left off. He tried to keep his job but finally Lehman, a fellow Democrat of the reform stripe took Dodge off as supervisor of the vice investigation and appointed an eager, fresh-faced former federal prosecutor named Thomas Dewey, a Republican, as a special prosecutor.

With a mandate from Albany and with the acquiescence and cheerleading of City Hall, Dewey put together a staff working out of lower Manhattan. His target: the rackets, notably, gambling and prostitution. It was the latter that seemed the most intriguing line of inquiry. Over the years the sex trade had been organized along lines in which men known as "bookers" provided madams with fresh girls for their brothels. Prostitution had always been a big business in New York and the supply of women who needed the work seemed a constant. The bookers provided fresh talent from an endless reservoir.

In the early 1930s a group of men who were low-level gangsters

forced the bookers into a union or a combination in which they had
to fork over some of their earnings to the hoods. The madams were
coerced into using bookers affiliated with the gangsters and in return
had the protection of the gang in case of the need for bail bonds,
lawyers, and other favors. It was classic cartel-style organization,
the kind which the Italian and Jewish gangsters had practiced for
years in other businesses: ice, grape supply, laundry, coal, and the
like.

A round of arrests broke up the booker cartel about a year before
Dewey assumed office, but there were others to fill their shoes.
After launching his investigations, Dewey learned that new men
were coercing the bookers and madams. To try to build a case, he
had his staff of investigators arrest prostitutes and madams in an effort to convince them to talk. To keep the women in custody and
away from the pressures of the combination, Dewey asked for and
got high bail for the suspects in amounts they couldn't post, even
with the help of corrupt bail bondsmen. That kept them insulated
from the mobsters. It was a case of Dewey trying tactics of persua-
sion, using a soft approach, which assured the women that they
wouldn't be facing long prison sentences if they agreed to cooperate. Many did talk and as a result, on February 1, 1936, Dewey's
staff fanned out around the city and arrested more women, as well as
four men suspected of controlling the prostitution racket.

Dewey and his staff tried to squeeze the new suspects to find out
if there were people higher up, bigger racketeers or even politicians
who might be involved. But things didn't go easily. The witnesses
were either too smart or too afraid to talk. The break came with a
Brooklyn man named David Miller. After losing his job as a police
officer in Pennsylvania on charges he ran a house of prostitution,
Miller came to New York in 1929 and started selling dresses door-
to-door. Some of Miller's clients turned out to be prostitutes and
eventually he went into their business with another man. The operation earned Miller a lot of cash but then some toughs came by to say
a combination of sorts was being formed and that he had better join
up. To convince Miller, the goons roughed him up. He decided to
run away to California only to return again in March 1935 and reen-

ter the prostitution business as a booker. It was then that Miller decided to pay the combination $50 on a weekly basis and have his prostitutes pay $10 a week as well. Miller played along with the arrangement until he was caught in Dewey's dragnet.

At first, Miller couldn't or wouldn't tell Dewey who the bigshots were at the top of the food chain in the prostitution business. But over time, Miller let out intriguing morsels of information, hearsay at best, but which suggested Luciano was linked to the prostitution racket. This was the first major indication that Luciano might be involved, and it made Dewey pursue every available lead to bolster what admittedly were thin connections to the Mafia boss.

In early 1936, a special Manhattan grand jury was working feverishly under Dewey to indict Luciano and others on charges they ran a $12 million a year vice ring, which at today's dollar value adjusted for inflation would have been $211 million. But with his political and police connections, Luciano got wind that he was about to be arrested and ran away, ensconcing himself in the friendly environs of Hot Springs, Arkansas. The town had turned into a gambling Mecca of sorts with scores of clubs and casinos and plenty of pretty and available women. Local law enforcement was very accommodating and pliant. Costello, Owney Madden, and others discovered the locale as a vacation spot and a place where cooperative politicians assured that they would not be harassed by the cops. Costello and his wife Loretta made numerous trip to Hot Springs, no doubt hooking up with Madden, who by that time had left New York in the face of looming legal troubles including suspicion of murder, to "retire" in a way. Madden did that by running his own casino and becoming a respected public figure of sorts.

In Hot Springs, Luciano thought he was safe from Dewey's clutches. But Dewey petitioned officials in Arkansas to extradite Luciano, a move that the mob boss fought with a small army of lawyers and it was said a $50,000 attempt to bribe the state's attorney general. But the legal maneuvers could only work so long, and Luciano had played out his string. A New York detective of Italian ethnicity who was working for Dewey was the one who had the honor of serving Luciano with a warrant on April 3 for his arrest.

Frank Costello (FAR RIGHT) in Hot Springs, Arkansas,
in the 1930s with some unidentified gentlemen.
Costello often visited the resort town for vacations and gambling.
(Photo courtesy Noel Castiglia)

The stone house owned by the Castiglia family in Westport, Connecticut.
The estate was a favorite getaway for Frank Costello and his wife,
Loretta, as well as other relatives of Domenico Castiglia, a cousin.
(Photo courtesy Noel Castiglia)

Frank Costello and his wife, Loretta, enjoying a moment on the patio of their home
in Sands Point, during an interview with *Newsday* columnist Jack Altshul in June 1950.
The photograph was taken by *Newsday* photographer Edna Murray.
(Photo courtesy Newsday LLC)

Frank Costello, on left, with women identified as two of his sisters
and a man who was unidentified. The inscribed photograph was found
in a family collection by Costello relative Noel Castiglia.
(Photo courtesy Noel Castiglia)

Photo depicting noted New Orleans restaurant owner Diamond Jim Brocato standing behind Frank Costello and his wife, Loretta, at Brocato's famed La Louisiane in the French Quarter. At lower left, raising a glass of wine, may be Meyer Lansky. *(Photo courtesy Joseph Brocato)*

Mugshot of Johnny Torrio, the fabled gangster from Chicago,
who along with Costello chaired a meeting of mobsters in Atlantic City in 1929
in which they sorted out bootlegging business and convinced Al Capone
to take a "vacation" by getting arrested. The ploy was for Capone to go away
for a short while to tone down the violence in Chicago.
(Photo courtesy Library of Congress)

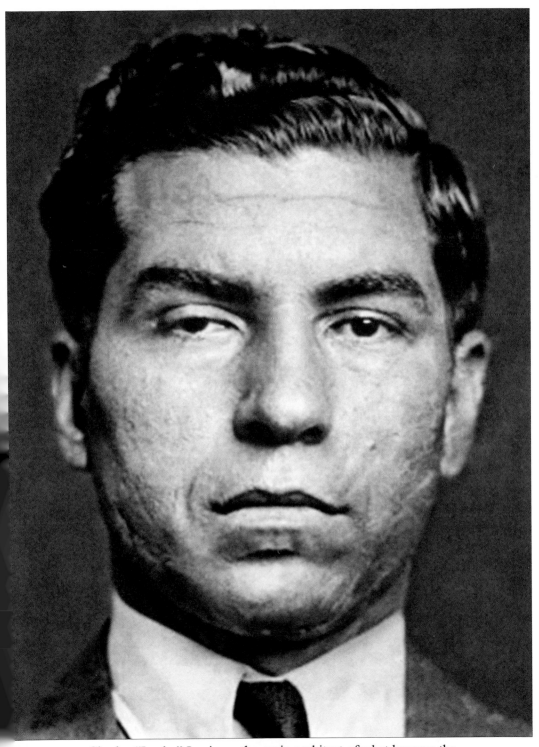

Charles "Lucky" Luciano, the main architect of what became the
Five Families of New York City, boss and close friend of Frank Costello.
He is shown in an NYPD mug shot.
(Photo courtesy Wikimedia)

Thomas Dewey, former Governor of New York and the prosecutor
who secured a conviction of Luciano in the 1936 vice case.
Dewey tried but failed to implicate Costello in wrongdoing.
Dewey later pardoned Luciano and allowed him to be deported to Italy
after World War Two because of the gangster's efforts to help the war effort.
(Photo courtesy Library of Congress)

New York City Mayor
Fiorello La Guardia,
who became the nemesis
of Frank Costello
by going after his
slot machine businesses
in the 1930s.
La Guardia is shown here
looking at a giant catch
at the Fulton Fish Market.

New York City Mayor
Fiorello La Guardia
lecturing on the evils
of organized crime.
*(Photos courtesy
Library of Congress)*

Cops in New York City pouring alcoholic beverages seized during
a Prohibition raid down the sewer. During Prohibition,
the city had as many as an estimated 30,000 speakeasies,
which were stocked by the smuggling operations of
Frank Costello, William V. Dwyer, and others.
(Photo courtesy Library of Congress)

Frank Costello and his wife, Loretta, enjoy a smoke in the living room
of their home in Sands Point, in June 1950. The photo was taken during
an interview the Costellos had with *Newsday* columnist Jack Altshul.
The photo was taken by the newspaper's photographer, Edna Murray.
(Photo courtesy Newsday LLC)

short time thereafter Mr. Carpenter and Mr. Schneider came out of the house. Mr. Schneider was carrying certain books, files and other papers which he took from Mr. Carpenter's home.

Frank Costello

Sworn to before me, this

75 day of February, 1926.

Signature of Frank Costello on a statement he gave during his 1926 federal bootlegging case.
(Author's collection)

The Costello family mausoleum in St. Michael's Cemetery, Queens, New York. Note the initials "F" and "C" on the bronze door. Cash dealings over the construction of the mausoleum led to Costello's conviction on federal income tax charges.
(Author's collection)

Louis "Lepke" Buchalter, a major mob figure in the 1930s and 1940s, as well as an associate of Frank Costello, shown here after his arrest in New York. The man on the left of the picture, to whom Buchalter is shackled, is identified as FBI Director J. Edgar Hoover.

Owney Madden, a bootlegger, nightclub owner, and associate of Frank Costello. Madden, a major Irish racketeer of his day, was beset by legal problems and left New York City for Hot Springs, Arkansas, in 1933. He died there of natural causes in 1965. *(Photos courtesy Library of Congress)*

A jaunty Meyer Lansky exiting a Manhattan courthouse in 1958.

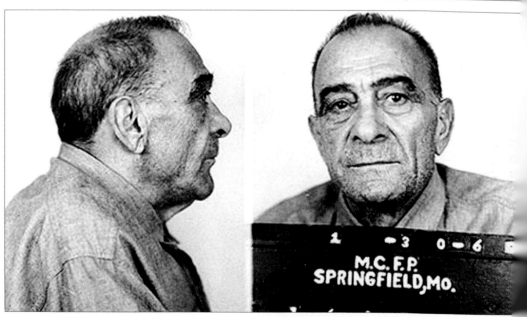

Vito Genovese, the man who nearly had Frank Costello killed and supplanted him as boss of the old Luciano crime family, shown in a prison mug shot after his conviction on a federal narcotics case.
(Photos courtesy Library of Congress)

Chicago crime boss Al Capone, seen in a mug shot taken in a federal penitentiary. *(Photo courtesy FBI)*

Frank Costello pruning a tree at his Sands Point home during a visit in 1950
by *Newsday* reporter Jack Altshul and his wife Edna Murray, who took the photographs.
The negatives for the *Newsday* photographs were among those
found during a search of the newspaper's old negatives.
(Photo courtesy Newsday LLC)

Luciano was said to have been speechless when served with the papers and then got angry with the detective.

"You! You're a hell of an Italian!" said Luciano.

"Sure, I am," the detective replied. "I am a hell of an Italian."

On April 17, Luciano was sent back to New York to face the charges.

The trial of Luciano and his co-defendants began in June 1936, less than two months after he had been extradited to New York. It was a hard-fought case by all sides. Dewey brought in a parade of witnesses and in his opening statement to the jury said that it was Luciano who took over the vice racket in 1933. He did that, Dewey said, by driving other men out of business, forcing them to pay up to join his syndicate or leave town.

As he did with the Mafia families generally, Luciano organized the business, creating a thriving operation that had more than 200 brothels in the city staffed by over 1,000 women, Dewey said. The pressure was applied to bookers who sent prostitutes to brothels, to either buy their way into the syndicate for $10,000 or leave town. The men were persuaded by the tap of a gun butt to do the right thing, the prosecutor stated. The weekly fee for any booker who joined the combination was $100 a week.

The first witness to tie Luciano into the syndicate was an ex-con named Joseph Bendix who had done time in Sing Sing prison. Bendix said that he wanted a job as a collector of cash from the brothels and finally met Luciano at the Villanova restaurant on West Forty-sixth Street to ask for the job. Luciano thought the job was a bit beneath Bendix and chided him for asking only for $35 a week.

"If you are willing to work for $40 a week, it's okay with me," Luciano said, according to Bendix. "I'll tell Little Davie [Bertillo] to put you on. You can always meet me here."

Like some of the prostitutes who testified, Bendix had baggage impacting his credibility, in his case an attempt to obtain a lighter sentence by telling prosecutors he had information about $1.5 million in stolen securities, information that prosecutors decided was worthless. The women, all of whom were looking for leniency from the court and in some cases were drug addicts, testified about seeing

Luciano in person or heard that he was supposed to be the head of the syndicate.

As the trial progressed, Luciano and the other nine defendants (three others had pled guilty during the case) tried to upend the government case by showing that Dewey was trying to threaten them with long prison sentences to falsely implicate the Mafia boss as the czar of prostitution. Finally, Luciano himself took the witness stand to deny he was involved in the scheme. The results were disastrous. Under four hours of brutal cross-examination by Dewey, Luciano was forced to admit he had been a bootlegger, had lied in the past to police and had peddled narcotics as a youth. Luciano admitted he knew gangsters like the late Joseph Masseria, Louis "Lepke" Buchalter, and Bugsy Siegel. But when he denied knowing Ciro Terranova, the fabled "artichoke king," Dewey showed the jury telephone records from Luciano's suite in the Waldorf-Astoria that showed calls from there to Terranova's house in the Bronx.

Early in the morning of June 7, 1936, a Sunday, Luciano and eight of his co-defendants were convicted of compulsory prostitution. The jury needed only about six hours to reach its verdict. Luciano appeared to show no emotion, but others clenched their fists, trembled, or sneered. Dewey put out a statement that Luciano was "the greatest gangster in America" and that he controlled narcotics, policy, loansharking, the age-old Italian lottery, and rackets in industries like the garment center.

Dewey had done the job he set out to do, get the conviction of a top racketeer. But over the years many would criticize his tactics, saying it prompted witnesses to give perjured or carefully sculpted testimony to get Luciano at any costs. According to Sciacca, during an interview he had with the madam Polly Adler in 1955, she baldly stated that she knew some of the witnesses Dewey used in the case against Luciano and that his staff "put words into their mouths and gave them all of the information they needed to tell a convincing story." Adler added, according to Sciacca, that "those girls lied because they'd been threatened by Dewey, they admitted that quite freely." Also years after the Luciano trial in 1972, Frank Hogan, one of Dewey's aides, who later went on to become Manhattan's longest-serving district attorney, admitted that under modern rules of criminal procedure and jurisprudence Luciano might not have been convicted. Back in the 1930s, defendants had no right of discovery of evidence before trial so they couldn't investigate prosecution witnesses or get access to various versions of the statements they gave investigators, admitted Hogan. Back then it was trial by surprise and sometimes ambush.

But Luciano was convicted under the law as it was in 1936 and as inadequate and as unfair as the rules of law were then by modern standards, that was the lot he was cast. When it came time to sentence Luciano, Judge Philip J. McCook gave him a term of thirty to fifty years. Upon hearing that, Luciano's eyes flickered, but he remained composed. He promised to appeal, a process that took months and in the end was futile.

With Luciano now out of commission as boss, and with his top lieutenant Vito Genovese having hastily fled to Italy with $750,000 crammed into his luggage to avoid an arrest for murder, command of the crime family fell to Frank Costello, the man who claimed to be legitimate and who fancied himself as nothing more than a businessman. But in reality, Costello was the gangster under the radar who not only had tight relationships with Luciano but also with powerful mobsters like Joe Adonis and Meyer Lansky, like-minded powerful men who didn't need the status of being a mob boss to feel secure in what they did.

Costello had some legitimate businesses—real estate and automobile sales and service—but his big money had come first from the Prohibition bonanza and then from the slot machine operations, which, depending on where he operated, were either illegal or somewhat legal, depending on how much he could pay off the cops. With his respectability, Costello was a somewhat reluctant prince of the Mafia, a man who stepped into the shoes of Luciano when needed—and 1936 was a time when the mob needed Costello's steady hand on the tiller.

It was only a year earlier that Costello and Luciano had seen how easy it was for things to spin out of control with some of their colleagues in crime. Take the case of Dutch Schultz, the Bronx beer baron and gambling boss, otherwise known as Arthur Flegenheimer. A German-American Jew, Schultz was a volatile character, particularly when his life and livelihood was threatened as often proved to be the case. In one instance, Dewey, wearing the hat of a Manhattan federal prosecutor before he became special state prosecutor, tried to prosecute Schultz on income tax evasion. Schultz's lawyers got a change of venue from Manhattan by claiming he couldn't get a fair trial in New York City, and the case was transferred for trial to the upstate town of Malone.

Once in Malone, Schultz did his best to influence public opinion by donating to charities and helping children. The local citizenry ate it up and in 1935, Schultz was acquitted on the federal charges. The jury verdict made La Guardia apoplectic and he promptly threatened to have Schultz arrested if he ever came into New York City limits again. Beset by big legal bills, worried about his future, and with his rackets hurting, Schultz had beseeched Luciano and the Mafia commission to have his nemesis Dewey killed. Luciano and the others thought Schultz was nuts for wanting to kill the prosecutor, and in turn a team of assassins shot Schultz and some of his sidekicks in the Palace Chophouse, a Newark restaurant, on October 23, 1935. Schultz survived the fusillade long enough to receive the Last Rites as a Catholic (he had converted to the religion earlier) before finally dying of his wounds on October 24. He was thirty-three years old. Burial for Schultz was in Gate of Heaven Cemetery in Westchester. Although it is a Catholic place of interment, Schultz's mother asked that he be buried in his Jewish prayer shawl and his yarmulke.

Such was the volatile world of the Mafia of which Costello was now a leader. Prosecutors like Dewey were on a tear, and La Guardia was acting like a little Napoleon on a mission to rid the city of racketeers. As carefully as he tried to be, Costello was now at a point in his life where he could find himself in trouble because of the actions of others. Costello found out the hard way in the very strange case of the theft of jewels from Mrs. Margaret Hawksworth Bell in Coral Cables, Florida. It was one of the strangest episodes in Costello's life and came close to costing him his freedom.

CHAPTER TWELVE
"I KNOW EVERYBODY"

IF WRITERS LIKE DAMON RUNYON and Dashiell Hammett needed a good, true-to-life detective to give inspiration to their stories they would have been happy with what Noel C. Scaffa had to offer. A dour man with black hair, a short-trimmed moustache, and a thick nose, Scaffa was one of those private gumshoes who constantly found himself in the newspapers and sometimes in trouble with the law, an occupational hazard from the way he did things. Scaffa was known as the "Great Retriever," the man who could find stolen jewels and get them back, often with no questions asked. Cops didn't like him all that much and Scaffa got arrested numerous times as he worked his magic in the underworld, often skirting the edge of the law.

Born in Sicily and arriving in New York in 1891, Scaffa's family seemed well off until the financial panic of 1907 wiped out his father's wealth. The old man died the next year and to support himself and his family, Scaffa took a job as a clerk in Maiden Lane, the insurance canyon in lower Manhattan where all the big firms had offices. At the age of twenty, he joined the Pinkerton Agency, the premier detective shop. He got his first big case quickly when the great tenor Enrico Caruso and his wife left their East Hampton home on Long Island for a trip to Cuba and discovered on their return that thieves had made off with $450,000 in jewels.

Scaffa was assigned the Caruso case, mainly because the Caruso servants spoke only Italian, a language the detective was familiar with since he was a child. Despite his efforts, Scaffa couldn't solve the case or recover the jewels. He told his bosses that the case could have been solved if the company had connections within the world of thieves and fences who regularly trafficked in stolen jewelry.

While he couldn't break the Caruso case, Scaffa realized that a good detective needed connections in the world of thieves if there was ever to be any hope in finding stolen jewels. He started his own detective agency around 1921, and while he took all kinds of cases to pay the bills, he developed a cache for recovering bangles and baubles. Apart from real estate, jewelry was one tangible thing the rich liked to flaunt. By doing so, they were advertising their assets to thieves and making themselves prime targets for rip offs.

From his days with Pinkerton, it became clear to Scaffa that thieves really didn't want to keep the jewels but would hold them for ransom, parting with them if they were able to be paid a portion of what the stones were worth. Scaffa reckoned that since insurance companies would pay the owners only about 60 percent of the value, the thieves would part with the stones if they got paid part of the remaining 40 percent of value. Once the stones were returned, the company wouldn't have to pay 60 percent, just 30 to 40 percent—to the thieves—to make the recovery.

Scaffa got to try out his modus operandi for the first time in a big way when thieves hit the Fifth Avenue apartment of Jessie Donahue. Lost in the break-in were diamonds and other stones worth a reported $650,000, but with insurance covering only up to $114,000. While police worked the case relentlessly, Scaffa, representing one of the insurance companies, waited with a sandwich and cups of coffee for a telephone call he guessed would come. It did. The caller asked for the "man in black," the nickname for Scaffa because of his preference for dark suits. About a week after the robbery, Scaffa walked into the lobby of a Manhattan hotel and met with a man identified in news reports as Sam Layton. Both men exchanged packages and then about two weeks after Mrs. Donahue had lost her jewels they were returned by Scaffa to the insurance companies. He never identified the mysterious Layton. The cops charged Scaffa with compounding a felony, and after a mistrial the case was dismissed.

After his success in the Donahue case, Scaffa's reputation as the go-to man for the recovery of jewels spread. Scaffa got involved in other big recoveries and over the years was said to have found $10 million in stolen property, mostly diamonds. He became a celebrity, the object of awe and envy. He frequented Broadway nightclubs—he was single—and rubbed shoulders with the likes of Costello and others in the underworld. Scaffa seemed to have a formula for success in his peculiar line of work. But his methods would wind up getting both he and Costello in trouble.

It was January 26, 1935, a time when Costello was making good money in Louisiana with the slot machines. In nearby Coral Gables, Florida, two low-level thieves from Brooklyn named Nicholas Montone and Charles Cali broke into the hotel suite at the Miami Biltmore of Margaret Hawksworth Bell, manhandled her, and robbed her of over $185,000 in jewels, including four strings of matched pearls, a diamond bracelet, and a 32-carat diamond ring. Montone was armed with a nickel-plated revolver and Cali with a .25 caliber automatic pistol. Her older, millionaire boyfriend Harry Content tried to stop the heist but also got robbed, losing a watch and $100 in cash. Both victims were gagged and tied to chairs. Clearly, Bell got the worst of the deal in terms of the monetary loss.

The theft was a big story because Margaret Hawksworth Bell was what was known in the tabloids as a "society" dancer who performed in various follies and reviews, often done in hotels. She was slim and attractive, and at the age of eighteen caught the eye of Content, then fifty-two years old. Content saw her during a performance in a Manhattan hotel and was smitten. The problem was that the older Wall Street investor was already married, and his wife wouldn't give him a divorce. Margaret, being younger and wanting to get married, wed a young Army captain in 1927, only to see the marriage end a year later. In 1930, Margaret married James Bell, described in the newspapers as a millionaire broker and polo player. They divorced after five years.

Margaret Bell and Content had finally resumed their relationship in 1935 after the death of his wife and Margaret's recent divorce. Having so much experience in marriage and divorce, Margaret was one of those ladies who acquired an impressive collection of jewels over the years, and in the circles she traveled—aside from real estate—stones were the one tangible item of property and status that was coveted. Both she and Content had plans to get married when the robbery occurred. Bell had worn some of the stones to the race track the afternoon before she was hit, advertising to the world and to any enterprising thief who wanted to know that she had some fancy jewelry with her.

The high-profile nature of the Bell and Content relationship gave the crime extra reason to be high on the radar of FBI director J. Edgar Hoover. His investigator soon discovered that the suspects Montone and Cali, who were both identified leaving the hotel by a doorman, had ties to the nightclub worlds in both Miami and New York, notably upstate Saratoga Springs. Hoover then brought up Scaffa's name as a pivotal player in the recovery of the gems while other law enforcement officials said the case involved "figures notorious in the New York underworld."

Just four months after the robbery in Coral Gables, Montone and Cali were convicted in Miami. But as Hoover had indicated, the case had more to it than those two defendants. FBI documents disclosed that the agency was digging deeper into the case and had become suspicious of both Scaffa and Frank Costello. Although Cali was arrested in Miami, Montone had fled after the robbery to New York and stayed four days at the Warwick Hotel before finally being arrested. During his stay at the Warwick, Montone had called Costello's telephone number, according to the records. Costello apparently helped hire a lawyer to represent Montone.

What put the case high on Hoover's list was the suspicion that private detectives like Scaffa were in collusion with jewel thieves in which reward monies for the stolen items was, as one FBI memo stated, "procured through false representations to the policy holding insurance companies." The FBI had come across numerous cases up and down the Atlantic seaboard and what gave the agency special interest was the passage of the "National Stolen Property Act," which essentially made it a crime to move stolen items in interstate commerce.

In the Bell case, FBI suspicion fell upon Scaffa because of problems with his story about how he located the jewels. Bell's jewels were found in a railroad station locker in Miami shortly after the theft. Cops had been given the key to the locker by Scaffa, who said he received it from a man he didn't know. FBI officials also had heard, but had trouble confirming, that Costello had advanced some of the money used in the heist by some of the principals. By May 29, 1935, Hoover was getting a flurry of messages from his subordinates about the progress on the case against Costello, Scaffa, and others. The messages were coming to him about once an hour, which in the era before email and texting was fast.

It was actually on May 29 that Scaffa and two other men, Al Howard and "Broadway Charlie" Stern, were taken into custody by FBI agents. They were taken in on charges related to the federal stolen property statute. Scaffa suffered from the added indignity of being hit with a perjury charge as well. Costello was also being sought, but according to one FBI memo written by Hoover was hiding out after he caught a tip he was being sought. Costello eventually did turn up on May 31 and, accompanied by an attorney, surrendered to federal authorities. It was then that the FBI got Costello to make a detailed statement about his life and how he did business. Coming some sixteen years before he testified to Congress, Costello's statement to the agents, while self-serving in ways, gave them a peek at what he was all about. He was a man who played things close to the vest.

For a start, Costello identified his occupation as that of a "betting commissioner," someone who took wagers from bettors at a race track and placed the bets with a bookmaker. Costello claimed he had no other businesses and denied any connection with Alliance Distribution Company, a Manhattan liquor distribution company.

"I have no bank account and have not had one in twelve to fifteen years," Costello said. "I have no safe deposit box. My wife has no bank account or safe deposit box."

Costello said that his rent for his apartment at 241 Central Park West was $241 a month, something he could afford on an income of $16,000 a year. He was a man who dealt in cash, Costello explained. He admitted knowing co-defendant Al Howard for over fifteen years and had loaned him $5,000 to start up the Piping Rock nightclub and gambling establishment in Saratoga, New York. In return for the loan, Costello said he got 20 percent of the profits. Howard and he were also associated earlier in running the Brook Club, another casino in Saratoga. These comments by Costello in particular about his ties to the Piping Rock would become relevant fifteen years later when U.S. Senate investigators raked him over the coals about his businesses—both legal and illegal.

Although the FBI reports had certain names redacted, it appears that Costello admitted to the agents that he knew either Montone or Cali and that one or both had worked at the Piping Rock and had been around Broadway over the years. One memo in particular, addressed to Hoover and written by a high-ranked FBI official, spelled out what the agency believed it knew about Costello's ties to the theft: Montone had contacted Costello at a Turkish bath right after the heist. It was the Montone connection that raised suspicions about Costello with the FBI. In his own statement, Costello admitted seeing Montone after he fled to New York and meeting the thief in the Turkish bath of the Biltmore Hotel. Seated in the steam room, Costello remembered Montone asking for some money, so he gave him $30—a twenty-dollar bill and a ten-dollar bill. For Costello, such generosity was part of his character and why he found himself in such a mess.

"I want to tell you something," Costello finally told the agents. "Here is the position I am in. I am here all my life and I know everybody and I'm inclined to help almost everybody if possible with no interest, personal, financial, or otherwise. When they are in trouble, sick, or need rent and I got it, I help them, and I believe it is my reputation. This is my only interest in this whole situation and I have nothing else to say."

The meetings, the loan to Montone, the insinuation that Costello had fronted some of the money for the heist, were all bits of circumstantial evidence which the FBI pondered. Costello was a known slot machine profiteer and gambler, that much was certain. But did he play a role in the Bell jewelry theft? Records show some in the FBI thought the evidence against Costello was slim. But as would often be the case in his life, officials wanted to pursue Costello at all costs, even if the chances of conviction were 50-50. One memo to Hoover from his staff admitted that one official believed the case against Costello was "very weak," but the grand jury insisted upon indicting him.

On May 31, Costello, Howard (Contento's alias), Stern, and a fellow name Pasquale Tesoriere were arraigned in New York on federal charges stemming from the Bell jewel theft. They were charged with conspiring with Montone and Cali to transport the stolen jewels over state lines. Scaffa was charged earlier with the conspiracy and later would be hit with perjury.

"They are honest men. They have never welshed," said Moses Polakoff, the attorney for Costello, as he asked for a low bail. "The fact that a man is engaged in bookmaking at the track, if he plies the vocation honestly, is not to be held against him."

Prosecutor F.W.H. Adams said the defendants were gamblers and singled out Costello as being someone with no legitimate source of income. In fact, everybody in the case didn't know how to make an honest dollar, added Adams. Nevertheless, Costello and Contento had bail amounts set at $7,500 and $10,000 respectively while Stern and Tesoriere had to stay in a federal jail facility.

Aside from Costello, Scaffa was the next headline-making target of the FBI. In September he went to trial and was convicted of perjury before the grand jury. The trial judge indicated Scaffa didn't play any role in the actual theft. His crime was that he lied about what had happened to the Bell jewels and falsely claimed he didn't know how the stones got into the locker in Miami. Scaffa's sentence wasn't long; he got only six months. But the legal troubles prompted New York State on October 1, 1935, to revoke his private detective license. Once a highly sought-after gumshoe, Scaffa had lost his celebrity and was believed by some to be a liability and a man who could no longer be trusted. Scaffa was never the same man afterward and died from a heart attack six years later at the age of fifty-three. If he was the big gem retriever of his day and reputed to have recovered stones worth over $10 million, Scaffa didn't die rich. His estate was valued at $30,000. There were rumors that he also left behind a black book containing the names and hangouts of many of the underworld's thieves and fences.

And what of Frank Costello? From the beginning, the FBI knew it had a slim case against him in the Bell jewelry caper. The case didn't get any better as time passed. On June 4, 1937, a full two years after he was first arrested in the case, the indictment was withdrawn at the request of Manhattan U.S. Attorney Lamar Hardy. Whatever evidence the FBI had gathered against Costello was just too insignificant to provide a reasonable likelihood for conviction. Once again, when he faced a major legal problem, fortune was kind to Frank Costello and the charges went away.

CHAPTER THIRTEEN
"PUNKS, TIN HORNS, GANGSTERS AND PIMPS"

ALTHOUGH FRANK COSTELLO CONTINUED to dodge the bullet when it came to prosecutions and had tried to keep a low profile, by the end of the Depression he was clearly a much more visible character in the underworld. To the FBI he was a known gambler and ex-bootlegger who they didn't seem to know too much about. As far as Mayor Fiorello La Guardia was concerned, he was one of those "bums" and "punks" he was committed to drive out of his city.

In the face of La Guardia's juggernaut, Costello had made a tactical retreat when he moved his slot machine business to New Orleans and operated there with seeming immunity from the cops. However, as FBI files showed, Costello had significant gambling interests elsewhere in the country. There was his share of the profits from the Piping Rock and Brook Club in Saratoga Springs. He also had provided some money to his old friend Al Contento for the Embassy Club, a gambling establishment in Miami, although Costello would tell the FBI years later that he didn't take any interest or ownership of the club.

Back in New York, although La Guardia would crow that he had driven racketeers out of many industries, the fact was that Costello and others remained in control of the numbers rackets in New York City. FBI files reveal that Costello, along with Bugsy Siegel, Joe Adonis, and the ever-present Meyer Lansky were in charge of the numbers rackets. The numbers game had long been a staple of gambling in the city, and, in truth, the Mafia didn't have total control. For instance, in areas of Harlem, Stephanie "Queenie" St. Clair, a cunning and brash black woman, had significant control over some of the numbers operations there. With the help of her enforcer, Ellsworth "Bumpy" Johnson, St. Clair held off attempts by white gangsters like Dutch Schultz to push her out of the business. St. Clair outlived many of her rivals, and when Schultz was gunned down in Newark in October 1935, she was quoted as saying, "as ye sow, so shall ye reap."

With his operations outside of New York, Costello built connections to numerous gambling and numbers interests in other cities. FBI files show informants telling of Costello being active in Philadelphia and Baltimore, New Jersey, Iowa, and Chicago. The bureau was relying on more than just underworld characters to provide it with information on Costello, Schultz, and the other racketeers. FBI records show that on October 20, 1935, three days before Schultz was mortally wounded, the agency received information from a man affiliated with the *New York Post* newspaper—in what capacity remains unclear since the name was deleted—on a confidential basis. The source, who identified himself as "the informant" passed along a report to New York special agent in charge Rhea Whitley that identified Costello, Luciano, and Louis Buchalter as being "lieutenants" of someone who had control of the largest crowd in the underworld.

The claim by this mystery informant that Luciano and Costello were reporting to someone higher up the food chain of the mob is suspect for the simple reason that there didn't seem to be anyone in the mob of greater status. There may have been those of near-equal status like Albert Anastasia and Vito Genovese. But there didn't appear to be anyone above them. The man who was the informant may have been someone with particular entrée in his journalist duties— perhaps a newspaper columnist—to New York night life and the gangsters who inhabited it. That world was long the milieu that Damon Runyon loved to mine for characters, although the documents don't give any indication that Runyon was the confidential informant, unlikely also since he worked for the rival Hearst newspapers. In fact, the informant claimed to have been present during conversations with Costello who told him about the way he set up slot machines in New Orleans with the help of Huey Long. Perhaps as an indication of the bloodshed to come, the informant said in the report that when he mentioned the names of Costello or Luciano in conversation that Schultz frowned and refused to talk about them. The *New York Post* source also indicated that the mob had a "representative on the staff of Dewey" and that there was strong sentiment for Dewey to get rid of Schultz from the city.

Days after the report was passed along to the FBI, Schultz and two other associates were shot in the Palace Chophouse in Newark late in the evening on October 23, 1935. Schultz died the next day after lapsing into delirium. There was nothing more Dewey needed to do about Schultz. Meanwhile, the aggressive prosecutor, whom Schultz wanted to have killed, was free to continue going after Luciano and others.

After convicting Luciano, Dewey focused his attention on Costello by going after the liquor distribution industry. After Prohibition ended, Costello, Kastel, and others tried to keep their hands in the business of alcohol. It seems that Dewey had focused on the distribution business as an offshoot of his probe into the dealings of James Joseph Hines, a Tammany Hall leader in East Harlem who Costello was close with—and whose political ties will be dealt with a little later in this book. Hines was one of those steady political operatives who over the years had gained immense power in the Democratic Party and had been the bane of La Guardia, helping to defeat the Little Flower when he tried to get reelected to Congress in 1932.

The son of an East Harlem blacksmith who took care of the NYPD horses, Hines was described as a tall, thin-lipped man with a big physique, a jutting jaw, and cold blue eyes. Hines made a lot of money but never paid his taxes and in 1935 was forced to shell out for six years of back taxes. He also had a reputation for being on the take from gamblers like Schultz to the tune of $200,000 to protect their operations from arrest and prosecution. Hines was targeted by Dewey in 1937 as part of an investigation into labor racketeering, extortion, and restraint of trade in the bar and restaurant business. Hines wasn't charged in that case but his name came up in a trial of some labor leaders when one frightened waiter testified how he was told by one labor tough that "Jimmy Hines and The Dutchman," were behind an attempt to take over the waiters' union.

With evidence like that, Dewey focused on the restaurant business and liquor distribution. Owners of bars and restaurants had complained that low-level thugs in the employ of racketeers "persuaded" them, at the risk of bodily harm or worse, to buy liquor from certain businesses. The one company name that came up was that of Alliance Distributors, Inc., of 153 Fifth Avenue in Manhattan, a liquor distribution concern believed at the time to be one of the largest Scotch whiskey distributors in the nation of the King's Ransom and House of Lords brands. Costello not only received his mail at the company office but also frequented the place. However, in a 1935 debriefing with the FBI, Costello told agents that while he did stop by Alliance on occasion that he had no connection to the firm and insisted to agents that "my homes is my office." (In his 1951 testimony during a U.S. Senate hearing, Costello acknowledged that he had an agreement to get five shillings—about 20 pence—for every case of whiskey exported to the U.S. by Alliance. It was apparently a deal designed to get the liquor into bars and restaurants, but the arrangement fell through.)

While Dewey had success going after Luciano and others, his attempt to link Costello in a nefarious way to Alliance and the liquor racket was unsuccessful. A grand jury did indict in May 1939 an office manager at Alliance, a woman named Lilen Sanger, a thirty-year-old described as "stylishly gowned," on charges she lied about Costello and his connection to the business. She was also accused of lying when asked about attending a New Year's Eve party in Atlantic City where Costello was present. But at Sanger's trial, witnesses said she was always in another room when Costello stopped by the office suite and that she was never shown his mail. Sanger also testified that while she attended the Atlantic City dinner that she didn't know Costello was there and couldn't recognize his photo when it was shown to her in court. The three-panel group of judges, skeptical of Dewey's evidence, acquitted Sanger.

Costello was no longer a gangster with a low profile. But as the Alliance Distribution case showed, he seemed untouchable even for a tenacious prosecutor like Dewey. Unable to make cases against Costello, La Guardia and Dewey went after proxies, men close to Costello and with whom it was suspected he did business. Luciano was the most noteworthy target. Another was Frank Erickson, one of the city's biggest bookies. Born in 1896, Erickson lost his parents early in life and grew up in an orphanage. Working as a bookmaker from an early age, Erickson became adept at the business of taking bets from people about the outcome of sporting events—or any event for that matter—at agreed upon odds. Bookies set the odds, receive the money, and pay off the winners.

Erickson is credited with starting the first national wire service for gamblers, which allowed for synchronized betting around the country. Along with Costello, Erickson is also credited with setting up a system of laying off bets—spreading the risk among other bookies in case they had to make a large pay out—which became standard operating procedure in the business.

Records of the La Guardia administration show that the Mayor and William Herlands, his commissioner of investigation, put Erickson in their sights in 1939 since he was "reputedly one of the largest bookmakers and betting commissioners in the country." Erickson took betting action from around the country but primarily used his headquarters in Manhattan as a place to collect bets and pay off winners.

La Guardia and Herlands knew from law enforcement intelligence that Erickson had financial ties to not only Costello, but also Joe Adonis and other "underworld characters" like J. Richard "Dixie" Davis, the renegade lawyer for Dutch Schultz who was himself ensnared in plenty of illegality. But what also made La Guardia's blood boil was that Erickson had ties to a number of politicians and law enforcement officials, notably Brooklyn District Attorney William Geoghan, through friendship and gambling. Checks were found drawn by Erickson and payable to judges and police officers. Erickson also had a pistol permit, something Herlands thought was suspicious.

La Guardia had a tendency to fly off the handle with gamblers and all manner of gangsters, and when he learned that Erickson had handled bets from a particular acting police lieutenant wanted cops to arrest the gambler on sight. Claiming he had nothing to hide, Erickson agreed to testify to Herlands and police commissioner Lewis J. Valentine over a three-day period in April 1939. The transcript went on for over 300 pages.

Erickson acknowledged that he had been a gambler and bookmaker for over twenty years and had grown so big that his operation accepted bets on races at almost every track in the U.S. He also accepted wagers on hockey games, prize fights, and the World Series. As a way of trying to burnish his images with more respectability, Erickson said he was a "commission broker," a title Costello also used.

Asked about his underworld contacts, Erickson admitted to not only knowing Costello, but also Luciano, the elderly Johnny Torrio, Dixie Davis, and Joe Adonis. Since he had an office at 1480 Broadway in Manhattan, Erickson tried to show that he didn't take any bets there, where it would be illegal, but rather in a "wire room" in New Jersey. However, Herlands found records that showed how central the New York City office was to Erickson, serving as a clearinghouse for his large interstate operation.

But what really seemed to get Erickson into trouble was the way he handled his application for a New York City pistol permit, which he received in 1932, and allowed him to keep a revolver at his Tudor-style home at 105 Greenway South in Forest Hills, Queens. On the original application Erickson said he needed the gun to protect life and property, as well as that an "attempt had been made to kidnap applicant." But during his testimony, Erickson said it was his brother-in-law who had been kidnapped. He also listed on the application that his occupation was "retired," while he told Herlands that he was a bookmaker. Erickson also said he had never been arrested when in fact he had faced bookmaking charges at least five times, leading to dismissals or acquittals.

The end result of the testimony was that Herlands told La Guardia that Erickson could face prosecution on a number of grounds: violation of the gambling laws, lying on his pistol permit application, and being a "disorderly person" because he had no visible profession. La Guardia agreed and if he couldn't get a gambler like Costello he wanted to make sure his buddy Erickson was prosecuted.

Easier said than done. Erickson was charged with perjury, but when the case got to court a technicality got in the way of the prosecution. The two notaries who had notarized two of Erickson's permit applications couldn't remember whether or not they had taken a formal oath from the gambler. This failure in the proof troubled Queens County Judge Thomas Downs.

"Here is a man facing fifteen years in prison if he is convicted," said Downs. "How could I charge a jury on the testimony of [the notary] if he cannot remember whether he administered an oath or not? You cannot guess a man into prison."

Downs directed a verdict of acquittal and also indirectly criticized La Guardia's heavy-handed involvement in pressing the case, telling the prosecutor it wasn't his fault that the charges against Erickson had been brought.

"It is not your fault if someone in a fit of excitement wants to throw matters such as this into court," said Downs. "I am not going to let this case go to the [appellate court] and get scolded for incompetency because I am afraid of some one."

Erickson was free of the perjury charge, and La Guardia was apoplectic again. The Mayor went off on one of his anti-gangster tirades, ordering that Erickson be arrested as a disorderly person and insinuating bad things about Downs.

"Now there are just two kinds of public officials; those who want to put punks, tin horns, gangsters and pimps in jail or keep them out of the city. That is the kind I am," La Guardia said in a statement. "The other kind are those who want to keep them out of jail and in the city. If anyone wants to take that attitude that is all right with me, but we will not relent."

Predictably, Downs reacted angrily, and in a letter sent to La Guardia in June 1939 asked the Mayor point-blank if he was referring to him in his outburst after the Erickson dismissal. Downs got no response from La Guardia when he kept asking the same questions. (City archives show that in 1945, when he was no longer sitting as Mayor, La Guardia made a similar comment about Downs when the judge was running for reelection.) What did happen was that a Queens man, identified in city records as "F.P. James," wrote La Guardia claiming that Downs had been a race track bettor and had placed bets with a bookmaker bankrolled by Erickson. If true, the allegations would be political dynamite that La Guardia could have used to undermine Downs and cast doubt on his honesty. But city commissioner of investigation William Herlands looked into the allegations and wrote La Guardia, telling him that James had "given us an inaccurate, unreliable hodge-podge of facts containing scattered elements of truth" but nothing worth any official action.

Meanwhile, Erickson did battle again with the city over the charge that he was a disorderly person and vagrant who had no visible means of support. This is the kind of charge today that might fit many trust fund kids but under modern jurisprudence is an archaic concept. In Erickson's case it was ludicrous since he had plenty of money and assets, no matter how he obtained them. The vagrancy charge was also dismissed.

La Guardia's single minded, bullying actions in going after a bookmaker like Erickson, barring him from the city and pressuring judges, was the kind of stuff that if it happened today would have City Hall tied up in civil rights lawsuits for years and likely liable to pay out millions of dollars in damages. But La Guardia, emboldened by the public adoration he felt and the way people had soured against gangsters, wouldn't be deterred, no matter how petty he may have looked and how many times the courts ruled against him.

Frank Costello had moved his slot machine action to Louisiana to get away from La Guardia's clutches when City Hall in 1934 went on its crusade against gambling. Things seemed fine for Costello in the land of the Big Easy. He and Philip Kastel were raking in big money in profits, over a million dollars a year, and the authorities turned a blind eye for the most part to the presence of slot machines. Graft seemed endemic in Louisiana at that time in all sorts of public contracts and endeavors. For the slot machines it seemed a perfect environment for the business to flourish. Costello and Loretta visited the state frequently; her brothers Harold and Dudley took up residence there, as did Kastel and his wife while they maintained a nice summer home in Connecticut.

But Costello was a known quantity to the FBI and the Internal Revenue Service. For at least four years, from 1934 to 1937, the IRS installed taps on the telephones of people Costello had dealings with. The IRS even at one point put a tap on a hotel phone used by Costello and Kastel. The same was true for the New York State police and NYPD which passed along information to the federal tax people, some going back to Costello's bootlegging days. Auditors had been going over Costello's and Kastel's tax returns and thought they saw blood in the water. If there was any doubt in Costello's mind that he was under serious tax scrutiny, that disappeared in late August 1939 when he was called to testify before a Manhattan federal grand jury about the New Orleans slot machine venture he had with Kastel, who also testified. There were also a lot of questions about who had a piece of the partnership Kastel and Costello had set up to run the New Orleans slot venture.

Armed with what they thought was strong evidence that Costello and Kastel had evaded federal taxes with their New Orleans slots, the U.S. Attorney's Office in New Orleans indicted them both in October 1939. They also indicted the two Geigerman brothers along with James Brocato and Jacob Altman, both of New Orleans. The government charged that the group evaded over $500,000 in taxes—said to be the second-largest evasion case of its kind at that time—by falsifying ownership records of the Bayou Novelty Company slot machine venture. Costello surrendered in New York on October 9 dressed in one of his signature gray suits, and actually showed up at government offices thinking he had been called down to testify in another national crime inquiry. Instead he was arraigned on the Louisiana charges and held on $75,000 bail, which he raised the next day.

It would take seven months for the Louisiana tax evasion case to come to trial. In the meantime, back in New York City, Fiorello La Guardia tried to keep the pressure on Costello through the NYPD. In April 1940, La Guardia said he had picked up information that Costello was active along the waterfront and tasked the NYPD with finding out what they could about the situation. The waterfront was actually the turf of at least two mob families, the Mangano clan along the Brooklyn piers and Luciano's family in Manhattan, particularly around the South Street fish market. Based on what was found in city archives, the cops didn't find very much about Costello and the docks. In an internal memo, the Manhattan borough detective squad listed the basics about Costello, reporting his incorrect true name was "Saverio" and had records of various arrests, including the 1915 gun case and the 1935 Bell jewelry heist conspiracy, as well as the looming tax case in New Orleans. The police report was barebones and included an allegation that Costello and actor George Raft jointly owned the Hurricane Restaurant at 1619 Broadway.

The detectives noted that Costello was about to stand trial in New Orleans for tax evasion. The cops promised that detectives "assigned to duty along the waterfront, will continue to give this matter every possible attention." The police response was a bureaucratic kiss-off and with Costello in Louisiana, there wasn't really much else for the NYPD to observe about him along the waterfront. Yet, Costello had clout on the waterfront, notably through Joseph "Socks" Lanza, who controlled the Fulton Fish Market, and in Brooklyn with the Camarda brothers, especially Emil Camarda an important official with the International Longshoremen's Association. Camarda had control with Anthony "Tough Tony" Anastasio, of the so-called "Italian" locals of the ILA. Costello's ties to the docks would become important later on in the fast approaching period of World War Two. But he had more pressing problems facing him with the tax case.

Costello's trial for tax evasion, along with Kastel and the others involved in New Orleans slot machines began on May 6, 1939, and although it wasn't big news in the New York newspapers it was in Louisiana. The major local interest there was in the political angle surrounding the way Costello said he introduced slot machines into the state through Huey Long. But the evidence didn't support the government.

On May 15, 1940, a verdict of acquittal was ordered in favor of Costello, Kastel, and all the others. Frank Costello had managed to escape unscathed from another federal case. Since 1927, the box score read: Costello 3 and federal prosecutors 0. Costello left the courthouse and neither he nor his attorneys commented. The prosecutors for that matter were also mum. (In 1945, the U.S. Tax Court backed the defense position when it found that the IRS hadn't proved that Costello and Kastel were equal partners in Bayou. The Tax Court also found that Kastel was liable for the taxes on the entire amount he received from the company, regardless of what he may have shared with Costello.)

Back in New York several days after Costello walked free, NYPD commissioner Lewis J. Valentine wrote a letter to La Guardia to pass along some perfunctory police reports on Costello and made note of the results in New Orleans, in the process misspelling the judge's name and misidentifying the court where the trial took place. La Guardia didn't hide his contempt for Costello.

"Now that he has been acquitted down in New Orleans, keep a sharp eye on him," La Guardia wrote back to Valentine. "See that he is kept away from the waterfront and places of public gathering should he return to New York. I consider him a vagrant under the law and appropriate action should be taken."

There was no way of La Guardia knowing at the time but with war clouds looming in Europe, history would show that Costello's ties to the waterfront would actually prove useful in World War Two, when the U.S. military turned to the Mafia—Costello included—to help secure the port of New York against wartime sabotage and help with the invasion of Italy.

CHAPTER FOURTEEN
"I NEVER STOLE A NICKEL IN MY LIFE"

THE STORY, TOLD MANY TIMES about Frank Costello's political influence, related back to 1932 and the Democratic National Convention in Chicago. It was there, according to George Wolf, that his client entertained delegates in and around the Drake Hotel to work to assure the nomination of Franklin Delano Roosevelt as the party's presidential candidate. The political wheeling and dealing was just like back home in New York.

"Here in Chicago, what did it turn out to be?" said Wolf. "Guys running up and down hotel corridors day and night trading votes and offering jobs and threatening political revenge just like little old Tammany Hall."

In that case, Costello was very familiar with the machinations of Tammany Hall. After all, he was there in Chicago with none other than Jimmy Hines, the leader of Tammany. Their candidate Roosevelt secured the nomination and went on to win the 1932 Presidential election. All the boozing and schmoozing had paid off. Just to hedge its bets, other branches of Tammany backed Roosevelt's main rival Al Smith—just in case.

The story of how Costello became intertwined with Tammany and its power is one of the great mob stories of the era. In a town so solidly Democratic for decades, Tammany controlled government, the court, and cops. Public officials who sought office had to please the leaders of the organization and protect its interests. It was a culture of corruption with payoffs all around. It all seemed so appropriate. Everybody got a taste, and the criminals—on the street and in City Hall—were happy. It wasn't "honest graft," the kind George Washington Plunkitt, the Tammany orator, said was okay because it never hurt anybody. "I seen my opportunities and I took them," was how Plunkitt rationalized lining his bank account. No, these were the kinds of alliances that created the nefarious banks of another sort, the favor banks where politicians were promised support and money if they laid off the criminals and allowed them to go about their illegal businesses.

Costello had known that it paid to have political connections growing up in East Harlem. He was aware of how Giousue Gallucci, the onetime boss of Little Italy during Costello's youth, had added to his reputation on the street by being involved with politicians. He was seen as a man of influence with officialdom, as well as a chief criminal boss of the area surrounding 108th Street—as long as he was able to duck the assassin's bullet. It was unclear when exactly Costello got involved with the Democratic party. But it appears that at some point he became part of an organization known as The Tough Club, a Tammany organization on the West Side.

The relationship between the mob and Tammany was one that seemed to be shaped by the reality of their separate worlds. While Tammany was once a power with a great deal of financial resources, that had waned in the 1920s and 1930s. La Guardia had made merit selection for jobs a bedrock of his administration, thus undercutting the patronage Tammany was able to trade upon. Still, it was the Mafia, buoyed by Prohibition, which had the money the organization needed.

"Tammany Hall was poor and growing poorer, while the mobsters (despite La Guardia's crackdowns) were wealthier than ever," said Oliver E. Allen in his book *The Tiger: The Rise and Fall of Tammany Hall*. "Recognizing the value of protection, the gang leaders required—even demanded Tammany's aid. By now they were virtually calling the shots and Tammany could hardly refuse to listen since it desperately needed the money."

The Mafia projected its powers through Tammany's district lead-

ers. This was done either, as Allen stated, through the appointment
of Albert Marinelli at the behest of Luciano, or through the overall
corrupt lives some of the leaders lived. The case in point for the latter
was Hines, the man Costello accompanied to Chicago. Hines was
leader of a district that included the Upper West Side and Harlem. The
West Side was a major storage and shipping area for the bootleggers.
Harlem was an area in which gangs competed for the numbers operations, notably Dutch Schultz and Stephanie St. Claire, the brassy,
independent black woman who staved off many attempts by the Italians and Jews to cut into her territory or force her out of business.

Hines had no real clout with St. Claire. But with Schultz, Hines
found a steady stream of income in the form of protection money
paid by the gambler. The payments came in regular envelopes filled
with $500. What Schultz got in return was the knowledge that his
political friend Hines had co-opted the Manhattan district attorney,
William C. Dodge, by sanctioning his run for the office. It was a
very convenient relationship.

But after grand jurors became exasperated with Dodge's timid approach to serious organized crime, Thomas Dewey was appointed
special prosecutor and things suddenly changed for Hines. After indicting and convicting Luciano, Dewey turned his sights on Hines
and the result was just as devastating. Hines was a politician who
one reporter said seemed "impregnable to prosecution." Nevertheless, with Dewey running the grand jury, Hines was indicted in August 1938 for protecting Schultz and his gambling racket. Using the
threat of long prison terms to coerce their cooperation, Dewey got
two of Schultz's associates—George Weinberg and Harry Schoen-
haus—to become government witnesses. Their testimony showed
how rigged the criminal justice system had become under Hines.
The Tammany leader, the witnesses said, so controlled city magistrate Hulon Capshaw that cases were dismissed on Hines say-so,
with Capshaw telling him, "I have never failed you yet, have I
Jimmy?"

Witness upon witness told of the close ties between Hines and
Schultz. Frances Flegenheimer, the widow of Schultz (who had been
assassinated in 1935) was an eighteen-year-old hat-check girl when

she married the Dutchman. She told of how Schultz and Hines had met in a Manhattan speakeasy known as The Stable in November 1932 and disappeared in the back for about a half hour. When both men came out and Hines left, Schultz told his wife to "forget about seeing Jimmy Hines in here tonight." Schultz went on the lam shortly after the meeting, but his wife said he still provided her with cash.

Dodge, like Capshaw, wasn't indicted in the case. But the witnesses told how pliant the prosecutor had been. Hines described Dodge as "stupid, respectable and mine," while he bragged that NYPD's division in Harlem was under his thumb. But those were warm ups. Other witnesses showed how blatantly corrupt Hines had been by the way he had cops demoted because they wouldn't lay off Schultz's gambling parlors. Then Dewey pulled another rabbit out of the hat when he called a surprise witness, John Curry, the former Tammany leader who was thrown out through Hines's power plays in 1934. On the witness stand it was Curry's turn for revenge when he told the jury that it had been Hines who demanded that Dodge be Tammany's candidate for Manhattan district attorney in 1933 and that NYPD commissioner James Bolan reassign cops in the 65th Division who had been causing problems for criminals and numbers operators.

Hines was shown to be a man who was used his naked political power to protect the criminals and his friends, as well as line his own pockets, the kinds of things the public and reform politicians like La Guardia had screamed about for years. On February 25, 1939, after only seven hours of deliberation, a Manhattan state jury convicted the once untouchable Hines on all counts. "That's the breaks of the game," Hines said after the verdict. He would appeal, but the case finished his political career. The newspaper trumpeted the Dewey victory. "Democracy Cleans Its Own House," *The Evening Post* said in one editorial, to be followed by "Bankrupt Tammany Must Now Be Liquidated."

Frank Costello didn't come up in the Hines trials, despite his own ties to Tammany. Federal authorities were breathing hard trying to make a tax case against him in New Orleans over the slot machine busi-

ness. But in New York, Costello remained untouchable, although not totally unnoticed. His name did come up when La Guardia released a report about Frank Erickson's gambling empire. The fifteen-page
document prepared by William B. Herlands, then the city commissioner of investigation, listed Costello as one of the "underworld
characters" Erickson had a relationship with. Herland's list included
Joe Adonis and Schultz's old and now disbarred lawyer Richard
"Dixie" Davis. Still, Costello was out of reach of La Guardia or any
of the local prosecutors.

Costello had built his power base not only on gambling and his
command of the Luciano crime family but also on his ties to Tammany. He held no official position in Tammany: it would have been
ludicrous and foolish if he had. What Costello did do was to cultivate close ties and friendships to a number of Tammany's district
leaders, the men who commanded the local political clubs tied to the
main organization. One district leader was Dr. Paul F. Sarubbi, and
another John DeSalvio (also known as Jimmy Kelly). Two others
were Abraham Rosenthal and Clarence H. Neal Jr.

With its powerbase eroding and the embarrassing revelations
about Hines's blatant corruption, Tammany went through some
leadership changes at the top in which Costello played a major role.
A former Congressman, Christy Sullivan, had taken over as boss of
Tammany in 1937 but bore the responsibility for some significant
election reverses, including the reelection of La Guardia, the organization's nemesis. So, in 1942, Sullivan was voted out and Michael J.
Kennedy voted in as boss by Tammany's executive committee.
Costello influenced the four district leaders he was close with—
Sarubbi, DeSalvio, Rosenthal, and Neal—to back Kennedy. As historian Allen later reported, the committee had Costello as its guest
the day of the vote, a man some in the organization called "the
boss."

Costello's power behind Tammany had been generally obscured
from the public, which had no inkling of what went on in the smoke-
filled rooms and private restaurant meetings where he excelled at
making his influence felt. Those politicians who knew of Costello's
reputation in the underworld also knew he was a major mob boss.

But they also were taken in by his smoothness and his persuasiveness, Costello's style of doing business. He had cultivated an image as a gentleman above suspicion.

The secrecy that surrounded Costello's political role suddenly stripped away when Manhattan's new district attorney, Frank Hogan, decided to place a wiretap on Costello's home telephone in mid-1943. Hogan had succeeded Dewey as district attorney in 1942, after the racket-busting prosecutor became Governor of New York. The exact reason for the placement of the tap on Costello was never made clear but likely stemmed from his various mob associations and intelligence about his secret business dealings in the Manhattan nightclub world and the suspicions of him holding a hidden interest in the Copacabana and other venues.

Normally, wiretaps don't become public unless they are part of a court case or other proceeding. Costello was never charged with any crimes as a result of the fruits of the Hogan wiretap, which appears to have ended in November 1943. But on August 28, 1943, Hogan released details of one recording, which had captured Costello talking with Magistrate Thomas A. Aurelio, a judicial candidate in the upcoming election for a spot on the New York County Supreme Court.

"Gangster Backed Aurelio For Bench, Prosecutor Avers," blared *The New York Times* on a front paper headline the next day. In a public statement Hogan admitted that while Costello's backing of the candidate wasn't a crime, the prosecutor made clear that his sense of decency was offended by the ties that existed between the gangster and Aurelio.

"Although the facts developed so far do not disclose the commission of a crime, this affront to the electorate and the threat to the integrity of the judiciary called for action on my part," said Hogan as he released the materials. The prosecutor admitted that he was publicizing his evidence in the hopes that Tammany's leader Michael Kennedy—an ally of Costello as it turned out—would take action to repudiate Aurelio's candidacy.

Had a prosecutor in modern times released piecemeal evidence of political meddling from a wiretap, the action might be considered a crime. But Hogan was operating at a point in history when the city had been primed, by La Guardia's words and deeds, to hold gangsters in disdain. It was as if anything goes in the fight against the mob. The disclosure would bring grief and embarrassment to Costello and Aurielio and lead to the further slide in Tammany's power and prestige.

Just what did Hogan capture on the wiretaps? The evidence Hogan revealed in a transcript was of a conversation Aurelio had with Costello the morning of August 24, four days before the prosecutor told the world about the existence of the wiretap. It was a call that candidate Aurelio made to Costello's private, unlisted home telephone, and he seemed jubilant over getting the nomination.

The transcript described the conversation:

> AURELIO: Good morning, Francesco. How are you, and thanks for everything.
> COSTELLO: Congratulations. It went over perfect. When I tell you something is in the bag, you can rest assured.
> AURELIO: It was perfect. Arthur Klein did the nominating; first me, then Gavagan, then Peck. It was fine.
> COSTELLO: That's fine.
> AURELIO: The doctor called me last night to congratulate me. I'm going to see him today. He seems to be improving. He should be up and around soon and should take the train for Hot Springs.
> COSTELLO: That is the plan.

That initial piece of the conversation was Aurelio recounting for Costello what had happened during the nominating convention. The doctor he referred to was apparently Dr. Sarubbi, a district leader who was Costello's personal physician as well. It appeared that Sarubbi was recovering from an illness and was planning to go to Hot Springs, Arkansas, a resort where Costello himself liked to take the waters.

Later in the conversation, Aurelio mentions a man whose name was deleted from the transcript but whom Costello should do something for because "he certainly deserves something."

"Well, we will have to get together, you, your missus, and myself and have dinner some night real soon," said Costello.

"That would be fine," answered Aurelio, "but right now I want to assure you of my loyalty for all you have done. It's undying."

"I know," replied Costello. "I will see you soon."

On its face, the conversation Costello and Aurelio had that day was innocent of any suggestion of wrongdoing. But for Hogan, it was a question of Costello's disreputable character and the suggestion—which the prosecutor never proved—that Aurelio knew of Costello's bad reputation when he accepted his support in getting the nomination. The intimacy and influence Costello seemed to have with Aurelio, as shown in the one conversation, seemed an affront to the judiciary and law enforcement. Hogan had the job of derailing Aurelio and in the process undercutting any political power Costello had, while trying to make him a pariah.

Hogan recounted Costello's criminal record, admitting he only had the one gun-possession conviction as a young man, and noted his arrests on federal charges. There was also Costello's reputation as a "racketeer and gangster," as well as his notoriety as "czar of the slot machine and gambling racket and as a banker and money man for innumerable gambling enterprises." On top of all that, Hogan noted Costello's close ties to Luciano and Joe Adonis as well as Jewish gangsters Louis Buchalter, Jacob Shapiro, Abe "Longie" Zwillman, Meyer Lansky, and Bugsy Siegel. For an added kick in the pants, Hogan said that federal authorities had Costello on a "blacklist" of narcotics traffickers. He was referring to some vague rumblings federal narcotics officials had picked up that Costello was somehow involved in drug trafficking, although there was nothing concrete.

The reaction from the political establishment was predictable. Kennedy proclaimed that all the judicial candidates were chosen solely on merit and their "high, professional reputation." There had been no pressure to put Aurelio on the ballot.

"No pressure or influence of any kind from any source was exerted on me or on any of my colleagues on the executive committee," said Kennedy, referring to the Tammany committee. But if the charges by Hogan about Aurelio having taken Costello's help were true, then the candidate's nomination should be "repudiated," said Kennedy.

Aurelio was the most unlikely whipping boy for the reformers. After graduating law school in 1918, Aurelio had worked as an assistant district attorney before Mayor Jimmy Walker appointed him a magistrate in 1931. La Guardia reappointed him to the post in 1935 and said that "his work on the bench and his age are all in his favor." La Guardia also noted that Aurelio had "not abused the police," indicating he sided with cops who were going after criminals. In short, he seemed a competent law-and-order magistrate.

Similar condemnations came from other Democrats and Republicans, as well as smaller political groups like the American Labor Party, bar associations, and good-government groups. There was no way that Aurelio, or Costello for that matter, would be able to weather the storm of indignation swirling around them without any consequences. As a result of the Hogan revelations, the Appellate Division in Manhattan, the court that supervises attorneys and admits them to the practice of law, was going to hold a disbarment hearing on Aurelio after a formal complaint had been made by the Association of The Bar of The City of New York. Disbarment was the only way to keep Aurelio off the ballot since he refused to withdraw and too little time remained before the upcoming election for any party to get a new candidate.

The court set a schedule of public hearings in October for the disbarment action and subpoenaed a number of people, including Aurelio and Costello. Faced with a new legal challenge and more scrutiny, Costello needed a good lawyer, and for that he turned to George Wolf, an attorney whom he knew vaguely since he had represented one of the defendants in the old bootlegging cases years earlier. As Wolf recalled in his book, Costello summoned him to his apartment at 115 Central Park West with a telephone call on September 13.

Wolf described the impressive setting he found at the apartment:

His apartment was a seven-room penthouse on the eighteenth floor, obviously furnished in extremely good taste by a fine decorator. The living room was enormous, with antique gold hangings with scalloped valances, lamp tables of beautiful mahogany, antique lamps, and a wood-burning fireplace with a Howard Chandler Christy oil portrait above it.

Costello was wearing a conservative dark suit and impressed Wolf as being a "swarthy man, with black hair brushed straight back from his forehead, brown eyes and creases around his thin lips. His nose was sharp and gave him a sort of Cyrano de Bergerac profile."

Wolf kept a diary and noted that in their meeting Costello admitted giving help to Aurelio by telling the then-magistrate to get the support of Italian organizations and speak with Kennedy, the head of Tammany. Also, according to Wolf's account, Costello said he also urged Aurelio to get La Guardia's support and for the Mayor to speak to Kennedy. Costello noted that he spoke to Kennedy but that Aurelio had said his case was hopeless.

Wolf said he pressed Costello on why private politicians would come to him for advice on a candidate and how he had such power in the party, questions which Costello avoided answering at that time.

"Look, Mr. Wolf, I told you enough. You want to find out more, go talk to Abe Rosenthal, Clarence Neal, Dr. Sarubbi," said Costello, Wolf recalled.

Wolf took on Costello as a client and would be his counselor at law for most of the rest of the Mafia leader's life. Wolf had one bit of advice for his client: tell the truth. The only thing that can get you into trouble was lying under oath. If Costello needed assurance about his new lawyer, Meyer Lansky gave it to him: "You got yourself a good lawyer there."

The first order of business was the disbarment hearing against Aurelio, and the event turned into a spectacle. Hogan indicated he thought it would take four days to present evidence to the presiding referee, a former Appellate Court and Court of Appeals judge named Charles B. Sears. Hogan was certain that disbarment of Aurelio would be the end result. Hogan's strategy was to show Costello's criminal life, the bootlegging and the gambling, and all the disreputable Mafiosi and gangsters the man knew. He planned to do that through Costello's own words.

Costello took the stand in the disbarment case on October 26, 1943, and was described as being modest in the way he admitted helping Aurelio get the nomination but that he was able to do so because of having helped Kennedy become leader of Tammany Hall. Because of that, said Costello, he was able to hold Kennedy to his promise to help Aurelio get the nomination.

Hogan dug into Costello's background, the usual stuff that was already known about his days as a bootlegger and gambler. Yet at one point Costello pointedly told Hogan that he had held an honest job a number of times, from the time he was arrested on the gun charge in 1915 to the present day where he was involved in the manufacture of Kewpie dolls.

"I gamble yes, but I never stole a nickel in my life," an indignant Costello said at one point.

The slot machines he had weren't all bad, he said. A bettor can always get something: "They do have slugs, but you always get a mint."

Hogan couldn't resist dragging up Costello's friends in the mob, and Costello didn't duck the questions. There was Arnold Rothstein, who Costello knew well and lent "quite large" amounts of cash. Gangsters like Frank Nitti, Lucky Luciano, "Trigger Mike" Coppola, Louis Buchalter, Joe Rao, Jerry Catena, Owney Madden, and Anthony Carfano were all "very good friends" or else "acquaintances."

As far as Costello was concerned, a promise was something to be kept, be it in the Mafia or politics. When Kennedy seemed to be cooling off toward Aurelio's candidacy, Costello told Hogan that he confronted the Tammany boss and chided his manhood.

"I asked him, what are you, a man or a mouse?" related Costello. "You made a promise and should live up to it. You're the Tammany Hall leader—you're the boss—and your word should be your bond. You ought to declare yourself."

In the end Kennedy did say he was going to back Aurelio, said

Costello. He related that he had other meetings with Neal, Sarubbi, DeSalvio, and Kennedy at nightclubs and restaurants. As a courtesy to Costello, referee Sears held a secret hearing to allow Costello to relate the names of respectable people he knew. They were acquaintances of ten to twenty years whom Costello met for an occasional round of golf or a drink.

Costello's testimony proved what was already known to law enforcement—that he was an old bootlegger and gambler. Did he have notorious friends? Certainly. He also reminded everyone that he had respectable associates as well. Did Costello have political power because he was a gangster? Hogan's questioning and Costello's answers danced around the issue and left it to the imagination of where his power really came from. But the prosecutor knew he had scored points by showing to the world what Costello was about.

"Hogan merely smiled, apparently satisfied with the spectacular testimony he had drawn forth," Wolf later recalled. "It would alert both government and civic leaders that a criminal with nationwide underworld connections controlled the Democratic Party at every level in New York."

Aurelio's day as a witness was more important because his future depended on it. Costello wasn't facing any charges, at least not yet. But Aurelio could see his progression to a vaunted judgeship come to a disgraceful end if Sears ruled against him. Described by one newspaper account as being a "meek-mannered, puffy-cheeked individual with a mild voice," Aurelio told Sears that his chance at a judgeship came out of the blue when he was at a meeting with Kennedy, who was not yet Tammany leader, and others at the New York Athletic Club. It was then that Kennedy, who was vying for control of Tammany, said "If I was the leader of Tammany Hall, there's the man I would have nominated, Tom Aurelio."

Encouraged by Kennedy's remark, Aurelio said he then went about trying to get the nomination, talking to veterans' groups, prominent Democrats, as well as La Guardia, in the weeks before the judicial convention. It was Joseph Lescalzo, an assistant district attorney in Queens County who introduced him to Costello in February 1943, remembered Aurelio.

"That was the first time I ever saw or heard of that man," Aurelio said.

Aurelio recounted a meeting at Kennedy's office, which other witnesses had testified about, in which the Tammany boss took him outside of the room and told him: "Your leader is behind you, but I want you to know that I'm promising you nothing. It's too early. I am considering it."

As the summer went on, Aurelio testified that he became concerned when another candidate might be emerging for Supreme Court and asked Costello about it. Costello responded, said Aurelio, by saying "everyone believes you are going to get the nomination" and that it was "in the bag."

How then did Costello know Aurelio had a good shot at the nomination? Did he coerce leaders like Kennedy and the others at Tammany? Or was Kennedy too frightened of what he may have heard about Costello's role as boss of the crime family to act contrary to his wishes? At least one witness testified that Costello was consulted for approval of prospective patronage appointments. It was fair to speculate on either question, but the simple fact was that there was no proof on either of those points presented by Hogan. In the end it just seemed to be innuendo based on Costello's career as a gangster.

Aurelio's attorney was about to ask him about the infamous telephone call to Costello when referee Sears adjourned the hearing for a short recess. The hearing had not brought out any direct evidence that Aurelio knew of Costello's past and in the face of that flaw in his case, Hogan ended his presentation. Other witnesses admitted knowing about Costello and his slot machine empire but Aurelio denied knowing about Costello's criminal ties or bad character.

Less than a week after the disbarment hearing ended, Sears put a stake in the heart of Hogan's effort to crush Aurelio. In a 7,000-word report dated October 30, 1943, Sears said that there was no question Aurelio sought out the aid of Costello to get the Democratic nomination for the judgeship. It was also clear that, as Sears noted, "Frank Costello is a man of bad character, an associate of malefactors" who himself was convicted of a crime and violated the law.

But Hogan didn't prove that Aurelio knew of any of Costello's character flaws, Sears stressed.

"The defect in the proceeding is that the record is wholly barren of any fact showing [Aurelio] had knowledge of Costello's bad character, or information to put [Aurelio] on inquiry with respect to his character," said Sears. "The testimony of Costello's bad character and bad reputation is not sufficient to establish [Aurelio's] knowledge in the face of his positive and unqualified denials."

As a candidate for office, it wasn't Aurelio's obligation to search the record of every person who gave him political support, said Sears. That would be just too harsh a rule, he added. Nor should Aurelio have been obligated to withdraw from the nomination once he learned of Costello's bad record. Sears noted that Costello was "apparently living a respectable life in a respectable neighborhood," referring to Central Park West. It also was significant that he knew people like Kennedy and Dr. Sarubbi, who happened to be Costello's personal physician.

"To require him to renounce his career because he learned of unworthy support would be an extravagant penalty for an act for which he bore no moral responsibility," concluded Sears. In the end, Sears recommended against disbarment, and the Appellate Division in Manhattan voted unanimously to affirm his decision. The case for disbarment was over, a defeat for both Hogan who presented the evidence and the white-shoe Association of The Bar of the City of New York. With the disbarment attempt behind him, as well as a failed eleventh-hour effort by the Democratic and Republican parties to yank him from the ballot, Aurelio had a clear shot to election day.

On November 2, 1943, Aurelio got the final vindication he needed when he won the seventh spot on the Supreme Court list, beating his nearest rival by nearly 50,000 votes. After the results became known, Aurelio avoided any public statements and retreated to the seclusion of his home in Manhattan. The victory was secured despite editorials in *The New York Times* that said that Aurelio was Costello's candidate and lambasted the jurist as being too irrespon-

sible and too reckless for not inquiring about the character of
Costello. Having survived the storm over his ties to Costello, Aurelio remained a jurist for over two decades without any more controversy or any blemishes on his record. He retired as a justice from the
Appellate Division, a prestigious court.

However, controversy and bad publicity were going to follow
Frank Costello around for a long time. Hogan's grand jury petered
out with no charges against Costello, raising the question of whether
it was all just a fishing expedition, which in the end finally salvaged
something to show with the Aurelio wiretapped conversation. Years
later, Hogan admitted during testimony in a federal court case that
the probe of Costello indeed had ended in late November 1943.

After the hearings, Wolf took Costello to one of his client's favorite spots, the Madison Hotel cocktail lounge. Although Costello
once had anonymity, with the headlines about the Aurelio hearings
fresh on the newsstands, the attorney said he couldn't help notice the
glances and whispers of the other patrons. Here was Frank Costello,
racketeer in their midst.

Costello went to great lengths to keep the respectable people he
knew out of the public testimony and for the most part succeeded
when Sears allowed him to talk about those friends in a closed-door
session. But he was still angry at the way Hogan had dredged up all
the gangsters who had crossed his path. Over drinks, Wolf said that
was done in an effort to show that Aurelio had to know Costello was
a big crime boss.

"What kind of crap is that," Costello responded, remembered
Wolf. "Boss of all crime! I am a gambler, period. I'm a business-
man. Just because I run into these guys at the track and the Copa,
Hogan makes a federal case out of it."

Costello never hid his bootleg and gambling past. But he considered himself now beyond that. Like Jay Gatsby, he wanted to be
considered respectable.

"Who is the boss?" Wolf recalled finally asking his client.

"Hell, you know better than anybody else," was Costello's response.
"Charlie Lucky. You're the guy getting him out of 'college.'"

CHAPTER FIFTEEN
"WHAT THE HELL ARE YOU FELLOWS DOING HERE?"

THE "COLLEGE" CHARLES LUCIANO WAS ATTENDING after his conviction for the prostitution racket was the inhospitable New York State prison in the upstate village of Dannemora. The facility is sometimes known as "little Siberia" since, located some twenty miles from the Canadian border, it faces bitterly cold winters and a deluge of snow. Known officially as the Clinton Correctional Center, the facility is often referred to simply by the village name: Dannemora.

That Luciano was sent to Dannemora was no accident. He was far away from his associates in the crime family, and getting to see him in the prison was an arduous journey. Luciano was effectively in isolation at such a remote location. But his closest friends and associates like Frank Costello did make the occasional trip to see him. Luciano could have spent the rest of his days at Dannemora until a series of events, all related to World War Two, came together in one of the strangest and unusual wartime operations. It all started with a welder's torch on the Hudson River docks of Manhattan in February 1942.

The *SS Normandie* was a French cruise liner that had been docked at a pier in the Hudson River where it had been sequestered since the start of World War Two. When she took her maiden voyage in 1935, she was considered the fastest and largest ocean liner afloat. But invoking the obscure legal doctrine of *angary,* the U.S. government seized the vessel for use during the war and rechristened it the *USS Lafayette*. The ship was in New York City at Pier 88 where she was being reconfigured and outfitted as a troop ship when at about 2:30 P.M. on February 9, a fire broke out. A careless welder ignited some life vests that contained flammable kapok. Through a series of mishaps and miscalculations, the fire spread. Because of a large amount of water sprayed on to the *Lafayette* to stem the fire, the vessel developed a dangerous list and early on February 10 capsized. The headlines talked of possible sabotage by Axis agents and in the wartime environment a story like that had traction, despite the fact that an investigation showed that the mishap was the result of human negligence and incompetence. The U.S. also had fears of German U-boats learning from spies about convoy operations.

With the New York waterfront one of the largest in the country and as the best port to supply U.S. military efforts in Europe and Africa, the Navy, fearing that it had gaps in its intelligence on the docks turned to the one group who knew the port better than any other—the Mafia. In the months before he took on Frank Costello as a client, George Wolf remembered that Luciano's attorney, Moses Polakoff, called him to say that Naval Intelligence, notably through the offices of Cmdr. Charles Haffenden, wanted Luciano's help, and the help of other mobsters, to guard the waterfront from espionage.

It sounded like a wild scheme. But Manhattan District Attorney Frank Hogan assigned a top aide, Murray Gurfein, to work with the military and to develop underworld sources who could help Haffenden. Of particular usefulness would be information about refueling activities of rum runners who might be tipping off the German navy and leading to losses of Allied shipping. There was also suspicion that fishing boats were helping German submarines replenish supplies and recharge their batteries so they could stay close to the U.S. coastline and torpedo Allied ships.

Waterfront gangster Joseph "Socks" Lanza, a member of Luciano's family and an official with the United Seafood Workers' Union, was the first to be approached for cooperation. With his contacts, Lanza knew a great many people working in the fish market as well as captains of fishing boats, bargemen, and seamen on the Atlantic coast. He and his attorney met Gurfein at 135th Street and

Riverside Drive, with the arrangements set up cloak-and-dagger style. Lanza, a power along the Manhattan waterfront, was already under indictment and wanted secrecy for the meeting because he was worried about being spotted talking to a member of law enforcement, something that might cast suspicion that he was working as an informant.

Aware that his help wouldn't mean that Hogan could make any promises about the criminal cases Lanza faced, the gangster agreed to help Haffenden. Lanza helped get union cards for Navy undercover agents so they could travel as crew on fishing boats. Civilians working for the Navy were also given union cards so they could keep jobs with companies that trucked fish from Long Island to the Manhattan market. Fishing vessels helped bring back debris from the ocean, including spent flares and human body parts, for examination by the Navy. But Lanza's influence was limited to the fishing industry and he admitted that his status as a defendant in a pending criminal case made some suspect he was working for the police, thus limiting his usefulness.

"Socks decided to cooperate anyway, but shortly afterward he told Haffenden 'certain elements' wouldn't help unless they got word from Charlie Lucky [Luciano]," Wolf said years later. "One of these 'certain elements'—unnamed, of course—was Frank Costello, who wanted Luciano back in charge so he could resume his own businesses without the responsibility that came with the title Boss of all Bosses."

Lanza made clear that Luciano could help because, as he told Gurfein and others, Luciano still had clout and could get valuable information. "The word of Luciano may give me the right of way," Lanza said at one point. He also said that if Luciano was on board with the idea, he would send out the word to Adonis, Costello, and others to help. Gurfein approached Polakoff who was at first reluctant to get involved since he had not spoken to Luciano since his last lost appeal. But Gurfein appealed to the attorney by saying it was something very important and Polakoff agreed to arrange a meeting with Lansky, a man whom Luciano trusted.

During a meeting at Longchamps Restaurant on Fifty-eighth Street in Manhattan, Gurfein made his pitch to Lansky who agreed to help any way he could. But the Jewish gangster also sounded a note of caution: Some Italians still liked Mussolini and any approach to them had to be done carefully. Would Luciano help? Sure, said Lansky, his entire family—parents, brothers, sisters, nieces, and nephews were in the U.S. To make it easier to gain access to Luciano, the state agreed that he be housed in a less onerous place than Dannemora and transferred him to Great Meadow Correctional Center, a maximum-security facility near Albany. Great Meadow was about three hours from Manhattan and considered plush accommodations compared to Dannemora.

Polakoff and Lansky traveled to Great Meadow and met for the first time with Luciano on May 15, 1942. "What the hell are you fellows doing here?" a surprised Luciano said as he was brought to the prison warden's office for the unexpected visit. (As Luciano later remembered the first meeting, it was actually at Sing Sing prison with Costello and attorney George Wolf present. Everyone talked over a spread of kosher pickles, Dr. Brown's Celery Tonic, and cold cuts.) Polakoff and Lansky told Luciano how the Navy needed his help and the crime boss agreed to go along. Luciano asked that Lanza make a trip to Great Meadow so he could tell the waterfront boss who to see and what to tell them back in New York. But, Luciano had one condition: he wanted his cooperation to be kept a secret, particularly since the government wanted him to be deported at some point.

"When I get out—nobody knows how this war will turn out—whatever I do, I want it kept quiet, private, so that when I get back to Italy I am not a marked man," said Luciano. He clearly felt uncertainty at that point about who would be in power in Italy when hostilities stopped and didn't want to be outed as a secret agent of the U.S. government. A beating or even a lynching were things on Luciano's mind when he asked for assurances of secrecy.

From May 1942 until August 1945, a stream of visitors from the mob visited Luciano in prison, with Lanza and Lansky being the most frequent. Polakoff was always present but apparently just sat off to the side as the crime boss talked with his old cronies. To keep some secrecy, only Polakoff's name showed up on some of the visitor log entries, with the notation that he came with one, two, or three unnamed visitors. Frank Costello had only one recorded visit to Great Meadow, on August 25, 1942, where he was part of an unusual group of seven men who visited along with Polakoff. Of course, it was entirely possible that Costello visited at other times, but his name not recorded, as was often the practice in this byzantine arrangement.

It was back in 1939 that Mayor Fiorello La Guardia told his police commissioner Lewis Valentine that if Costello was active along the waterfront that the cops should do their best to keep him away from the docks. It looks now like the police didn't bother Costello's activity at all and for the war effort that might have been a very good thing. After the war, Lanza recalled that when Luciano came on board with the project and talked to Costello, Lanza found he got more assistance from the right people.

"Costello was helpful in the way that he would O.K. me to go and see people where I got the right of way through Charlie," said Lanza, who used Costello's influence by claiming that Costello was in favor of the project. When he had to, Lanza spoke to Costello who told him the clandestine efforts on the waterfront were "a good thing and you go along with it." One of Costello's friends, a gangster named Jim O'Connell, served as a go-between for both men.

A part of Haffenden's plan was to get longshoremen union cards for his undercover operatives, and he did that by using some of Costello's and Adonis's dockland contacts. The Camarda brothers on the Brooklyn piers and two Irishmen on the West Side of Manhattan alerted their men on the waterfront to look out for sabotage and espionage.

With more resources and contacts coming from the likes of Costello and Adonis, Lanza was able to expand his waterfront contacts and eventually locate seamen, particularly Italians, who knew things about the coastline and geography of Sicily. This was not an idle academic exercise. The Allied strategy was to invade Sicily and then drive up Italy into the underbelly of the Axis. It was though the Italian contacts on the New York docks that Naval Intelligence learned about friendly contacts in Sicily, including local Mafia bosses, who could be trusted to help the Allied invasion when it finally happened in the summer of 1943.

Operation Husky, as the Allied invasion of Sicily was known, began on July 9, 1943, and lasted for over a month. It was costly in terms of lives with an estimated 5,500 U.S., British, and Canadian soldiers killed, along with over 9,000 Italian and German forces. The number of wounded on all sides totaled over 60,000. After the war, a report done on the significance of Luciano and his friends' cooperation with the U.S. war effort stated that the contacts in Sicily given to Allied forces were helpful. Two naval commanders in particular were quoted as saying that the Mafia contacts they were able to make in Sicily through the intelligence Haffenden got from the American underworld were "valuable contacts" and that they were "extremely cooperative."

Organized crime experts and pundits would debate for years the importance of Luciano's—and by extension Costello's—cooperation in the Allied effort. Clearly, the work was of some importance, particularly in girding the waterfront and providing avenues of intelligence. The naval commanders who worked on the ground in the invasion of Sicily found the contacts with the local Mafiosi to be useful in counterintelligence activities. After the Allies pushed the Germans out of Sicily, local civic administrations were formed on the island and some had Mafiosi like Calogero Vizzini as mayors, said Gaia Servadio, in her book *Mafiosi*. But, there should be no mistaking the fact that it was the hard slugging of the Allied forces, led in part by General George Patton, which drove the opposing forces out of the way and cleared the path to the Italian mainland.

Even before the first amphibious landing crafts hit the beaches of southern Sicily, steps were being taken to have Luciano's assistance in the war effort amount to something for his personal benefit. In late 1942, with Luciano's cooperation in full swing, Polakoff called attorney George Wolf, the lawyer who at that point was still several months away from having Costello as a client. According to Wolf, Polakoff told him all about the cooperation Luciano had given the Navy, which was in itself an astonishing tale. But Polakoff now wanted to take things further for his old client: a motion in court to reduce Luciano's sentence. Toward that end, Polakoff visited Dewey, who at that point was now Governor of New York State, having ridden the adulation he gained as a rackets buster all the way to Albany. Dewey was well aware of the cooperation Luciano had been giving the military since he had been kept in the loop by law enforcement. Dewey's advice to Polakoff was that an attorney not connected to the original criminal case make the motion, and Wolf said the governor suggested him as a possibility.

Wolf said that he was at first leery about representing Luciano. But Dewey told him privately: "George, I will see to it that no reflection will be cast upon you in representing Luciano on this motion." With that assurance, Wolf said he took on the case.

It was early February 1943 that Wolf filed his motion for a reduction in Luciano's sentence with New York State Supreme Court Judge Philip J. McCook, who presided over the original trial and sentenced Charlie Lucky in 1936 to thirty to fifty years in prison. Wolf wanted to tell the court in detail what Luciano had done to aid the war effort because he felt that might appeal to Judge McCook, who himself was a veteran. Polakoff wanted to take a different approach in order to protect Luciano from retaliation if he were ever deported to Italy and because the U.S. was still at war. Eventually, the lawyers agreed to simply state in the motion papers that Luciano had been "cooperative in the war effort."

On February 8, Wolf appeared before McCook and argued that the government didn't want the explicit details of Luciano's cooperation made public. McCook cut the attorney short, telling him he had a plan to handle any sensitive discussions.

"I am willing to see in private any person who is willing to submit himself under oath or not as I see fit, and tell me privately matters that ought not to . . . made public either on account of the war now in progress or because of the interest of the public as expressed by the District Attorney," said McCook.

Wolf agreed to call Haffenden and Gurfein on short notice and had both men appear that very day before McCook in his private chambers. Both men told McCook, in general terms, what Luciano had done to help the Navy, taking care not to reveal anything about cases that could hurt the military. Three days later, McCook released his opinion and also tiptoed around the issue of what Luciano specifically did to help the Allied cause.

Luciano, said McCook, "probably" attempted to assist the Navy and "possibly with some success." But whatever Luciano did do, it wasn't enough to justify a reduction in his sentence, said McCook in his ruling. However, the court held out hope for Luciano, saying that if he continued to assist the authorities—if he was in fact doing so— and remained a model prisoner that there was the possibility of executive clemency in the future from the Governor. The decision, while a denial of the motion for a reduced sentence, was a clear signal to Dewey that he had the power to do the right thing. At that point the invasion of Italy had not yet begun, and the end of the war was over two years away. For Frank Costello, he would have to wait a bit longer to relinquish the crown as crime family boss. He also had his own personal affairs to deal with.

CHAPTER SIXTEEN
GO WEST, YOUNG MAN

FRANK COSTELLO HAD DONE A PRETTY GOOD JOB of staying out of the public eye, even when faced with his own legal problems. He avoided surfacing during the effort to get Luciano a reduced sentence. But after the Allied forces overwhelmed the German and Italian forces in Sicily, attention on Costello seemed to be constant. A world war was going on, but the newspapers salivated for stories about the big gangster.

After the Aurelio story broke, with evidence that Costello, the big gangster, had backed his candidacy, his attorney believed that his image needed some refurbishment. Toward that end, Wolf said he came up with the idea of having Costello purchase some Wall Street real estate—what better part of town to be a property owner—as part of some grand gesture to help charitable causes.

"I told Frank my intention was to legitimize him to the extent this could be possible," remembered Wolf. "He loved the idea."

Wolf planned to have Costello pay his taxes—something history would show the attorney ultimately wouldn't be successful in achieving—and to make a good investment in real estate. Wolf pitched Costello the idea of purchasing three parcels of Wall Street property making up 79 Wall Street. As it turned out, the owners were having financial problems and needed to unload the parcels, which, according to FBI records, encompassed 79-89 Wall Street, 148-152 Pearl

Street and a building at 114 Water Street. The properties were as-
sessed at $512,000, a minuscule amount compared to today's assess-
ments, which would be in the hundreds of millions of dollars.

Wolf's idea was to have Costello take over the properties, rent out
the offices, and turn over the rental income, above expenses, to charity. It was a way of burnishing Costello's reputation and making him
seem a beneficent man, not some sleazy gangster. Costello's reaction, as remembered by Wolf, was one of excitement.

"You done it, George," said Costello. "Wait until those creeps in
Sands Point hear that their shady neighbor is the president of a Wall
Street corporation. I like it, George. Beautiful."

The deal went off without a hitch. News reports said that Costello
plunked down $500,000 in cash and secured a mortgage of $249,000.
FBI records showed that the 79 Wall Street Corporation was incorpo-
rated on April 21, 1944, with Wolf, his daughter Blanch Wolf, and
businessman Harry Shapiro listed as directors. Costello was president and his wife Loretta the vice president and secretary. The corporation listed Wolf's office at 30 Broad Street as its address.

Costello's reference to his snooty neighbors in Sands Point was a
reference to the quiet, exclusive community on the North Shore of
Long Island where he and Loretta had purchased a home right in the
middle of a world populated by millionaires. According to a report
in *The Brooklyn Eagle,* the couple took title to the property on Barkers Point Road on May 18, 1944, for $30,000, paying $15,000 cash
and taking out a mortgage to pay for the rest. The seller had been an
oil company executive and his wife who were going off to Mexico.
The house, now known as 5 Barkers Point Road, had twelve rooms
and sat on about two acres of land. There were horses nearby, and
Long Island sound was literally around the corner and a comfortable
walk from the house. Costello's neighbors were the Guggenheims,
Vanderbilts, and others of the wealthy class. He had arrived, in a
sense, in a world of respectability.

Sands Point was the fictional setting for *The Great Gatsby,* and
the point was not lost to well-read people like Wolf and anyone else
who had an appreciation for F. Scott's Fitzgerald's masterpiece set
in the 1920s, when booze and money flowed during Prohibition.

Costello's house was in the mythical "East Egg," the tony section of the North Shore, across Manhasset Bay from "West Egg" where Jay Gatsby had his mansion in the novel. Like Gatsby, Costello had made much of his fortune from bootlegging.

But unlike Gatsby whose longing for East Egg was because that was where the love of his life Daisy lived, Costello was chasing status. While Gatsby had the green light at the end of Daisy's dock to symbolize the unattainable, the nearby Alva Vanderbilt Belmont beacon at the end of Lighthouse Road served the same purpose in Costello's life. Costello was able to buy into Sands Point and he liked the notion of being a country squire in a place where corporate executives lived. When a local girl named Margaret stopped by to sell Girl Scout cookies, Costello was generous and bought as many as ten boxes, although her mother was stunned when she saw his name on the receipt. Costello had beach rights through the local neighborhood association and was rumored to have attended barbecues. But as would be made clear to him throughout his life, the rich and respectable people Costello so much wanted as neighbors were very different. He was a kid from an East Harlem slum who grew up to be a preeminent gangster. He discovered that the world wouldn't let him forget.

Costello couldn't forget his criminal life because he wasn't able to leave it, no matter what his attorney did to try and sanitize him. La Guardia's anti-racketeering campaign had driven some of the gamblers out of the city. In Costello's case, he shifted some of his business to New Jersey where he and Joe Adonis opened up a place called the Big Hall in Cliffside Park, a community by the Hudson River.

Close to New York City via the George Washington Bridge, the Bergen County section where Cliffside Park was located had become a gambling Mecca of sorts for the New York mob. In fact, just north of the bridge was the Riviera, a nightclub situated high above the Hudson on the Palisades and run by Ben Marden. With its sliding domed roof over the dance floor, dining room with walls that could retract and a private back room that seemed a perfect place for gambling, the Riviera attracted all sorts of New Yorkers—gangsters and plain folks—who drove over the bridge on the weekends for the two-minute ride to the club's circular driveway. Costello, Adonis, and Moretti were said to have patronized the club. The Riviera was long suspected of being a gambling haven, and Marden was called to testify about that before a federal grand jury and asked if the Murder Inc., gangster Louis Buchalter owned the gambling concession at his club. Marden, who went on to become a benefactor of Albert Einstein College of Medicine, denied that Buchalter was involved. No charges were ever brought against Marden or the Riviera for gambling offenses.

Adonis was another Italian immigrant who had become a Mafia power in Brooklyn following the death of Frankie Yale in 1928. Born near Naples in 1902, Adonis's real name was Giuseppe Antonio Doto. There are numerous stories about how he took on the surname "Adonis." One held that he made the change after reading an article about Greek mythology while another story was that he was given the name by a Ziegfeld Follies girl he was dating. In any case, the name stuck although he sometimes used the alias "Joe DeMio."

Like many of the men who earned their stripes in the underworld, Adonis made early money in bootlegging and gambling. Federal officials also believed he was involved in narcotics trafficking. But one of the big notches on his belt came with the assassination of old boss Joseph Masseria in 1931. Adonis, so the stories went in the underworld, was reputed to be one of the shooters in Masseria's murder. His actions put him in good stead with Luciano and with Costello.

Costello remained a resident of New York State but Adonis moved around 1945 to Fort Lee, New Jersey, a mere stone's throw from Cliffside Park and virtually a neighbor of another powerful gangster, Albert Anastasia who also took up residence in the same town. Gambling operations flourished in New Jersey gambling laws were very unevenly enforced. Old-timers recalled stories of how Bergen County residents would rent out their telephones to gamblers so they could place bets. The residential phones were handy because NYPD plainclothes detectives became adept at finding the telephones of the more established gambling parlors and tracing the calls made to places like the old Jamaica race track. Calls being made from private homes didn't easily prompt suspicion.

But the problem was that all this North Jersey gambling was taking place in wartime, when there were restrictions on the use of gasoline. New York police and agents from the Federal Office of Price Administration started in the summer of 1943 to question the way fuel was being used by certain limousines. The investigators halted the limousines that had been rented to carry card and dice players across the George Washington Bridge from Manhattan to a place in Fort Lee known as "The Barn," a gambling den between Hoyt Avenue and Central Road, a few hundred yards from the Riviera's spot on the Palisades.

A continuing anti-gambling offensive prompted New Jersey's attorney general and governor to go after operations in Bergen County. Allegations were raised that Costello and Adonis were in command of the dice games and horse betting in Bergen. Both Adonis and Costello had their own problems with their Cliffside Park gambling operation. The place was targeted for a raid in June. But, when the cops arrived they found it had been cleaned out: neither Adonis nor Costello were anywhere to be found.

Back in Manhattan on June 14, 1944, Costello took a cab ride to the Sherry-Netherland hotel on Fifth Avenue. Costello quickly discovered that he had left an envelope containing $27,000 in cash on the backseat of the cab. Although the source of the money was never shown, Van Riper, the attorney general of New Jersey would later claim that the cash came from the Cliffside Park gambling operation. Upset that he had misplaced the envelope, Costello tried in vain to trace the cab. Meanwhile, cabbie Edward Waters discovered the envelope in the back of his vehicle and being an honest man took it to the police station on Sixty-seventh Street where the money was vouchered and waiting for someone to file a claim for its return.

But with the owner being Frank Costello, the saga of the missing money was not going to be resolved quietly, particularly after City Hall got involved. As Costello's attorney George Wolf recalled, his client at first didn't want to get the money back, apparently fearful of legal issues if the police knew the cash was his. But Wolf told Costello that if he *didn't* claim the money, it would look like he was trying to hide something.

"Damn that stupid cabbie," remarked Costello, according to Wolf. "Why didn't he keep the money."

Both Wolf and Costello drove to the police property clerk's office to explain that the envelope with the cash was Costello's. Then, as Wolf remembered things, the telephone rang with a call from La Guardia who ordered the beleaguered clerk not to turn over the cash to "that tin horn bum" or risk being fired.

Costello then sued to get his money back and, as might have been expected, the matter was not going to pass unnoticed. The city, at La Guardia's insistence, refused to turn over the money, claiming it was "outlaw" money Costello received from gambling or another kind of illegal activity—the Mayor wasn't sure which. The city wanted the money to go to the police pension fund.

"What I am interested in," said La Guardia, "is where did the bum get it and where was he taking it?"

Wolf had said Costello got the money in his role as president of his Wall Street realty company. Costello told the property clerk that $15,000 of the cash had been given to him by Wolf to close out a real estate deal with the rest having been borrowed from someone he didn't want to name to solve a cash flow problem brought about by paying an $8,000 installment on his federal income taxes. Costello got more specific, claiming the $15,000 had come from old gambling partner Philip Kastel and over $11,000 from his brother-in-law Dudley Geigerman.

With La Guardia and the police able to use nothing but innuendo and suspicion that the money represented the proceeds of a crime, Costello was on firm legal footing to get the cash back. But there was another problem: an IRS lien of $27,000 for back taxes. Manhattan State Supreme Court Judge Carroll G. Walter ruled that Costello was indeed the owner of the money but also directed that $27,000 of it be turned over to the IRS. Costello got back $127, his forgetful moment in the cab having cost him a great deal.

Turning to La Guardia's attempt to grab the cash for the pension

fund, Judge Carroll all but called the Mayor a thief. "I cannot toler-
ate the idea that the Police Department may keep a citizen's property
for no better reason than its own innuendo that perhaps the citizen
acquired the property in a gambling transaction," said Walter. The
judge said if there was evidence that the cash represented the proceeds of a crime, he might consider the city's position. But in this
case, there wasn't any, said the court.

Although Costello won a pyrrhic victory, cabbie Edward Waters
did better. Costello gave him a $500 reward and some war bonds
which had a maturity value of $3,500. The newspapers generally ran
sympathetic stories about Costello after the ruling on the lost
money. But no sooner had one controversy been put to rest in his life
than Costello faced another one raised by his constant nemesis:
Mayor Fiorello La Guardia.

The Copacabana on East Sixtieth Street in Manhattan was the
nightclub of choice for Frank Costello and everyone else in his
crowd. It was because of the attraction the Brazilian-themed club
had for Costello and his ilk—as well as suspicion that he had a secret ownership interest—that La Guardia went after the business in
an attempt to revoke its cabaret license, which it had since it opened
in 1940. City Hall used the fact that the Copacabana crowd, including its manager Jules Podell, were involved in gambling, consorted
with unsavory characters, didn't pay city taxes and, in the case of
Podell, concealed criminal records when applying for licenses.

La Guardia's action was also aimed at drying up another source
of revenue for the mob. He believed that Costello and his gambling
crony Frank Erickson had interests in a number of night spots and
wanted that to stop. The Copacabana wasn't the only club City Hall
thought Costello had an interest in, although officials weren't certain about just what dealings he had in the place beyond his frequent
attendance. Previous attempts by La Guardia to show that Costello
had a secret interest in the Hurricane Restaurant failed to turn up
anything concrete.

To get at Costello's reputed interest in the Copacabana, the city
convened a special hearing in which a NYPD deputy commissioner

presided and tried to show that denizens of the club like Joseph Adonis and Costello were involved in gambling elsewhere. It was an indirect approach. Testimony showed for instance that Adonis had been a customer at the Piping Rock Restaurant in Saratoga Springs, an establishment to which that Costello had provided money, and had spent his nights in the gambling casino at the back of the restaurant playing gin rummy. The back room at the Piping Rock had roulette wheels, dice tables, and chemin-de-fer, a version of the French card game baccarat.

"Joe Adonis was in the casino every night of the week," said an undercover detective who visited the Piping Rock. Most of the time, Adonis spent time playing gin rummy with entertainer and comic Joe E. Lewis, who performed in the restaurant. A spotter at the door of the casino screened customers, and Jack Entratter, a club impresario, made sure that the Copacabana crowd was cleared to enter the casino, the detective noted.

Jules Podell was also grilled on the witness stand and admitted having done a short stint in jail for the illegal sale of whiskey in 1929 and that Costello had an interest in the Piping Rock. The most damaging evidence for Podell were records that showed he had five bootlegging arrests and one for grand larceny, matters that he hadn't noted on his pistol permit application in 1934.

Podell's attorney said the whole case was a smear against his client. But a city official responded that the government was trying to show that the Copacabana was trying to keep secret that Podell and others were connected to it. Of course, Costello was the main object of the investigation, and his lawyer said that the whole licensing review was motivated by La Guardia's intense hatred and desire for revenge.

When called as a witness in the Copacabana case, Costello fought the subpoena in court. He also flat-out refused to testify "on advice of counsel," and the city tried to get Costello held in contempt. His attorney used as evidence of La Guardia's hostility the Mayor's various statements that Costello was a "bum" and a remark about a year earlier during the Aurelio incident by police commissioner Lewis J.

Valentine. It was then that Valentine said that Costello "is not a local bum but an international thug. I don't know where he will go when he dies or if there is a hell deep enough."

But after about two weeks of hearings, the Copacabana affair ended with a compromise settlement on September 30, 1944. The club's current cabaret license was revoked and a temporary six-month license granted. The club agreed that the city had a valid claim for $37,371 in back sales and business taxes. More important, the Copacabana said it agreed that "whatever interest Frank Costello may now have or have had in Copacabana . . . either directly or indirectly is completely terminated and severed." Costello, the settlement said, wouldn't have any management activity or derive any income from the club in the future.

The Copacabana settlement was a carefully worded document. The club didn't say that Costello, in fact, ever had an interest in the club. To be sure, the club's recorded owner, Monte Proser, said in the agreement that as far as he knew Costello has not and never had any interest in the Copacabana. La Guardia extended his nightclub push to the point where he put an estimated 1,100 nightclubs around the city on "probation," granting them temporary licenses as their ownership interests and operations were vetted by the police and other agencies. Surprisingly, given the potential disruption of their businesses at a time when the city was awash with soldiers and sailors on leave, many nightclub owners voiced approval of the Mayor's action since it assured that clubs were owned by legitimate people and not gangsters.

La Guardia had clearly hounded Costello over the years. But Costello not only pushed back against City Hall but adapted as needed. He shifted the slot machines to Louisiana where that business thrived for a few years and he diversified with the Beverly, the nightclub that became a fixture in Jefferson County. He had real estate interests as well. Then again, he sat as the caretaker boss of the Luciano mob, getting his cut of the proceeds of the action of other gamblers and their rackets.

As 1945 approached, Frank Costello was still standing. He had avoided a number of attempts at federal and state prosecutions over the years. Dewey had gone on to the governorship and had his eye on the White House. Meanwhile, La Guardia was approaching his political twilight. He had been reelected mayor twice and carried the city through World War Two. But as the election of 1945 gathered steam, La Guardia lost his zest for the game of politics. He was also showing signs of illness: severe bouts of lower back pain, which were a symptom of the pancreatic cancer growing inside him. La Guardia had enjoyed at least some support from President Franklin D. Roosevelt over the years but with the president's death in April 1945 and Harry Truman's taking on the job, La Guardia's closeness to the Administration diminished. Up to a point, he believed he could win reelection but decided not to run again.

The election campaign of 1945 was a convoluted one in which various candidates tried to earn a spot on the ballot. One thing was clear throughout the political maneuvers and that was the fact that Frank Costello still seemed to hold tremendous power inside Tammany Hall. Although wounded over the years by La Guardia and the prosecution of Jimmy Hines, the "Tiger" as Tammany was called still had some bite. Whoever held sway of Tammany still had clout in the city and there was no doubt that Costello was such a person.

As soon as it became clear that La Guardia was not standing for reelection, an intricate political game got underway. One person who was in the race was William O'Dwyer, not to be confused with old bootlegger William V. Dwyer who worked with Costello. O'Dwyer had run previously against La Guardia in 1941 so he had some experience in the game, and from his background was the strongest candidate. An immigrant from Ireland, O'Dwyer had once been a candidate for the priesthood in Spain but washed out, sailing to the U.S. in 1910, and upon landing in New York took a job as a $9 a week grocery clerk. Then he worked as a mariner, hod carrier, and a bartender at the Vanderbilt Hotel before finally joining the NYPD in 1917. He went to law school and became an attorney in 1923, becoming a city magistrate and then in 1938 was elected Brooklyn District Attorney. During World War Two he was commissioned a major in the Army and assigned to the Inspector General's office to investigate kick-

backs and corruption on Army contracts. He was promoted to Briga-
dier General and then by President Roosevelt to the War Refugee
Board.

O'Dwyer was familiar with the workings of the mob from his investigation of Murder Inc., the criminal combination that worked as
a team of executioners for the underworld in the city. As prosecutor
he secured numerous convictions of the killers and their associates,
namely Louis Buchalter, who in 1944 was the last major New York
gangster to be executed. But as good a record as O'Dwyer had
against Murder Inc., his record seemed tainted when his chief witness, Abe Reles, fell to his death from the Half Moon Hotel in
Coney Island, where he was being safeguarded as a witness. Police
determined that Reles died when he tried to get out of the room by
climbing down a rope of bedsheets, although conspiracy theorists
maintained either the cops or the mob killed him.

O'Dwyer knew Costello and visited him at his home where, he
would later recall, there were plenty of other Democratic politicians
present, including Tammany head Michael Kennedy and the organization's secretary Bert Stand. O'Dwyer never hid the fact that he was
friendly with Costello although years later it would come back to
haunt him. As George Wolf, Costello's attorney later said: "Frank's
candidate was Bill O'Dwyer."

Opposing O'Dwyer was Judge Joseph J. Goldstein, a Democrat
who was actually running on the Republican-Liberal-Fusion ticket,
a move that further muddied the political waters. Goldstein was starting from a weaker position in the race and in the month before the
election lashed out, perhaps in desperation, to claim that O'Dwyer
was really just a puppet of Adonis and Costello. In public statements,
Goldstein said that Adonis, who was Brooklyn's public enemy no. 1,
was able to tell the Brooklyn Democratic leadership that they had
to take O'Dwyer. When it came to Costello, Goldstein said that the
O'Dwyer nomination "was engineered by Frank Costello, Joe Adonis
and Irving Sherman," the latter being a shady businessman with close
ties to Costello. Given the fact that O'Dwyer acknowledged a friendship with Costello and had visited him in a meeting with other party
officials present, Goldstein's remarks seemed not far from the mark.

As earnest as he was in trying to link O'Dwyer with Costello, Goldstein's campaign was sabotaged by La Guardia when the Mayor pushed his own candidate, Newbold Morris, who was president of the City Council and ran under the "No Deal" party ticket. Morris would dig into Goldstein's support. At the election, O'Dwyer won easily, pulling 1,225,000 votes, to Goldstein's 431,601, which was not much better than Morris's 408,348. O'Dwyer's margin of victory was nearly 700,000 votes over Goldstein. Costello and his political associates had engineered another significant victory. He was still a king maker in New York.

But, as Tammany historian Oliver E. Allen later wrote, any expectation that the Hall would have easy sailing with O'Dwyer at the helm was short-lived. O'Dwyer gave Tammany some patronage requests but soon started criticizing the organization. Then, according to Allen, O'Dwyer engineered the ouster of county leader Edward Loughlin and his replacement by Frank Sampson, with orders to rid Tammany of underworld influence. O'Dwyer secretly told Costello of Sampson's mission, noted Allen, who added that the new county leader was effectively defied by Tammany's executive committee, led by Carmine DeSapio who happened to be a friend of Costello.

One meaningful anecdote about Costello's continuing power came from Wolf who related how his client gave him copies of signed resignations of Tammany leaders, as well as a few judges, with the instructions "If anything happens to me, you know what to do with these." Although Wolf said he didn't know what Costello was talking about, the letters of resignation would play out in another political scenario some years later.

With his political influence stable for the time being, Costello turned his attention to his old friend Luciano. It was May 8, 1945, that the imprisoned Luciano took to heart Judge McCook's recommendation and filed a petition with Governor Thomas Dewey for clemency. The date was significant because it also was V-E Day, signifying the Allied victory against Germany. Dewey referred the petition to the state parole board, which began a lengthy investigation, interviewing Lansky, Polakoff, Luciano and others and likely included Costello and Lanza about Luciano's efforts to help the war effort. The mob men cooperated with the parole officials. But when it came time to get statements about Luciano's work from naval intelligence officials, including Haffenden and Gurfein, their superiors declined to give that permission.

The parole authorities were stuck. They had gleaned much from Lansky and others about Luciano's efforts. But the Navy effectively shut down cooperation on the investigation which could parole Luciano and cut short his heavy prison sentence, which had at least twenty and as much as forty more years to run. If he wasn't given parole, the only way out of prison for Luciano was in a coffin. Finally on December 3, 1945, the parole board recommended that Luciano's sentence be commuted for the sole purpose of deporting him. Dewey mulled the recommendation for a month and on January 3, 1946, decided to agree with the board and commute Luciano's sentence for deportation.

"Upon the entry of the United States into the war, Luciano's aid was sought by the armed services in inducing others to provide information concerning possible enemy attack," said Dewey in a message explaining his decision. "It appears that he cooperated in such effort though the actual value of the information procured is not clear. His record in prison is reported as wholly satisfactory."

For good measure, Dewey also commuted the sentences of five others, all of whom were to be deported. Among them was Mock Tick Tong, who was sentenced to death in 1925 for murder in a Chinatown tong battle but subsequently was commuted to life in prison. Dewey ordered him deported to China. The four others who had their sentences commuted were ordered deported to Italy, England, Greece and Spain.

In his biography, Luciano claimed to the authors that he had originally demanded that he be given parole for his cooperation but that Dewey stood firmly against that. Luciano also claimed that Dewey agreed to go easy on city racketeers and that he, Luciano, secretly contributed $90,000 in untraceable funds that was funneled to Dewey's campaign. Luciano didn't specify which campaign but presumably the 1944 Presidential race, which Dewey lost.

It took just about a month for Luciano to be moved around for deportation. He was taken from Sing Sing prison to Ellis Island on February 2 where he was visited by Costello and Polakoff. Costello brought Luciano his baggage and what were described as personal items. Authorities went to great lengths to note that Luciano's guarded room on the island was just like any other: a chair, a bed, a toilet. Costello and Polakoff left promptly. But Luciano was not to leave from Ellis Island. He was moved to Bush Terminal in Brooklyn where he was to pick up passage on the victory ship *Laura Keene,* an old, 7,000 ton freighter.

Luciano was under guard during the final days he remained in the U.S. But it was reported that on Saturday night February 9, two days before the *Laura Keene* sailed, that six men, possibly including Albert Anastasia, the major waterfront gangster, had a farewell spaghetti and wine dinner on the ship. In his book about Costello, Wolf described a more ornate feast, with Costello, Joe Adonis, Meyer Lansky, Anastasia, and a few lesser lights arriving with hampers "crammed with wines and liquors, lobster and caviar—and no doubt money." Wolf claimed a few judges and politicians attended, although *The New York Times* reported that only a half dozen men came to the party.

On February 10, 1946, the *Laura Keene* left Bush Terminal for Italy with a cargo of flour and a solitary passenger—Luciano. Federal immigration officials traveled on the ship as far as Ambrose Light, the beacon that marks the beginning of Ambrose Channel, the main shipping lane into New York harbor. It would take about two weeks for the *Laura Keene* to get to Genoa, Luciano's first stop in his old country. Back in New York, Costello was no longer just a caretaker boss. With Luciano out of the country, Costello was *the* boss of the family and one of the most powerful gangsters in the country.

CHAPTER SEVENTEEN
CUBA LIBRE

LUCIANO MAY HAVE BEEN EXILED TO ITALY but that didn't mean he didn't retain power and influence with his Mafia family. It wasn't long before Luciano got in touch with his men—Costello, Anthony Carfano, Lansky, and others—to plan his next move. Transatlantic telephone calls served as Luciano's best way to keep in touch, and it seems that the federal government didn't monitor them all that closely. If he couldn't return to the United States, Luciano had a very convenient base to operate from some ninety miles from American soil: Cuba.

Through the influence of Sicilian Mafia boss Don Carlo Vizzini, Luciano was able to get an Italian passport and travel documents. It was in late September or early October when Luciano boarded a plane for the Western Hemisphere. He is said to have traveled an indirect route to Brazil, Venezuela, and Mexico City before finally landing in Camaguey, Cuba.

"I had the police chief, a couple of senators, even the president himself in my pocket," Luciano would later brag. "The whole thing was set up for me by Meyer Lansky."

Of course, Cuba had long been a playground and business center for the American Mafia. Lansky had been a major player and ran a number of the casinos on the island. As portrayed later in the film *The Godfather: Part Two*, Cuba was an open country for the mob and the lure of the Mafia money for politicians like Fulgencio Batista was powerful. With money, the Mafia had effective sway over much of the government and allowed Cuba to be a gangster sanctuary. His road to Cuba made with corrupt payments to assorted politicians and officials, Luciano decamped to the fabled Hotel Nacional.

Luciano had work to do in Cuba and it was Lansky who arranged for him a large meeting in Havana with many major players in the American Mafia. There is some uncertainty about the exact date: government records in the National Archives indicate it was in early 1947 while mob historian Allan May puts it in December 1946. In any case, the participants represented the high echelon of the mob. Frank Costello and Meyer Lansky were the only two gangsters of note on the government list. But May's list, as well as Sciacca's compilation, were more extensive and have Anthony Carfano, Thomas Lucchese, Vincent Mangano, and Vito Genovese representing the major powers from New York. From Chicago were the Fischetti brothers, Rocco and Charles, as well as Tony Accardo. Carlos Marcello, Costello's casino and slot machine partner from New Orleans, also made the trip. The lists were impressive.

Two non-mobsters in attendance, according to the government list, were Luciano's attorney Moses Polakoff and the young, popular crooner Frank Sinatra. Polakoff may have been present to discuss with Luciano his legal and immigration situation. Sinatra's role was that of an entertainer who, according to his biographers Anthony Summers and Robbyn Swan, made the flight to Havana from Miami on a plane with Chicago gangster Rocco Fischetti in February 1947 and was seen exiting the aircraft on newsreel footage, giving more credence to the view that this giant mob confab was in early 1947.

"Giving Frank the maximum benefit of the doubt, it would seem that he made some very bad decisions at a very sensitive time in his personal life and his career," Summers and Swan would say about Sinatra's trip to Havana. "This was his walk on the wild side with the Mob, with the men he had come to admire for all kinds of reasons, both inexcusable and understandable."

Sinatra wasn't there to take part in any mob conclave: he was just the entertainment. There had long been stories about Sinatra and the help the mob gave him, including the story that Costello and Willie

Moretti got the singer a gig at the Rustic Cabin in New Jersey and were otherwise instrumental in pushing Sinatra's career. But Summers and Swan said there was no proof that Moretti and Costello set up the Rustic Cabin deal but noted that FBI and federal narcotics agent files talked about reports that Costello had been a big pusher of Sinatra's career, assigning the Fischetti brothers to chaperone him in the business. In Havana, Luciano, Costello, and the rest hunkered down to talk about their businesses. Federal narcotics officials were aware that something was up because a local Cuban newspaper had printed the story earlier about Luciano's arrival. Agents surveilled with the aim of seeing if Luciano was involved in narcotics traffic coming out of Cuba to the U.S. and might be trying to control the mob from the island. However, while the agents faithfully watched the comings and goings of the mob retinue—be it to restaurants, beaches, or brothels—they couldn't determine with any certainty what the meeting was all about.

As it turned out, one subject was the unhappiness of everyone over the way Bugsy Siegel had been acting. Siegel had gone to California to take care of rackets there and eventually it was suspected that he was skimming from the mob and its Hollywood union business. But there had been another problem for Siegel, one that had the potential to implicate Costello and cause him harm as well. Siegel had come up with the idea in the late 1930s of building a gambling Mecca in Las Vegas, Nevada, a state where gambling was legal. Many in the mob were cool to the idea, but Siegel convinced Costello to invest. Following Costello's lead, others went along and threw in money as well.

Siegel's idea was to build a plush hotel known as the Flamingo and hire big name entertainers to draw crowds. On paper the idea sounded like a good one. But Siegel, who may have been a good bootlegger, was a disaster for the project. He made unrealistic demands for construction materials, which were in short supply due to the war. Cost overruns mounted and when the Flamingo was ready for its opening night, December 26, 1946, the project was many millions of dollars—mob dollars as it turned out—over budget. Nevertheless, Siegel had planned a big opening night, with Hollywood stars to be flown in to fill up the casino. The stars were on the plane ready to fly in to Las Vegas when foggy weather grounded them. They were no-shows on Siegel's big night, and the Flamingo reportedly lost $500,000 in its first two weeks. The debut was a big bust.

No matter how valuable loyalty and other personal traits may be in the Mafia, it exists to make money and when that goal is threatened the consequences can be deadly. Costello's attorney George Wolf had tried to keep his client out of trouble but with the financial problems caused by Siegel's overspending and mismanagement of the Flamingo project, the lawyer learned how much Costello now risked. He had staked his own money on the venture, enticed others to throw in cash and now was the object of recrimination when things were not looking good. Wolf remembered fearing for Costello's safety.

"What happens if you can't raise it?" Wolf remembered asking Costello about the money his old friends wanted back.

"Part of it's already happened," Costello replied cryptically, recalled Wolf.

With Luciano in Havana, the mob men complained to him personally about the money that was lost. There were stories that some wanted Costello killed as punishment. When he got to Cuba to see his old friend, Costello knew he faced a critical point. Luciano had been his old friend, the man he had entrusted with the command of the crime family. But money is all important in the Mafia, and Luciano told Costello he had to get the money back somehow.

"Otherwise I can't hold them back," Luciano warned Costello, according to Wolf's account.

There was also another condition, remembered Wolf. Luciano told Costello to retire as head of the ruling Mafia commission and let Vito Genovese take the seat. When Costello got the money back, he could take over the chair on the commission again.

"What happens to Bugsy?" asked Costello.

"Him I can't help," Luciano answered.

Costello survived the Flamingo fiasco. He apparently recouped the lost money, and as Wolf would later say went into hock to do it. The hotel even went on to make a profit after Siegel closed it for three months and then reopened. But by then Siegel's cause, as Luciano said, couldn't be helped. The night of June 20, 1947, after a dinner at Jack's restaurant in Santa Monica, Siegel returned to the mansion he had in Beverly Hills with dinner companion Jack Smiley. Siegel's gal pal Virginia Hill, for whom he bought the home, was out of town. Both men sat at opposite ends of a sofa and Siegel began to read a copy of *The Los Angeles Times*.

Suddenly, shots rang out and glass from a living room window shattered and sprayed around as bullets from a carbine fired by someone from the outside found their mark on Siegel's face. One round hit him in the left eye while another struck the right cheek and sent the other eye out of his skull and on to the carpet. Siegel paid the price for screwing around with the Mafia's money. The news photos of the crime scene showed Siegel reclining on the sofa, his face bloodied and his left eye socket empty. In a strange juxtaposition, a small statue of a nude woman, her arms stretched overhead, can be seen in the foreground of one of the photos taken by the press photographer.

Luciano was sitting pretty in Cuba. He could beckon Costello, Adonis, and anybody else he needed to make the ninety-mile jump from Miami to Havana. Luciano felt free in Cuba and traveled around without a problem. But his freewheeling activity turned out to be his problem. When newspaper columnist Robert Ruark traveled on vacation to Cuba he saw Luciano in a restaurant. The chance discovery led Ruark, who was also a hard drinking, big game hunter who liked a good scoop, to dig around and write stories about Luciano, as well as Sinatra, in Cuba.

Ruark's reports, and others it sparked, couldn't be ignored by the U.S. government. By the end of February 1947, Harry Anslinger, head of the United States Treasury Department Bureau of Narcotics, asked that the U.S. stop the shipment of medicinal narcotic drugs to Cuba until Luciano had left the country. Anslinger suspected that old Luciano cronies were making trips back and forth from Florida to Cuba to traffic in the drugs the U.S. had been sending to the island nation. The Cuban government was told of Anslinger's suspicion but did nothing, he said, prompting the Americans to take matters into their own hands.

Luciano was considered so dangerous to narcotics enforcement officials in the U.S. that the American government finally restricted the export of legitimate narcotics to Cuba for as long as Luciano stayed in that country. Officials also thought it was an "interesting coincidence" that in the months Luciano was in Cuba the U.S. witnessed the importation of $250,000 worth of European heroin. Acting quickly, Cuban officials arrested Luciano and two bodyguards at a villa he had been living at in the exclusive Miramar section of Havana and sent the group to a special camp across Havana bay.

About a week after his arrest, Luciano filed a writ to get his release so that he could leave the country. His Cuban attorney charged that the arrest was a "political persecution" by a faction in the U.S. because Luciano had been "anti-Nazi." But such protest was merely for show. Luciano was not going to be allowed to stay in Cuba, and after Cuban president Grau San Martin signed an order for Luciano's deportation as an undesirable alien, the mob boss was placed on the Turkish ship *Bakir* on March 19 bound for Italy. He paid his own first-class fare of $300 and spent his time on the voyage playing cards with tourist-class passengers. Once back in his ancestral land, Luciano was promptly jailed and held for an investigation into how he had been able to travel so clandestinely. It wouldn't be the last anyone would hear about Charlie Lucky.

CHAPTER EIGHTEEN
TAMMANY TALES

BACK IN NEW YORK, FRANK COSTELLO was finding out how toxic his name had become. The Aurelio scandal had put him in a nasty spotlight. Mayor La Guardia, NYPD commissioner Lewis Valentine, prosecutors Dewey and Hogan had all dragged up Costello's name any chance they could. Of course, there was little they could point to in terms of a criminal record because, aside from the 1915 gun case, which sent him to jail for just under a year, Costello had never been convicted of anything. But his reputation as a slot machine king, a major bootlegger back in the day and his role as Luciano's man had earned him the label of gangster no matter how hard he tried to appear legitimate to his neighbors in Sands Point.

Every up and coming mobster in New York during the 1920s had something to do with bootlegging. It was an acceptable thing to do since the public, and many in government, saw Prohibition as a half-assed, dumb policy. Those who sold booze and trafficked in it were local heroes. But after Prohibition took a stake to its heart with the passage of the Twenty-first Amendment, the liquor flowed and bootlegging was obsolete. In his biography, Luciano said that the mob stockpiles of liquor were winnowed down by donations to churches and synagogues as a way of building good will in the neighborhoods and creating a source of revenue for the institutions. Yet those who had profited from hooch and dealt with the mob found that their old ways would come back to haunt them. Such was the case of businessman Irving Haim.

Born Irving Haimowitz, Haim had a long career in the liquor trade. In the 1920s he was involved with Sherwood Distillery Company of Maryland, a firm that in 1923 had its federal alcohol permits revoked because it had violated the Prohibition laws. To survive, Haim did business with Costello and Kastel, and the relationship was mutually beneficial and went beyond the typical bootlegging action. Good whiskey always had a market in the U.S.—be it during Prohibition or after—and Haim came across a very good opportunity in Scotland.

In the nineteenth century, Edradour distillery was formed as a cooperative venture of some local Scottish farmers. The operation was said to be one of the smallest of its kind and, as writer Charles McLean noted, relied on water from a moor that was "rich in peat and granite." Economic issues forced the descendants of the original founders to sell the distillery in 1933 to William Whatley & Co., whose owner had previously bought JG Turney & Sons to sell to the export market. As McLean explained in an article about the history of distilleries he wrote a few years ago in *The Herald* newspaper of Glasgow, Turney used Edradour Scotch in its blends which it sold under the brand names House of Lords and King's Ransom.

At some point—it was unclear when—Whatley designated Costello as its American sales representative for the two brands at a rate of just over 3,000 pounds a year, or $25,000 dollars at the estimated exchange rate of the time. (Costello later said the deal was never consummated.) Then in 1937, McLean reported, Haim, who had been teamed up with Costello for years during Prohibition, bought the holding company that owned Whatley and in essence became the owner of the storied distillery. The purchase, it would later be revealed in U.S. Senate testimony, was financed through a New Orleans bank and secured by Haim, Kastel, and Costello, with a few other suretors. (The distillery was sold in 1986, according to McLean.)

During his days as a bootlegger, Costello had reportedly done business with Joseph P. Kennedy, the father of future President John F. Kennedy. During testimony in 1943 before a state liquor panel,

Costello said that not only was Phil Kastel and Haim involved in the Scotland deal but also "Joe Kennedy." Wolf, who was present at that testimony, asked Costello if he meant the Joseph Kennedy who was the former Ambassador to England. Costello's response, said Wolf, was "Hell, no . . . Joseph Kennedy, the old bootlegger in Toronto. I known him twenty-five years."

While Haim's ties to the scotch industry through the purchase of an old distillery might have seemed quaint, his connection to Costello hurt his businesses. It was in 1948 that Haim's International Distributors, one of the nation's larger wholesale liquor distributors, had its license with New York State up for renewal. It had the exclusive distribution rights to a number of brands of whiskey including House of Lords and King's Ransom scotch. The license was issued by the State Liquor Authority and the agency found evidence that Haim and his firm had falsely answered questions on its original license application. In particular, SLA attorneys said Haim hid the fact that he had been prosecuted in the Sherwood Distillery matter back in 1923 and didn't disclose his ownership interest in another distillery.

In terms of Costello, the SLA attorneys wanted to disapprove the renewal of the license because Haim knew him and his old sidekick Phil Kastel. Taken together with the false statements found in the application, the SLA used the Costello-Kastel connection as icing on the cake and refused to renew the license of International Distributors. A lawsuit was then filed by Haim to overturn the ruling.

It was up to Manhattan Supreme Court Justice Morris Eder to sort the whole mess out. In one sense, Haim made it easy for Eder because of the various falsehoods in the paperwork. The omissions and lies were so blatantly obvious that Eder said the SLA was in its rights to deny the renewal application. But when it came to Costello and Kastel, the court didn't hide its concern that the pair's notoriety wasn't an important issue. The main thing was that Costello had almost a spotless record as far as the criminal justice system was concerned.

"Much was said upon the argument concerning Costello, who was referred to as Public Enemy No. 1, but it seems strange that if such has any foundation in fact, that no action has been taken in that regard by the police and public prosecutor, or by any public authority, with all the resources at their command, to protect the public," said Eder.

At one point in court Eder said, "Mr. Dewey was the district attorney, Mr. Hogan is the district attorney. Yet nobody seems to indict him for anything. What is wrong with this man? If he has done anything wrong why don't they do something about it."

If Haim's ties to Costello were the only thing, Eder would have overturned the SLA decision and given International Distributors its license back. But the lies were enough and Eder let the agency decision against Haim stand.

Despite the fact that the Aurelio affair had exposed Costello's influence over Tammany Hall, his power did not seem to diminish in the immediate post-World War Two years. The reformists and good-government types would wring their hands and call for merit selection of judges. But Costello somehow seemed to keep his position as a man of influence. No matter what his enemies in government would say about him, Costello seemed to have staying power.

Nineteen forty-nine was an election year in New York City. It was also a year in which Frank Costello learned first-hand, to his embarrassment, how no good deed goes unpunished. With Wolf's prodding, Costello had been sending any profits from his Wall Street real estate holdings—minus expenses—to charities. It had been the attorney's self-professed way of burnishing Costello's image, making him seem more benevolent and caring. As would later be explained in news articles, Costello had given so much money to the Salvation Army that he was among its 200 biggest contributors. The organization asked them all to serve as vice-chairmen for its upcoming fundraiser, and about 123 accepted, including Costello when he was asked that year by Walter Hoving of the Hoving Corporation to serve as a vice-chairman of the men's committee of the Salvation Army 1949 fund-raising campaign. It seemed like something that fit right into the game plan of making Costello respectable.

As a member of the committee, Costello invited people to attend the fund-raising dinner, set for January 24, 1949. The donation was $100 per person. He put together a list of his own guests, which included judges and politicians. But when Wolf saw a few of the other names on the list of invitees, he blanched in horror. They were some of Costello's mob cronies.

"I remonstrated with Frank, I pleaded," Wolf recalled. "Nothing I said could change his mind. Those so-called 'gangsters' were his friends. Furthermore, forget the Waldorf. The dinner would be held at the Copacabana."

Wolf said he warned Hoving about Costello's past but the businessman was unfazed, believing that there was simply no way that anybody could be criticized for charitable work. But when it came to somebody like Costello, there was a lot of baggage he carried no matter how good his intentions. The dinner went off as scheduled and, as Wolf later wryly put it, "The Mayor and the politicians mingled with gangsters in their finest outfits; nary a gun in sight."

Reporters and photographers got wind of the event and staked out the door, photographing those who attended: city council president and future mayor Vincent Impellitteri, Manhattan Borough President Hugo E. Rogers who headed Tammany Hall, state Supreme Court justices and others from the bench. Also present was Dr. Richard H. Hoffman, a psychiatrist who had treated Costello over his feelings of social inadequacy and recommended that he associate with a better class of people. Wolf later came out and gave the press a short list of some of those attending. Costello turned over about $10,000 in contributions to the Salvation Army, some $3,500 from the dinner proceeds and another $6,500 of his own money.

The resulting publicity showed how things had backfired. With so much attention on Costello, and little on the amount of money raised for the charity, he and officials of the Salvation Army decided it was best for him to resign as a vice-chairman. Through Wolf, Costello let it be known that he was afraid the adverse publicity would hurt the fund-raising. He bowed out. The Salvation Army said that it would not return any of the donations.

As embarrassing as the Salvation Army matter might have been, the year promised to have more surprises for Costello, some not of his making. As 1949 progressed, a major election was looming. Mayor O'Dwyer was running for reelection and it was no secret in politics that he had been an associate of Costello through Tammany, having sought his help in 1945 when he ran after La Guardia bowed out. Just the mention of Tammany and Costello made some of O'Dwyer's enemies see red. Some lambasted the Mayor, saying he was too close to the gangster element and had allegedly been soft on racketeering. Others, like Clendenin J. Ryan, heir to a business fortune and a staunch foe of O'Dwyer, took their hatred to another level.

Long before Watergate, the strangest and most brazen attempt at political surveillance occurred in those months leading up to the November 1949 election. It is one of those scandals that is all but lost to history but showed how virulent politics could be in New York City. This was a period in which wiretapping was illegal but under the quirks of the law could be performed by private detectives if they secured a legal order by applying to a police official above the rank of sergeant. This could lead to a flurry of surveillance, both legal and illegal.

Ryan, who had been an aide to La Guardia at City Hall, was convinced that political corruption was rampant in New York and that none other than Frank Costello and Mayor O'Dwyer held the city in a "vicious grip" of crooked machine politics. To find evidence of corruption, Ryan hired John G. Broady, an attorney, former prosecutor, private investigator, and "inveterate wiretapper," to start an investigation. As Manhattan District Attorney Frank Hogan would later explain after revealing what the two men were up to, Ryan and Broady talked about doing some "legal" wiretapping as part of their private probe. Broady also employed the services of a former NYPD detective named Kenneth Ryan as well as Edward M. Jones, who had at one time worked for the U.S. Treasury Department.

Ryan and Broady tried to interest others in their investigation, including some state judges and a prominent white-shoe lawyer named Paul Windels who had offices on Wall Street and had been a former top city lawyer under La Guardia. But Windels and the others thought the idea was impractical and sparked by some rehash of old stories from the newspapers. Still, Broady wouldn't be deterred and, as Hogan later alleged, prepared to place illegal wiretaps all around. Astonishingly, taps were discovered on Mayor O'Dwyer's telephones at City Hall and the home of Manhattan Borough president Hugo Rogers.

As in the case of the bungling Watergate burglars decades later, the entire bugging operation unraveled when a police officer discovered the tap on Rogers's telephone. This was uncovered when a police officer whose normal duties were to check telephones of city officials in an effort to guard against unlawful surveillance discovered a tap on the home telephone of Rogers. Hogan got involved in the case and his staff along with O'Dwyer displayed for reporters the bulky bugging equipment allegedly used in the scheme. At one point, O'Dwyer and police commissioner William P. O'Brien questioned Ryan early one morning at City Hall. The Mayor even promised ex-cop Ryan that he would put in a good word for him with Hogan if he came clean. Ryan excused himself to go to the bathroom and then fled City Hall undetected, leaving his tan top coat and hat in O'Dwyer's office. He also left leaving his new Mercury sedan in the City Hall parking area. He returned a few days later after hiring a lawyer.

Clendenin Ryan, the millionaire and no relation to the fleeing ex-detective, had been a nettlesome presence at City Hall for months. He formed something called the Clean Government Committee, published a weekly newspaper called the *Public Guardian,* and badgered O'Dwyer with questions, sometimes about Costello being the "real boss of New York City" but often about mob cases he thought the Mayor had bungled while acting as Brooklyn District Attorney. As far as Costello, Ryan said he was O'Dwyer's "commissioner in charge of vice and corruption." Offended by Ryan's outburst, one detective from the Mayor's office told the millionaire at the courthouse one day, "It's too bad your father didn't leave you brains instead of money."

The wiretap scandal made for great newspaper headlines and fed the political gossip mill. Ten Democratic members of Congress even came to City Hall to talk with O'Dwyer behind closed doors about the case. In the end, Ryan wasn't charged. In June 1949, with Broadly and others under indictment, Ryan decided to bow out of the election fight, believing that anti-Tammany—and thus anti-Costello—forces led by Judge Samuel Seabury could take care of things and attempt to oust O'Dwyer with a fusion candidate in the election.

Two years later, after the case had been more or less forgotten by the press, Hogan asked for the case against Broadly and the others to be dismissed. Hogan was forced to admit that his case had a fundamental weakness: the suspects were arrested before they actually illegally intercepted any telephone conversations. In other words, Hogan had jumped the gun. Of Clendenin Ryan's charge of public corruption, Hogan said cryptically that his office was conducting an investigation into "the existence of corruption" just like Ryan had tried to do.

If it did nothing else, the wiretap fracas and Ryan's comic attempts to go after O'Dwyer had the effect of keeping Costello in the political consciousness. In early spring of 1949, the Fusion Party asked Ryan to substantiate his charges about Costello controlling City Hall and for O'Dwyer to tell the public what he had done to rid city government of any "malign influences," which was a nice way of referring to Costello and the mob. But, then on May 25, O'Dwyer stunned the city by announcing he wouldn't seek reelection. As he spoke to reporters at City Hall, the Mayor gave no reason and when pressed wouldn't explain his decision. Asked if he might agree to run if drafted O'Dwyer answered "ridiculous."

But in politics the ridiculous has a way of becoming the reality. On July 13, 1949, after first rebuffing pleas by President Harry Truman and others, O'Dwyer decided to run for reelection after all. He explained his flip-flopping by saying he originally thought the five major county Democratic leaders would back Frank Hogan as a mayoral candidate. But when that didn't happen, O'Dwyer said he decided to seek reelection.

With O'Dwyer back in the race, Costello also reemerged as a factor because the political opposition brought his name up every chance it got. Newbold Morris, the Republican-Liberal-Fusion candidate, mocked O'Dwyer's statement that New Yorkers under his mayoralty had a "richer life."

"Richer for whom, Mr. O'Dwyer?" Morris asked in one speech. "For Frank Costello and every other mobster, every extortionist, every racketeer from Costello on down?"

Morris attacked the "graft-ridden political machine" he said was behind O'Dwyer, a reference to Tammany Hall, and all of the mobsters behind it. Ratcheting up the rhetoric, Morris went on in other speeches to say that Costello was the real boss of the Democratic machine and that so long as O'Dwyer was in City Hall, the mob felt safe.

"If you want a Tammany nomination for office in this city, it's wise to get the word of Frank Costello," Morris said. "If Costello wants you to get the nomination, you get the nomination. If he doesn't want you to get it, you just don't run for office on the Democratic ticket in this city."

To prove the point, Morris pointed out that Roosevelt's son, Franklin D. Roosevelt Jr., when running in a special election for Congress, was turned down by the Democratic Party. Roosevelt finally admitted that Costello was the real boss of the party, said Morris. The Fusion candidate also pointed out that Costello's pit bull in the press, Genoroso Pope, publisher of the Italian language *Il Progresso*, was a supporter of the Mayor. Morris apparently didn't know it at the time but Pope had received financial backing from Costello in the past and, as will be dealt with later in this book, would agree later on to go soft on stories about the mob.

As much as Morris beat up on O'Dwyer for the Costello link, the Mayor himself noted that he had cut out Tammany from many of his key decisions, including political appointments. In the end, the 1949 election results were more a vote in favor of O'Dwyer and the way he seemed to efficiently run City Hall, rather than a vote against him over Costello and the Mayor's silence about the issues his opponent raised.

O'Dwyer polled 1.266 million votes, some 141,000 votes more

than he garnered in his 1945 win. He won all the boroughs. Morris received over 956,000 votes and Vito Marcantonio, running under the banner of the American Labor party, received just over 356,000. For all of the political remonstrating about Costello, the issue of the mob and Tammany didn't shift the electorate. But William O'Dwyer wouldn't be finished with Frank Costello in his life, not by a long shot.

CHAPTER NINETEEN
"I'M A NEIGHBOR
OF YOURS"

IN EARLY 1950 FRANK COSTELLO WAS LIVING among the people he wanted to be like. The apartment on Central Park West, the house in Sands Point—these were the places that exuded status and class. After being beaten up in the newspapers by politicians as the gangster who controlled Gotham through Tammany Hall, Costello was desperate to show he was a man of culture and accomplishment who belonged among the wealthy and not just some dark-skinned Mediterranean immigrant who sounded like a tough guy. After all, Costello was a man of leisure who had the wherewithal to spend his days lunching in the Waldorf-Astoria, taking steam baths at the Biltmore Hotel, and dining in the best restaurants.

Costello played the media card in his game of acceptability. The story goes that Costello looked across the Peacock Alley in the Waldorf and saw a familiar face, that of Alicia Patterson, founder and editor of the Long Island newspaper *Newsday*. Founded in 1940, *Newsday* had steadily built itself into the biggest and most substantial newspaper on the island and would over time slowly force its competition out of business. The other New York dailies didn't give *Newsday* a serious battle over circulation in Nassau and Suffolk counties because *Newsday*'s household penetration rate would eventually reach 60 percent. This situation was different in the five boroughs where *Newsday* at the time had minuscule circulation.

If Costello was looking for a big media outlet to talk to there were certainly others with a larger audience. But Mrs. Patterson happened to live in Sands Point in a large Norman-style mansion high above Long Island known as *Falaise* with her husband Harry Guggenheim, the former ambassador to Cuba and the scion of a wealthy family. The property Patterson and Guggenheim had in Sands Point, with its dozens of acres, dwarfed Costello's country squire house on Barkers Point Road. But Costello wasn't intimidated as he walked across the hotel lobby and approached Patterson.

"I'm a neighbor of yours in Sands Point," Costello said as a way of introducing himself to Patterson. "Why don't you and your husband come to my house for cocktails some time. Maybe you'd like to invite me to your house."

Patterson likely didn't know it at the time but her extended family seems to have had a tenuous connection to Costello's clan through the old bootlegging days. Her brother-in-law Isaac Guggenheim also owned a palatial estate in Sands Point known as Villa Carola. After Isaac died in 1922, a group of bootleggers took to off-loading $90,000 worth of what was called "Chinese whisky" at a dock on his property facing Hempstead Bay. The incident in April 1924 led to the arrest of several men, including Costello relative Edward Aloise of Astoria, all of whom were caught trying to move the booze in a bucket brigade formation to waiting trucks. Cops confiscated the liquor, as well as three trucks, and the local police chief said it was the biggest single haul made on Long Island.

Back on Long Island, the next day after her meeting with Costello, Patterson had lunch with her columnist Jack Altshul, broaching to him the idea of an interview with the mob boss. Altshul was skeptical that a normally press shy Costello would really consent. But the next day, Patterson told Altshul that Costello agreed to an interview. On a Saturday morning, Altshul and his photographer wife Edna Murray, who was at the time eight months pregnant, paid Costello and his wife Loretta a visit to his home in Sands Point. They got quite a scoop.

There were more than enough reasons for Costello to open the door to the two *Newsday* journalists. Just about a month earlier he had appeared voluntarily before a U.S. Senate subcommittee that quizzed him about what he knew about national gambling syndicates. Costello was evasive on some things but was being candid when he told the committee members that the public wanted to gamble and that it was difficult to control. Asked about his influence with politicians he said, "I couldn't even get a parking ticket fixed."

Costello came out of his house to meet Altshul and his wife, and extended a hand in greeting. He wore a short-sleeved tan sport shirt, darker slacks and what were described as "moccasin styled" shoes. He offered the couple a drink as he escorted them to the terrace where a radio was tuned to a Yankee-Athletics game. Inside the house the television, a relatively new device, was showing a Giants baseball game. The selection of the games wasn't because Costello was a compulsive sports fan.

"I'm bettin' on the Yankees and they're getting trimmed," said Costello. "Inside I've got the Giants on television and they're not going anywhere either."

"Saturdays are usually a big day for Frank," Loretta chimed in. "He's got a couple of games on television, a game on the radio and he'll go inside to watch the race from Belmont when that goes on."

Although Costello had no way of knowing at the time, Altshul was also an inveterate and troubled gambler. Colleagues remembered how he would bet on the most mundane things, like how a rain drop might fall down a train window. He also became obsessive, running out to Roosevelt Racetrack when he was supposed to be editing the newspaper at night and having his colleagues cover for him if the publisher called. So hearing about Costello's obsessive interest in sports results was something Altshul could understand. Over the years his betting would become an uncomfortable part of his life, and in 1981 he would go cold turkey and not travel to Atlantic City again.

At home on Barkers Point Road, the Costellos appeared relaxed and well into life in the suburbs. But, with his interests in Manhattan, Costello said he only really got out to Sands Point on the weekends. He couldn't take commuting into the city. Hot Springs in

Arkansas was where Costello went for weeks of golf, availing himself of the famous baths.

"I take the mineral baths you know and I come back feelin' like a new man," Costello said.

In Sands Point, Costello and his wife entertained, but it is highly unlikely that any of their well-heeled neighbors came to the parties. Observing him, Altshul couldn't help but remark on how unprepossessing Costello seemed.

"He is just under average height, under the paunch of a man of 54. Only a big star sapphire could give an inkling that here is a man reputed to own hotels, nightclubs, Wall Street real estate, gambling houses, slot machines," Altshul later wrote. "He looks not unlike George Raft in the cast of his features. His black hair is not as sleek as Raft's, is thinning and gray at the edges."

Costello walked around the property with Altshul. They walked up to a split-rail fence where two horses on an adjacent property came up to greet them. Costello pulled out an apple and offered it to a chestnut-colored horse, who refused to take it. A pinto pony took the half Costello offered. For a photo, Costello posed lounging in a hammock, a copy of a recent *Time* magazine in his lap which had him on the cover as a result of the recent Senate hearing.

Altshul perceptively noticed how cultured and refined the Costellos made an effort to appear to be. Loretta, who Altshul described as a "pleasant-faced, plumpish woman who talked in a soprano voice," seemed to speak "with a conscious effort to be grammatical." Loretta said she didn't do the cooking but had a maid to do that. Her living room had a number of pastoral paintings and a portrait of a nude girl

"Frank has a lot of artist friends," she said. "That girl is art. It's all the way you look at it, you know."

Despite all of the stories about late nights in the clubs, Costello said his evenings were, well, boring.

"You know, I haven't seen the late show at a nightclub in 15 years. I go in for the dinner show, leave about 10 o'clock. Most nights I am in bed by ten, ten-thirty," he said.

Finally, the talk got around to the investigation of the gambling syndicates and Costello admitted knowing gamblers, as did other people. Why should he be any different? His past criminal record was just a product of the times he grew up in.

"Look, whadda I need with a syndicate. I got all the money I ever need," Costello noted. "So, when I was a kid in Harlem, it was fashionable to carry a gun. So they passed a new law, the Sullivan law. And I did a bit. Only time. That makes me a criminal."

As far as his activities in Prohibition were concerned, Costello indicated that by bootlegging he just provided a service the public wanted. Drinkers were on one side of the bar while Costello sold the booze from the other side, making money.

Altshul couldn't resist getting Costello to play a short game of klabiash, a card game that originated in Europe. Costello said in jest that maybe he shouldn't play, just to save his reputation. They played and as it turned out Altschul won, to which Costello said "You're the champ."

As Altshul and his wife Edna were leaving, Costello asked the pregnant woman whether she was hoping for a boy or a girl. Edna answered she was thinking about a girl.

"You got it," he said with a grin. "Costello can rig anything."

About a month after the visit to Sands Point, Edna Murray Altshul gave birth to a baby girl Sara.

In the months before his interview with Altshul, Costello's appearance before the Senate subcommittee had also given him headlines. It was at his attorney's suggestion that Costello agreed to appear before the senators and talk about gambling and his views on proposed legislation. Wolf said he thought the opportunity would be a good chance for Costello to show he had nothing to hide and to further burnish his attempt to appear legitimate.

Traveling to Washington, Wolf recalled that his client was a Nervous Nelly as the hour of his testimony approached. They were breakfasting in the Mayflower Hotel and Wolf noticed Costello had hardly touched his meal, and when he did finish he took a napkin and polished his teeth. Dressed in a dark, conservative pin-stripe suit and a blue figured neck tie, Costello wanted to make a good impression and leave nothing to chance.

In Capitol Hill in the jammed committee room Costello indicated he had been out of the gambling business for over fifteen years but didn't think any law could wipe out the activity. The proposal to outlaw the transmission of gambling information in interstate commerce was doomed to failure, he said.

"You can't wash the spots off a leopard," Costello told the subcommittee. "If a man is a gambler, he'll find a trick. Local officials can stop it to a certain extent, but there'll always be some cheating."

Costello acknowledged working for years as a "betting commissioner," earning up to $30,000 in commission. In that job Costello said he took big wagers from bettors who didn't want to run down the odds and placed them with bookmakers, taking a 5-percent commission along the way. But that was all in the past, Costello said. Now he was into real estate, owned the Beverly nightclub in Louisiana and had some Texas oil leases with his friend Frank Erickson. Pressed to say if he had an interest in any gambling location, Costello pled the Fifth Amendment, although he admitted that there was a little gambling at the Beverly, the roulette wheels and dice games.

Asked why everybody called him a "big shot" Costello answered with a Cheshire Cat grin that the newspapers had an investment in him: "to them I'm number One."

Costello's testimony before the subcommittee didn't seem to damage him. But times were still dangerous for him. He and Erickson were on a list of 150 racketeers that was leaked to the press. On the rundown were Costello's old friends: Joe Adonis, Joey Rao, Waxie Gordon, Vincent Alo, Mike "Trigger Mike" Coppolo, and Anthony Carfano. Federal prosecutors said they would see if they could build criminal cases and it looked like they might start a nationwide sweep against the Mafia.

Unlike Costello, Erickson didn't fare as well from his Senate testimony. Called as a witness he went against the advice of his lawyer and answered questions. It proved disastrous. Erickson seemed evasive and lacking in candor. The substance of his testimony showed that he had indeed been involved in gambling and, as *The New York Times* reported, "had to admit that for the last thirty years he had violated the laws of every state." Added to his problem was that back in New York, Hogan and his staff seized Erickson's business and personal records from his office at 487 Park Avenue. The materials showed that he was partners with a number of racketeers in the Colonial Inn casino in Hallandale, Florida, an operation that netted its partners nearly $700,000 in profits one year. Erickson had a 5 percent share of the business but others also owned a similar amount: Joe Adonis, Meyer Lansky and his brother Jake, as well as Vincent Alo, who was described as a "reputed agent of Costello."

Although Costello wasn't shown to have a share of the Colonial, Erickson's papers showed that he had made some loans to Costello and his 79 Wall Street Corporation. Some of the loans appear to have been paid off. One document was a thank-you note to Erickson for his $1,000 donation to the Salvation Army, one of Costello's favorite charities.

Erickson was indicted by a Manhattan state court jury on charges of conspiracy and bookmaking. In the face of overwhelming evidence, Erickson quickly pled guilty to the charges on June 26, 1950. His attorney, in pleading for leniency, said that while bookmaking was considered an evil influence that it was a product of the public's desire, a position Costello had taken just a month earlier during the Senate hearing. The court sentenced Erickson to two years in prison and fined him $30,000, with the added provision that for an additional three-year suspended sentence he never again engage in professional gambling.

The case essentially broke Erickson as a man, stripping him of his role as the nation's biggest bookmaker. Meanwhile, Costello had his own issues. Word leaked out in June that Senate investigators were looking at a 1946 New York case in which Costello and the mob were linked to vice—which is another way of saying prostitution and gambling—and narcotics trafficking. Senator Estes Kefauver, the Tennessee Democrat and chairman of the committee doing the investigating, said the particular case involved six narcotics dealers in Harlem, while another investigator said at least two were members of the Mafia and thus white.

Costello denied the allegation that he was involved in narcotics and said he detested anybody who was. Yet with all of the publicity Costello had received in recent months, more and more he was emerging as the nation's preeminent gangster. It didn't matter that he claimed to only be a legitimate businessman whose days as a bootlegger and gambler were behind him. The drumbeat of headlines and statements about Costello's power continued.

There was also another development that didn't appear good for Costello. Politicians were becoming more vocal and assertive in putting distance between themselves and Costello. O'Dwyer, fresh from reelection in late 1949, decided to resign in 1950 for what were said to be concerns about his wife's health. He would take a less-demanding job as U.S. ambassador to Mexico. Taking over as acting Mayor was Vincent Impellitteri, the Democratic president of the City Council. O'Dwyer's leaving opened the field up for another mayoral election, and this time the candidates seemed unanimous in using Costello as a whipping boy, accusing their various opponents of being his stooge.

Impellitteri accused his opponent Judge Ferdinand Pecora, who was running on the Democratic-Liberal line of being the candidate backed by Costello. Impellitteri, who was running as the candidate of the Experience Party, based his claim on a conversation he had at City Hall with publisher Generoso Pope Jr., a friend of Costello, who had said the gambler had told him he was going to back Pecora, something Pope said he was going to do as well.

"I am not questioning Judge Pecora's character," Impellitteri said in a radio address. "But I do say he is no more than a respectable front for the lowest, vilest elements this town ever saw."

"If Pecora is elected," Impellitteri continued, "Frank Costello will be your Mayor, but the voice will be that of Pecora. Carmine DeSapio, the Tammany leader, and others allied with him in this campaign take their orders from Frank Costello, directly or indirectly." He referred to an old meeting in 1946 that Costello attended which allegedly was to decide which judgeships were going to be parceled out, a plot that he said failed when news of it leaked to the press.

Impellitteri also argued that Pecora's attendance in 1949 at Costello's fundraiser for the Salvation Army was also an indication the judge was in the pocket of the gangsters. Adding to the frenzy, Impellitteri ordered his police commissioner, Thomas F. Murphy, to round up all hoodlums on the spot to assure the electorate wouldn't be intimidated by goons.

Pecora fired back with a challenge to Impellitteri to a debate in which both men's qualifications for office would be on display and to hash out what he called the "false issue" of "Costelloism." Even Republican candidate Edward Corsi, who didn't really have a prayer in the up-coming election, got into the act. He chided Impellitteri, saying the acting mayor simply did nothing to go against Costello except to walk away from him at a social event.

In the end, Impellitteri won the election but not by a landslide. He pulled 1.16 million votes, to just over 935,000 for Pecora. Corsi got just over 382,000. It is hard to say just how much of a role the Costello factor played in the results. But what was clear as 1950 was coming to a close was that Frank Costello was a toxic figure in New York politics. The mantle of gangster may have worked years ago but now the public, led by increasingly vocal politicians of all stripes, was showing a strong disdain for the Mafia. Runyon had portrayed the Broadway hoods as likeable rogues. But now men like Costello, dubbed "the most influential underworld leader in America," were being portrayed as the enemy of the people. A year earlier, the American Municipal Association, which represented 10,000 cities around the country, had beseeched the federal government to do something about organized crime. For Frank Costello and the rest of the Mafiosi, the worst was yet to come.

CHAPTER TWENTY
THE BALLET OF THE HANDS

THE NIGHT OF APRIL 6, 1950, CHARLES BINAGGIO, the politically connected underworld boss of Kansas City, and his driver and enforcer
Charles Gargotta, were driven to a gambling den and after a short
while decided to borrow Nick Penna's car to go to Binaggio's political clubhouse. Binaggio, considered the heir to the town's political
boss Tom Pendergast, was an ex-con who had control over the city's
gambling rackets. Binaggio figured he and Gargotta would only
need about fifteen minutes to take care of some business at the First
District Democratic Club. They never came back with Penna's car.

Sometime around midnight, an assailant or assailants, shot both
men in the head inside the clubhouse on Truman Road, which had
recently been named after President Harry Truman. Cops found Binaggio dead seated in a swivel chair at the rear of the club. He had
apparently been talking to his killer when he was shot four times in
the head at such close range that powder burns were around the
entry wounds. His silver cigarette holder had dropped to the floor as
blood pooled around it. Gargotta had apparently been running away
when he was shot from behind into the left side of his head. In his
frenzy to escape, Gargotta tore at the venetian blind on the front
door. Robbery was quickly ruled out as a motive: Binaggio had $24
in his pockets, Gargotta had over $2,000. The only reasons police
came as quickly as they did to discover the bodies was that a cab
driver getting a bite to eat heard some running water inside the club.

Kansas City wasn't New York or Chicago in terms of the mob structure of the country. But it was a focal point for gambling in the Midwest and Binaggio was considered to be one of the local mob bosses. Both Binaggio and Gargotta were part of a nationwide race wire that communicated horse-race information around the country. They were also believed to be sharing proceeds with the old Capone mob in Chicago, as well as a gambling syndicate out of New York. A nationwide federal investigation had linked both men to Frank Costello.

The wake funeral for Binaggio was one of those affairs that was a testament to his local stature. Honorary pall bearers included a judge, politicians, former members of Congress, a sheriff and members of the local police board. Also carrying the $2,500 casket—pricey for that time—was local gangster Max Hablen. Newspapers reported that even Costello showed up to pay his respects although local police said they had not heard he had appeared.

The murders of Binaggio and Gargotta were the latest of over two dozen murders in Kansas City in the previous three years. What made the double homicide stand out was the fact that it seemed to link the world of politics and the mob in St. Louis, a combination which the local citizenry and the newspapers saw as an attempt by the underworld to gets its rewards for backing elements of the Democratic political machine. Given the fact that the city had only just weathered a storm of corruption, the civic leaders was outraged over the killings. *The Kansas City Star* said in an editorial that the killings represented a "National Challenge" and were a "major development in a national threat from organized crime." Binaggio and Gargotta were killed, the newspaper speculated, as a result of some internal warfare with other leaders in a national crime syndicate led by none other than Frank Costello.

The outcry over the killings reverberated in Washington, D.C., which had just begun to grapple with the problems of organized crime. After the American Municipal Association had a year earlier called on the federal government to combat organized crime, the Kansas City killings became a rallying cry for some against Washington's inaction. It was up to a relatively unknown senator from

Tennessee named C. Estes Kefauver to draft a resolution to create a special committee to investigate the issue. A bookish, bespectacled man with a thin face, Kefauver prevailed in his effort and was named chairman of the Special Committee on Organized Crime in Interstate Commerce, which had a working budget of $150,000.

Kefauver's committee launched on what would be a fifteen-month nationwide series of hearings in major cities going after what he called the "life blood of organized crime," gambling. Miami was the first city to be examined and soon after Kefauver visited Kansas City, a place he said had been struggling to get away from the law of the jungle. By early 1951, Kefauver was ready to move his committee operation to New York and that meant there was one person who would be the marquee witness: Frank Costello.

Some months earlier, Costello had appeared before a different Senate committee looking into gambling, and the event had been rather painless for him. Gambling was an activity Costello had been long associated with, and it was certainly no secret. But now the Kefauver committee posed a different problem. Its brief was wider and could delve into many aspects of Costello's life. Recent news reports said he was linked to narcotics trafficking and even murder. Costello's attorney George Wolf thought his client should waive his immunity and not claim the Fifth Amendment privilege against self-incrimination. But to cover his bases, Wolf asked Costello to ask some of his old friends what he should do. The answer was the same.

"They all advised him not to claim immunity, to tell the truth," Wolf recalled. "They thought by doing so he might end those rumors which dogged him about narcotics."

As was the practice with Kefauver, the committee heard from Costello in secret executive session on February 15, 1951, in Manhattan federal court, and as Wolf remembered it things went well. Kefauver asked Costello about his gambling, bootlegging, and slot machines, things that had been public record for years. At one point, the attorney said that Rudolph Halley, the counsel for the committee, asked if a photographer could take a picture of Kefauver interrogating Costello. Wolf agreed and in the session the Senator, for the benefit of the camera, questioned Costello and waved his finger at him. Costello, said Wolf, played the game and wagged his finger in what the attorney said was a joke back at Kefauver.

But Kefauver didn't take Costello's action as playful and instead jumped up in anger, telling the photographer to stop taking pictures and then shot an ominous warning at Costello.

"You've had your laugh, Mr. Costello, but you will live to regret this," fumed Kefauver as he walked out of the room, remembered Wolf.

Not long after the executive session ended, but before Costello had a chance to testify in public, Kefauver's committee issued an official interim report. The document was devastating to Costello, accusing him of being the No. 1 crime boss in the country, who was in charge of all rackets, including drug trafficking. The report, which was completed before any testimony had been taken in public in New York, said there were at least two major crime syndicates in the United States. One of them was a so-called "axis" between Miami and what was left of the Capone group in Chicago led by the Fischetti brothers and one Jake Guzik. The other was a variant that included ties between Miami and New York, headed by Frank Costello and Joe Adonis. The arbiter of any disputes between two alignments were to be arbitrated by Charles Luciano from his perch in Italy. The report stung Costello and Wolf. In discussing strategy for the upcoming public testimony of Costello, scheduled to begin on March 13, the attorney said that they had to be careful about one line of inquiry from the Senate: Costello's net worth.

"With a man like Frank Costello, a net worth statement would enable them [the government] to ask specific questions about the amount stated," Wolf explained years later. "That is why the net worth statement was so dangerous for Frank, especially. If he estimated a low figure, they could dig up evidence of expenditures to prove he had underestimated his net worth and was guilty of tax evasion. If he gave a high estimate, they would want to know just where all the money came from."

Costello told his attorney he didn't know what his net worth was. He was a man who professed to not keeping records, checking accounts, or investment funds. But given that he had diversified to become a businessman, it is more likely that he knew the value of his assets and any debts. Still, the strategy was that on the question of net worth, Costello was to take the Fifth Amendment and not answer if asked by the committee.

For the public sessions, which actually began in December 1950, the Senate committee began using television to broadcast the sessions. A relatively new device, television had begun to make inroads as a news medium, although its use was in its infancy. Two of Costello's closest associates—Joe Adonis and Willie Moretti—preceded him in testifying publicly. Moretti's session on December 14 seemed in some ways comical, and *The New York Times* ran a sub-headline that read "Moretti Praised by Committee for Rags-to-Riches Saga of Dice and Horse-Playing." But a day earlier Adonis had a much tougher time, refusing to answer any questions about his business or income.

Moretti didn't avoid talking about gambling and the horses, in fact he relished doing so. He recalled starting shooting craps as a kid in Philadelphia, graduating to horse racing, and taking a fling as a featherweight boxer before marrying in 1927 and settling down in New Jersey. His gambling income varied from year to year, swinging from $15,000 one year to $45,000 in another. In 1950 his only winnings were about $11,000 at the track since he was preoccupied with preparing for his appearance before the committee. Kefauver asked him how he made money at the track, and Moretti was ready with an answer.

"Bet 'em to place and show," Moretti explained. "You've got three ways of winning. Come out to the track some time and I'll show you."

Asked about the gangsters he knew, Moretti again was open in his answer, acknowledging decades of friendships with the likes of Capone, Luciano, Costello, Genovese, Erickson, and Kastel.

"Everything's a racket today," said Moretti. "Everybody has a racket of his own. The stock market is a racket. Why don't they make everything legal?"

Adonis didn't engage in any lengthy, friendly colloquy with the committee. Instead, he was more confrontational. He told the committee from the beginning that he would be taking the Fifth Amendment on most questions, although he did admit using a number of aliases. But each time he was asked a question of substance he took the Fifth.

Prodded at one point by Halley, the committee counsel, if he was afraid to answer questions, Adonis snapped back "I am not afraid of anything." Kefauver warned him that he would likely be cited for contempt of the Senate, which several months later was exactly what happened.

The formal New York City hearings for Kefauver's committee were set to begin on March 12, and the list of witnesses expected to be called included the upper echelon of the Mafia and associates: Joe Adonis, Frank Costello, Meyer Lansky, Joseph Profaci, Thomas Lucchese, Albert and Anthony Anastasia, Vincent Mangano. Also on the list were Frank Erickson and the mob moll Virginia Hill.

Frank Costello's long awaited public appearance before the Kefauver Committee took place on March 13, 1951. The setting was rather modest for such an event. Costello walked into the twenty-eighth floor hearing room in Manhattan federal court, which seemed too small for the crowd, which included television cameras and a battery of newsreel photographers. He wore a powder-blue suit and was, as always, impeccably tailored. George Wolf, his loyal attorney since the Aurelio scandal of 1943, accompanied him. From the beginning, Costello's appearance was contentious, with Wolf decrying the presence of the television cameras and asking that they don't photograph his client.

"Mr. Costello doesn't care to submit himself as a spectacle," Wolf told Senator Herbert R. O'Conor. "And on the further ground that it will prevent proper conference with his attorney, in receiving proper advice from his attorney during the course of the testimony."

Wolf was referring to the cameras possibly picking up his private conferences with Costello, of which there would be many, during the course of the testimony. Wolf also wanted radio coverage cut off for the same reason. O'Conor agreed to keep TV cameras off Costello but wouldn't bar radio coverage, saying the microphones could be silenced when Costello and Wolf conferred. While it wasn't known at the time, the TV cameras focused not on Costello's face but just his hands on the table, a shot that, as events bore out, would be more telling than any of his visage.

After Costello was sworn in and gave his address as 115 Central Park West, Wolf took over and read a statement on his client's behalf, which can only be characterized as one of protest about the interim report issued by the committee some days earlier. In his statement, Costello felt he was being ambushed by the committee. Back in February, Costello said he testified truthfully and candidly about his life in an effort dispel stories that he was the leader of a national syndicate in charge of vice. Based on what Kefauver had told him about his having answered questions "forthrightly" about his career [although with some vagueness about the Prohibition years], Costello felt he was going to get a fair shake from the Committee. That is until the interim report came out naming him the head of one of the two crime syndicates in the U.S.

"While I realize the committee's pretenses of fairness were empty words, I was not prepared for the shocking discovery that the report was completed before I had even begun to testify and that nothing I could have said or done would have changed it one iota," said Costello's statement, which had obviously been sculpted with Wolf's help. "I was informed that chief counsel not only admitted that the report had been prepared before I started to testify but that it was, to use the chief counsel's own language, 'based upon inference upon inference' and without a single shred of direct evidence against me, after over a year of an extensive investigation, aided by virtually every local and federal investigating agency in the United States."

Costello then went on in the statement to remind the committee that a "man is presumed to be innocent until his guilt is proved beyond a reasonable doubt." He then asked to have "this last opportunity of proving that your charges against me are unjustified and that they should be retracted." In the end, Costello begged that he be treated as a human being.

After Costello was finished, Chairman Kefauver countered him and said the charge that the controversial interim report was prepared before he testified was "absolutely untrue." The report was only completed a week before its release and weeks after Costello had testified in secret executive session. The fact that a witness appeared to testify in a "forthright" manner didn't exonerate him for any connection with "crime or contacts with other people who may have engaged in it," said Kefauver.

Pressed by Wolf, the committee counsel Halley admitted that he had told the lawyer that the report had been completed before Costello had testified. Halley said nothing Costello had said in the secret session caused the committee to change the report, although moments later Kefauver admitted that the report had been changed about ten days to two weeks before its release.

After the fracas over what Costello said was a bushwhacking, his testimony began in earnest, picking up from the time he came to the U.S. and over the way his name had changed. The colloquy Costello had with Halley over whether he ever used the surname "Saverio" [or "Severio" as the transcript stated] showed how frustrating getting a straight answer out of Costello was going to be.

> MR. HALLEY: Thank you very much. But can you tell us whether or not you know whether you ever used the name Frank Severio?
>
> MR. COSTELLO: I am willing to admit that I might have used it.
>
> MR. HALLEY: You are not willing to admit that you know very well that you did use it?
>
> MR. COSTELLO: Why should I? Isn't that answer good enough?

Halley reminded Costello that he was convicted of a crime under the name Saverio over thirty-five years ago, something Costello acknowledged. But when asked again if that was the name he used, Costello said, "Well, I probably did." The issue of what names Costello used over the years encompassed four or five pages of the hearing transcript. It had an added relevance when the questioning quickly turned to the names he used on his application for U.S. citizenship in 1925 and his activities during Prohibition. The answers Costello gave would get him into trouble later but suffice to say he appeared to lie or be wildly inaccurate on those points.

Halley asked Costello if at the time he filed his naturalization papers he was also involved in the "liquor business" to which he replied, "I don't believe so." When a skeptical Halley asked Costello again about liquor, he again replied he didn't believe he was. Halley was also frustrated in trying to get Costello to be specific about when he was involved in bootlegging, asking him when it was he purchased liquor smuggled in from Canada.

"Well, I couldn't tell you the exact time," said Costello. "Approximately around 1927, 1928, 1929, I don't know. The later years."

"It could have been as early as 1922 or 1923, could it not?" asked Halley

"No, I doubt it," replied Costello.

"You don't think you ever testified to that?" said Halley.

"Well, I might have," conceded Costello. "But not now. To my recollection, I don't think it was earlier than 1927."

Costello was either lying or had the most porous of memories because it was clear that he had engaged in bootlegging well before 1927. The Blackwell Mansion episode of 1922, his brother's trucking business, and the 1926 federal criminal case, all showed how extensive Costello's ties were to bootlegging. But what was going to prove troublesome to him was the fact that the two men he used as character witnesses on his naturalization application were also part of his liquor conspiracies and thus falsely attested to Costello's good character at a time when he was violating the law, the committee believed.

Wolf and Costello were ready for the question of whether they had brought along a copy of a financial statement spelling out Costello's net worth. Wolf believed that such a document would incriminate his client. Halley asked for it. Costello refused to give it to him.

"What is your net worth today?" Halley pressed.

"I refuse to answer that question," Costello responded

"On what ground?" asked Halley.

"I am going to exercise my rights that it might incriminate me," Costello told the counsel.

When he testified in executive session, Costello said he would provide a statement of his net worth. But after the scathing interim report came out, Costello and Wolf both agreed that it would be crazy to turn over such a document. In front of the cameras, Wolf and Halley sparred over the document, but in the end Costello wouldn't budge.

As the testimony droned on, the TV cameras couldn't show Costello's face. But they were picking up the audio of Costello's raspy voice and something else that would captivate viewers: what he was doing with his hands. Throughout the testimony, Costello would fidget, alternately rubbing his palms together, crumpling a handkerchief, picking up a glass of water, crumpling some paper or beating his digits on the table. It was a performance, as *The New York Times* television columnist Jack Gould called it "video's first ballet of the hands."

There were plenty of journalists crammed into the courtroom. One in particular was Helen Dudar of *Newsday*, the Long Island daily Costello had given a lengthy interview to a year earlier at his Sands Point country home. *Newsday* would always try to squeeze a nugget of Long Island-centric news from a story and Costello provided something important in his testimony about George M. Levy, a lawyer and golfing buddy of Costello's

Among his various interests, Levy had the racing franchise at Roosevelt Raceway in Nassau County, one of several such harness-racing operations permitted by the state racing commission. *Newsday* had a continuing interest in Levy, given his relationship to Bill DeKonig, head of the pari-mutuel racing clerks union. The Senate found among some of the tax returns Costello had turned over a payment of $15,000 he had received from Levy. As Costello explained it, Levy was worried about complaints that bookmakers were hanging out at his racetrack and the racing commission might pull his franchise.

"Maybe you can think of something," Levy asked him, said Costello.

"I says, 'Well, what can I do, George, I can spread the propaganda around that they're hurting you there and you're a nice fellow, and I can tell them that if there's an arrest made, it's going to be very severe,'" Costello explained to the committee. " 'I don't know how much good it'll do you, but I'll talk about it.' "

In restaurants around Manhattan like Dinty Moore's, in hotels such as the Waldorf-Astoria, in salons, nightclubs, or wherever he had the chance, Costello spread the word among bookmakers and anyone else within earshot about staying away from Roosevelt Raceway. It was all done for friendship with Levy, for which he got $60,000 for what Costello thought wasn't much of anything. The Senators were incredulous with Costello's explanation and the self-effacing way he described what meager effort he gave to Levy.

"Don't you think the real reason that this bookmaking stopped out there is the magic of the name Costello, and when they heard Costello was against it, the rats all ran to cover?" said Senator Tobey.

"I don't think so, Senator," said Costello.

"Well, they went, didn't they?" replied Tobey.

The committee also introduced a transcript of a wiretapped call between Levy and Costello in which the two, contrary to Costello's vagueness about whether there were any bookies at the track, indicated that the gamblers were a problem. They were such a problem that Levy was planning to bring in the Pinkerton detective agency to keep out the gambling riffraff. If anything, the transcript showed how opaque Costello's memory was, perhaps selectively.

Costello returned for a second day of testimony on March 14 and the discussion started off with questioning about his New Orleans slot machine venture with Philip Kastel. Eventually the questioning got to the issue of the $325,000 note Costello co-signed for Kastel's attempt to purchase the Scottish distillery, something Costello said he did for friendship. Costello was questioned for a long period of time about the distillery deal and the note, something that got him testy.

"I answered about the note forty times, Mr. Halley," Costello said to the committee counsel.

"Answer it once more," replied Halley.

"All right, let it be the last one," answered Costello.

Halley's reply: "Well, we will decide that."

The committee probed deeper in Costello's relationship with Dudley Geigerman, the $27,000 Costello had left missing in the New York cab in 1944, and his relationship with Johnny Torrio. But by 2:00 P.M. the committee recessed. The uncovered ground that Costello needed to be questioned on included his net worth, his criminal friends, and his political influence, all things that had the potential for causing a big showdown. The committee also stoked the fires by saying that Costello might have even committed perjury in his testimony.

On March 15, any hope that the hearings would get off on the right footing quickly came to an end. As Costello took his seat, his attorney said that the entire spectacle in the courthouse—the lights, the sound of the film cameras, the hustle and bustle of reporters entering and leaving the room—made it impossible for his client to concentrate and talk in private with his lawyer. There was also the problem that Costello was suffering from a throat ailment and was having increasing trouble in speaking. Adding to the burden on Costello, who was called a "defendant" by Wolf, was the fact that the committee viewed him as an "arch criminal" who should be prosecuted for perjury.

"Now he has reached the end, and the limits of physical and mental endurance. He cannot go on," said Wolf. "He desires to defend himself and wants the opportunity to do so. He asks that this examination be postponed to such time as he is physically and mentally able to continue, and in surroundings and under circumstances where he can testify properly and defend himself."

Kefauver stepped in and tried to make things better for Costello, offering to have the TV lights turned off or positioned differently and telling both he and Wolf that they could cover their microphones with their hands to avoid having their private conversations picked up. But as far as an adjournment was concerned, Kefauver said no, the show must go on.

Costello had other ideas. He wasn't going to put up with more testimony, not the way he was feeling.

"I am in no condition to testify," Costello told Kefauver. "You heard my statement through Mr. Wolf and I stand by it and under no condition will I testify here until I am well enough."

"You refuse to testify further?" a surprised Kefauver asked.

"Absolutely," shot back Costello.

Kefauver still didn't believe that Costello wouldn't cooperate and asked Halley to start asking questions. But the moment of high drama for the hearings had arrived. Acting like some street-wise criminal, Costello called the committee's bluff as if he were talking to some cop at the precinct.

"Mr. Halley, am I a defendant in this courtroom?" asked Costello.

"No," admitted Halley.

"Am I under arrest?" Costello inquired.

"No," said Halley.

"Then I am walking out," Costello said.

Kefauver tried to get Costello to sit down and told him that the committee had no power to punish anyone except for contempt. The chairman also tried to appeal to Costello's sense of civic duty, telling him he was a very important witness to the investigation. But Costello would have none of it and told Kefauver that while he respected him he was walking out all the same.

At the last moment, Wolf pulled out a doctor's note, from physician Vincent Panettiere. The doctor said that earlier that day he had examined Costello and found him to be suffering from "acute Laryngotracheitia" and should stay in bed for "several days." The note was a double-edged sword because Panettiere didn't say that Costello would need "several weeks" to recuperate as Wolf had indicated. To Kefauver, Costello wasn't in any danger and simply seemed to have a sore throat.

Halley tried to ask Costello more questions but it was a futile gesture. Costello said he wouldn't answer any questions for the moment, and when pressed finally said, "I still refuse."

Just before Costello and Wolf left the room, Kefauver said that Costello seemed to be using his throat as a ruse to get out of testifying and now risked being brought up on contempt charges. Further, the full Senate could order Costello's arrest and compel him to come back and testify. In the meantime, with the marquee witness gone, Kefauver and the committee called other witnesses.

It took the better part of a week, until March 19, for Costello and the committee to sort things out. A physician appointed by the committee had examined him and believed his throat ailment wouldn't prevent him from testifying for an hour or two. But when Costello did show up he seemed to be in better spirits and with a stronger voice. The questioning delved a great deal into his political ties and activities. The testimony rehashed the Aurelio case, which Costello said burned him and dissuaded him from supporting any more candidates. But Costello also admitted that he had friendly relations with the steering committee of Tammany Hall, yet at the same time saying, "I'm not a politician, I am a friend of politicians." How did Costello explain his ability to persuade politicians? He had no explanation to give.

Asked at one point in the hearings what he had ever done for his country, Costello summed it up in a few words, which got laughs, "Paid my tax."

As he had done earlier, Costello peppered his testimony with claims of "I just don't remember" or complaints about being unable to recall dates and events because he didn't carry a diary around. As things wound down, Senator Charles Tobey of New Hampshire told Costello that the committee was happy he had recovered his voice. "Mr. Costello is happy too," replied George Wolf.

CHAPTER TWENTY-ONE
"GET FRANK COSTELLO"

AFTER THE SCHOOL DAY ENDED at Bedford Elementary School in Westport, Connecticut, thirteen-year-old Noel Castigilia would squeeze in some hours of part-time work at a local flower company. On weekends and holidays he also caddied at the Longshore Country Club. But in March 1951, Noel's after-school routine changed dramatically as the Kefauver hearings got under way. Noel would rush home and turn on the television, catching what he could of the live sessions and then follow up with the film from the nightly news broadcasts. He had more than a passing interest in the work of the committee. Frank Costello just happened to be a blood relative, a first cousin twice removed.

The extended Castiglia family had settled in the Westport area around 1912 with the building of a fabled stone house at 50 Lyons Plain Road. Frank Costello's family, also part of the Castiglia clan, opted to live in New York City. But as was true with any large Italian family, the New York Castiglias, including Frank Costello and his wife Loretta, would visit the farm on long weekends or during the week with business associates. Most of those visits took place in the 1920s through the mid-1930s, stopping before Noel was born in 1937.

"I only heard stories about 'Uncle Frank' and had only seen him once as a small child at a funeral in New York City from a distance," Noel later remembered.

The family tales about Frank Costello that young Noel had heard growing up in Connecticut were not good ones. His father, Frank Castiglia, an electrical engineer who graduated from New York University in 1930, just didn't like Costello or his crowd of bootleggers, gamblers, extortionists, and overall gangsters. At one point, Noel's grandfather, Domenico, pulled a rifle on some of Costello's friends as they drove up to the farm house and told them to leave. Costello was unlikely to have been in the car, and it remains unclear to this day what had happened to precipitate the showdown. So, when the Kefauver committee convened and called Costello, Noel had to see the man for himself and take his measure. After all, there had been some good stories about Costello: his helping people in need, his visits to the ancestral town of Lauropoli where he contributed to the building of a school. As Noel watched what he saw on the television screen of just Costello's hands, he came to his own conclusions about Uncle Frank.

"It became clear soon to me that Uncle Frank was calm in appearance, but sweating bullets inside," Noel recalled many years later. "He was evasive, curt, gave wise answers, including some humorous ones like 'I paid my tax.'"

But what was especially telling to Noel were the things Costello didn't say but showed through what little the television screen was allowed to show. The constant wringing of the hands, the need to use a handkerchief to soak up the sweat on his palms, it all made Noel think that the worst he had heard about Costello was true.

"This is where I stopped trying to give him the benefit of the doubt," said Noel. "In my book, at the time he was a very intelligent gangster, political manipulator, excellent boss, police corrupter, pragmatic and generous when he needed to be."

Noel's view of his relative would mellow over time. He would see Costello as a survivor of a criminal jungle that was 108th Street in old Manhattan, a man who was his own power in New York City after starting with nothing. His friendships with Luciano and Lansky were special in the way it brought him to the pinnacle of wealth and political control, Noel said.

Noel was one of an estimated thirty million viewers nationwide who watched the hearings, with perhaps ten million in the New York metropolitan area alone. It was one of the nascent television industry's singular moments of real drama, combined with public service. As *New York Times* television writer Jack Gould noted, the hearings provided a "morning, matinee and evening performance," which became a mass preoccupation that "exceeded the annual Fall interest in the World Series."

As Gould wrote: "Housewives skimped on their household chores and offered no guarantee that dinner would be ready on time. Television parties were commonplace in many homes. Public officials, judges, business executives and secretaries crowded around available TV receivers in clubs and offices. Bars and restaurants did a thriving trade. Everywhere there was the stillness of an attentive audience."

Department stores saw shopping decrease when the committee was in session. That wasn't necessarily a bad thing for some. One grateful husband wrote Kefauver that when he and his wife visited Manhattan his spouse decided to stay glued to the television in their hotel room and not go on shopping sprees. At the office of Manhattan District Attorney Frank Hogan, the prosecutor sat in his office and watched with several judges. Libraries tuned in and movie houses in Queens and Brooklyn showed the hearings on large screens, letting the public in for free.

Costello wasn't the only witness who drew audiences. Former Mayor William O'Dwyer, who had taken the job as ambassador to Mexico, was on the stand for hours, defending his records as Brooklyn District Attorney prosecuting Murder Inc., and explaining his contacts with Costello during a meeting in the gangster's apartment back in the 1940s. O'Dwyer said he happened to be at the apartment in his role as a general in the Army investigating possible contract fraud. O'Dwyer came across so poorly in the hearings that he resigned his ambassadorship a short time later. One saucy witness was Virginia Hill, also known as Virginia Hauser, who talked about her days and nights with Bugsy Siegel and denied taking any gifts from Costello, Lansky, or Luciano.

But of all who testified, it was Costello who represented what Kefauver saw as the face of organized crime. When the committee issued its report in May 1951, among its findings were a confirmation of what had been said in its February report: Costello, Joe Adonis, and Meyer Lansky formed the "eastern axis" of a group of racketeers working throughout the country. Costello clearly had major influence over Tammany Hall through his personal friendships with Democratic Party leaders as well as some Republican leaders.

The committee also went after O'Dwyer, who was portrayed as being suspiciously tentative in going after the mob. The main criticism was that as Brooklyn District Attorney O'Dwyer didn't follow through on the Murder Inc. probe by failing to indict some of the leaders of the gang, as well as its chief killer Albert Anastasia. The committee also made a point of noting how O'Dwyer characterized Costello's political strength by saying, "It doesn't matter whether it's a banker, businessman or gangster, his pocketbook is always attractive."

Costello had frustrated the committee when he refused to turn over his financial records reflecting his net worth and made statements that seemed filled with perjuries. While there was a question about whether Costello could be deported for his activities, the committee believed that a conviction for perjury, as well as for violating the gambling laws in Louisiana through his Beverly Club, might just be the ticket to boot him out of the country.

In a sense, Kefauver gave federal prosecutors a roadmap of how they could now go after Costello after so many previous failed efforts. As his attorney George Wolf would later say, the government was now on a mission to "Get Frank Costello" and began putting the wheels in motion to target him on a number of fronts.

The first bad news for Costello came about three months after the hearing ended in July. A federal grand jury in Manhattan indicted Costello, Joe Adonis, and Frank Erickson for contempt of Congress. Adonis and Erickson were already in jail for gambling charges, so it was only Costello who had to go to the federal courthouse in Foley Square to get formally arrested and put in a jail cell. But Costello was only in custody for a little less than an hour when Wolf appeared with him at the arraignment and posted the $5,000 bail.

As Kefauver and Halley had threatened during the hearings,

Costello was charged for refusing to answer questions over his net worth and then on March 15, walking out of the hearings after complaining of a sore throat. Costello also wouldn't answer questions about his investments either. The charges against Adonis and Erickson alleged that their refusals to answer questions before the committee on Fifth Amendment grounds were also grounds for contempt of the committee. Erickson wouldn't even answer questions about whether he knew anything about baseball or basketball gambling pools.

Costello's trial on the contempt charges began in early January 1952, and the government called just a few witnesses. One of them was Dr. Douglas Quick, who treated Costello for throat cancer eighteen years earlier and had examined him before his testimony before the Senate committee on March 16. At that time Quick had determined that the acute laryngitis Costello suffered from still would have allowed him to testify to a limited degree.

In the courtroom and once again impeccably dressed, reporters noted that Costello seemed bored by the testimony, sometimes yawning or else letting his eyes wander around the courtroom. Wolf had recounted how the Senate committee sandbagged his client, reneging on the expectation that the committee would give Costello a chance to exonerate himself. The attorney went after Dr. Quick on cross-examination, getting the cancer specialist to admit that he had testified in the grand jury that he had mentioned the possibility of using a tracheotomy tube in Costello's neck because his vocal cords were so swollen. Another physician who had examined Costello, Dr. John Kernan, admitted that he wouldn't have permitted a patient in Costello's condition to testify at all.

"From my point of view, both physicians' testimony had been hurt badly by their admissions on cross-examination," Wolf later said.

In another twist, Rudolph Halley, who had been the committee counsel who had questioned Costello with such hostility, also appeared as a witness. But it seemed that all Halley added to the evidence was some testimony about the conditions of the hearing and Costello's demeanor. Costello hated Halley so much that he wouldn't even look at him when he testified.

On January 11, the trial judge Sylvester J. Ryan gave Costello's cause a blow when he ruled that Costello didn't invoke his Fifth Amendment right against self-incrimination in good faith when he refused to testify before the committee about his net worth. As Wolf saw it, Ryan had taken away the key part of Costello's defense, leaving him open for a conviction. As it turned out, Costello came very close to a conviction when the jury on January 15 reported it was deadlocked 11 to 1 in favor of a guilty verdict. The one holdout thus forced a mistrial, as well as a federal investigation into possible jury tampering, which went nowhere.

A retrial found Wolf sidelined by illness and Costello had a new attorney, Kenneth Spence, take over his defense. As Wolf later related, Spence, a white-shoe Wall Street lawyer, appeared to make some tactical errors in the defense when he really didn't offer any. Spence tried to reargue the self-incrimination issue and then didn't fight the government claim that Costello's sore throat wasn't bad enough to keep him from testifying. As prosecutor Myles J. Lane told the jury, "Costello was too stubborn to answer . . . He thought he was a law unto himself. He thought he was bigger than the United States Senate." Spence didn't even offer a closing statement on Costello's behalf.

Given the poor defense offered on his behalf, the jury convicted Costello of all ten counts of contempt in the indictment late on April 4, 1952. Costello showed no emotion at the verdict, and outside the courthouse had no comment for reporters. Judge Ryan had wanted to sentence him right after the verdict but Spence at least did something to justify his legal fee when he got the court to give him a few more days to argue for a mistrial.

Prosecutors were elated at the verdict. Costello, the nationwide boss of crime, had been convicted and was certain to get a prison sentence. In fact, Costello got a sentence of eighteen months in prison and a $5,000 fine on the ten contempt counts. He didn't have to surrender right away since he had an appeal pending, which was heard in May. While the appellate panel didn't seem sympathetic, the judges in July actually reversed seven of the ten counts of contempt, saying that some of the charges were redundant while three actually violated his privilege against self-incrimination. In the decision, written by Judge Learned Hand, the court believed it wasn't even a close question about whether Costello had the right to take the Fifth Amendment on questions of his net worth and his indebtedness. He certainly did have the right under the Constitution, said the court.

The Senate committee's branding Costello a leader of organized crime before he publicly testified and the obvious income-tax implications of the questions could create "a reasonable apprehension in the mind of the defendant that his answers might be incriminating," the court ruled. The court also threw out four other counts because they were duplicative. But with three of the contempt charges sustained, there was no way Costello would avoid prison.

When it came time for Costello to surrender to the U.S. Marshals, his attorney George Wolf accompanied him to the federal court in Manhattan. As Wolf remembered, it was a hot August 16, 1952, when Costello, sitting in a dimly lit courtroom, asked that the marshals take him away. One deputy came out with handcuffs, and when Costello saw that he said, "Hell, I don't need those." But protocol dictated that Costello be handcuffed just like all the other prisoners before he was placed in a van and taken away for a trip to a local detention center and then on to the Lewisburg Federal Correction Center for the beginning of his odyssey through a number of prisons.

In Lewisburg, Costello was given registration number 20125-NE. As was standard for all prisoners, Costello was written up in an admission summary, and some of the observations contained in the report were a telling narrative of his life and his personality. After having been reared in what the narrator—whose name is unknown—said was a New York City slum, Costello "has risen from this lowly status to a position of eminence in underworld circles." As to Costello's personality, the report said, "He impresses as being an individual of rather low cultural status, but possessing a considerable degree of native shrewdness." Costello would have vehemently disagreed with the first part of that statement but couldn't argue with the second part.

In Lewisburg, Costello was concerned about his own legal problems and didn't care much for any programs the facility offered inmates. But he wasn't a malcontent either and got along with other
prisoners and guards. As a fifty-nine-year-old inmate who suffered
from throat problems, Costello was only to be assigned moderate
physical duties.

Costello was only at Lewisburg for about a month when he was
transferred to the U.S. Penitentiary in Atlanta on October 10. He had
an initial interview to determine what kind of work he could do but
didn't have much to say. The officials decided to assign him some
light duty issuing clothing, under close supervision because of his
reputation. Costello proved to be a good inmate, causing no problems.

The stay in Atlanta lasted just over two months. The day after
Christmas, Costello was transferred to the federal correctional facility in Milan, Michigan. Milan was a low-security institution about
twenty miles south of Ann Arbor. Costello was sent there because in
a bizarre legal move, he filed a federal court petition to be freed
from custody on the grounds that the penitentiary wasn't the place
he should have been sent to. Since he had been convicted of three
misdemeanor offenses—contempt—Costello argued that he really
should be housed in a common jail, not a penitentiary. Costello
failed in that crazy bid to get free. The result was that he was moved
to Milan.

The correction reports of Costello's time in Milan showed that he
was an easy-going inmate. Costello wanted to be assigned to the
hospital wing so that he could receive frequent throat sprayings because of his chronic laryngitis, according to one FBI report. Instead,
he was assigned to work in the clothing room, again under close supervision. Although he wasn't any trouble, prison officials said that
the fastidious Costello had to be cautioned about having a dusty cell
and seemed "reluctant" to do the necessary cleaning. "He appeared
trying to live up to his reputation as a 'big wheel,'" one prison status
report stated.

Costello may have thought of himself as a big shot but the reality was that his status and reputation had taken many blows. In custody, Costello had trouble keeping on top of mob business back in New York. He was also under pressure from Vito Genovese who after his return from Italy in 1945 managed to escape a murder prosecution in Brooklyn after two prosecution witnesses wound up dead. Facing no more legal pressure—at least for a while—Genovese had steadily been expanding his influence in the crime family, to the detriment of Costello and his allies. As long as Costello was behind bars, Genovese had a greatly strengthened position in the Mafia.

CHAPTER TWENTY-TWO
"DEAR FRANK"

EXCEPT FOR THE TEN MONTHS Frank Costello had spent in jail in 1915 on the gun case, his wife Loretta had never gone for any long period of time without her spouse being nearby. The couple traveled together, most often to Hot Springs and Miami, and their lives seemed very comfortable. Two homes—the apartment on Central Park West and the house in Sands Point—allowed them to enjoy the best of city and country living. Costello didn't have a nine-to-five job and that meant on most mornings he could take breakfast at home before making the rounds of the barber's chair in the Waldorf-Astoria, the steam room at the Biltmore and evenings at the Stork Club and Copacabana. But when Costello was shipped out to federal prison in the summer of 1952, Loretta found herself living alone.

Frank and Loretta never had kids. Leonard Katz in his biography of Costello suggested the problem was one of Loretta's inability to conceive. As other couples without children do, the Costellos raised two small dogs, a toy poodle and a miniature Doberman pincher. Costello would sometimes walk the pooches in Central Park but more often that task was Loretta's.

Loretta certainly spent more time walking with her husband behind bars. Yet a woman of her financial means didn't want for friends. Cindy Miller, one of her closest friends, remembered recently taking her for walks in Central Park. The two women, Miller remembered, would sometimes lunch at "21." Miller favored Bacardi and diet coke and recalled how one day as she and Loretta lunched that a man claiming to be Mr. Bacardi told her she was drinking his liquor.

Another friend who filled the social gap in Loretta's life and saw that she didn't want while her spouse was away was publisher Generoso "Gene" Pope Jr., the Italian businessman who parlayed his family fortune to a base of political power of sorts. Pope's family relationship with Costello stretched back into the early part of the twentieth century. Pope's son Paul, in his book *The Deeds of My Fathers: How My Grandfather and Father Built New York and Created the Tabloid World of Today,* related how it was Costello who helped his grandfather, Generoso Pope Sr., when he had problems with competitors in the stone and cement business. Costello arranged for the senior Pope to meet with Tammany Hall politicians and got suppliers to Pope's Colonial Sand & Stone business to give it generous financial terms, recalled Paul Pope.

In the months before Costello went on trial for contempt of Congress, Generoso Pope Jr., wanted to buy the then failing *New York Inquirer* but didn't have enough money for the purchase. Costello gave Pope the $25,000 he needed for the down payment on the $75,000 price with no interest, reported Paul Pope.

"But there were a few strings attached," wrote Paul Pope. "The longest of them would be that Gene was not to mention gangsters or racketeers or organized crime in any way."

So at a time when other newspapers were reporting news of gangster arrests and Costello's role as a crime boss, the *Inquirer* would be silent. One of the writers for the Inquirer was Cindy Miller's husband John. Pope also reported Costello asked that the *Inquirer* run nice reviews and features about nightclubs he and his friends had interests in and that the newspaper attack the politicians who were going after organized crime. Generoso Pope would eventually transform the *Inquirer* into the *National Enquirer*, the newspaper that was the grandfather of tabloid journalism. While he was in the Milan facility, Costello wanted Pope to visit him and put the publisher's name on a visitors list as his "advisor," according to FBI records. It is unclear if Pope actually made any prison visits.

Under the terms of his incarceration, Costello was eligible for parole on February 14, 1953, a mere six months after he went to prison. His attorneys George Wolf and Joseph Delaney filed the necessary papers to request that Costello be considered for parole, and there was some optimism that he might be granted release as a telegram dated February 6 from Loretta indicated.

"Dear Frank, Saw Mr. Wolf. Parole Board seemed receptive. We are praying for the best. Mr. Delaney will visit you Friday. Don't worry. Lots of love, Loretta Costello," she said in her missive.

If his good behavior in prison was any indication, Costello had a good shot at being released. He did his job in the prison clothing plant and got along well with the staff, even if he did hold himself out as some sort of big shot. With all of the machinations going on in the New York Mafia with Genovese and others, Wolf thought his client was anxious to be freed for no other reason than to get back into the mix of La Cosa Nostra. But on February 20, 1953, the federal Parole Board denied Costello an early release in favor of what records stated was "continuing the subject's present plan."

Eight months later Costello's good behavior worked in his favor when he was ordered released on October 29, having served a year of his eighteen-month sentence. It was a tanned Costello, dressed in a pinstriped suit and sporting a fedora, who rode away that day just after 8 o'clock in the morning, driving off in a black limousine with his wife, one of her friends, and lawyers. Pursued by reporters in a high-speed chase through Detroit traffic, Costello would only say he wanted a "rest." At the train station, Costello and his party boarded The Detroiter for the overnight trip to New York. To avoid the press, Costello got off the train when it arrived the next morning at the Croton-Harmon station in Westchester County and then was driven to Manhattan.

Once back in New York City, Costello tried to have some peace and quiet. His doctor said he had some "pulmonary congestion," had lost weight, and ached from a viral infection. Since Manhattan was in a different federal court district from Nassau County where Costello had his Sands Point house, he had to petition the court to get permission to visit the Barkers Point Road manse, a request that was granted. A trip to the North Shore and its relative quiet was what he needed.

As good as freedom felt for Costello, the future held more legal entanglements. While he was at Milan, federal immigration officials had filed an action to strip him of his American citizenship and deport him. He also faced federal income tax charges accusing him of cheating the government out of over $73,000 in taxes from 1946 to 1949. Lawyers and courtrooms were going to be a constant in Costello's life after prison and there was no guarantee that he would stay out of a jail cell and, if he did, would be able to stay in the United States.

Frank Costello's next round of legal troubles were beginning well before he was even settled in Milan prison. It was in September 1952 that the U.S. Attorney General James P. McGranery said that he was beginning denaturalization proceedings against Costello. The grounds were that Costello had lied on his original application to become a U.S. citizen by not indicating that he had been arrested in his youth.

"I believe it is incumbent upon me to prosecute matters of this type involving unsavory characters," McGranery said.

But the truth was that the government had a thin case against Costello and needed more. So in early October, FBI records revealed that the Immigration and Naturalization Service went on a feverish search for dirt on Costello that could torpedo his citizenship. A crucial piece of information related to the background and whereabouts of Frank Alden Goss and Harry C. Sausser, the two men who were witnesses on Costello's petition for naturalization. Both Goss and Sausser had been old bootlegging associates of Costello and had been charged in the 1926 case that also snared William V. Dwyer. The INS wanted to try and prove that Goss and Sausser were disreputable characters and thus "incompetent" to be witnesses on Costello's petition to become a citizen.

The problem for the INS was that the files on the bootlegging case, which had been in the U.S. Attorney's Office in Manhattan, had "disappeared." Immigration agents tracked down Bruce Bielaski, the former special assistant to the attorney general who embarrassingly failed to nail Costello in the Prohibition case, but he apparently didn't have any files either. The INS was getting frustrated because, apart from some generalities about Costello's gambling and bootlegging activity, the agency couldn't find any specifics and saw that part of Costello's life being "a rather closed chapter." (The author found some of the federal court files through the National Archives, including papers that contained reference to Goss and Sausser as bootlegging defendants.)

The INS finally turned to the FBI. Agents did a records check to find what had happened to Goss and Sausser. The FBI also dug up old files on Costello from the jewelry-theft case involving private investigator Noel Scaffa. In that case, Costello, when he was arrested in 1935, gave federal agents a signed statement in which he explained his various business activities. Whatever the FBI found in the records search was enough because on October 22, 1952, the government filed a complaint in Manhattan federal court to begin denaturalization proceedings against Costello. The government charged that before the time Costello became a citizen on September 10, 1925, he had had a bad moral character, having violated the Prohibition laws, failing to file state or federal income tax returns, and conspiring to bribe Coast Guard officials. Officials also found, in part because of Costello's testimony to the Senate, that the aliases he used such as "Frank Saverio" weren't disclosed on his citizenship application.

The move to revoke his citizenship was a blow to Costello because he considered himself to be a patriotic American. When he was arrested for contempt, two other younger men were being processed for draft dodging and Costello berated them for ruining their lives. Friends knew him as a man who relished being an American, on his terms of course. When he toured Manhattan, he would talk about the historic buildings and the stories behind them. But there was strong evidence that Costello had lied on his application on a number of points. It was not going to be an easy case.

The denaturalization case would be put on hold after the Department of Justice in March 1953 filed an indictment against Costello for income tax evasion, claiming he didn't pay his fair share of taxes on money he made over a four-year period. The case was one of those strange ones in which the Internal Review Service, frustrated by Costello's lack of bank accounts and other records, had to reconstruct his income by looking at his expenses and then trying to estimate what income he needed—and didn't report—to support that lifestyle.

As it turned out, the government had help from an unwitting Loretta Costello. IRS agents John Murphy and Wilfred Leath had been poring over the Costello tax returns from 1946 through 1949 in the hopes of finding that the couple was spending more than they reported as income, which in those years averaged around $39,000. Loretta Costello had a check book and spent a fair amount of money on small luxuries, which added up to several thousand dollars. Then one day the agents came across a check for a little over $5 to a florist whose records showed that a small spray of plants had been sent to St. Michael's Cemetery in Astoria.

Had the agents followed the details of Costello's life they would have known that the family had plots at the cemetery. A visit to St. Michael's revealed the Costello family mausoleum, which was clearly visible from the road. As described in the book *Treasury Agent: The Inside Story* by Andrew Tully, agent Murphy discovered from the cemetery that Mrs. Costello had purchased the land for the mausoleum for $4,488, all paid in cash. The contractor who built the mausoleum talked readily to the agent but said he wasn't commissioned to build the structure by Costello but rather a gentleman named Amilcare Festa, who turned out to be a masonry and stone contractor in Astoria, with a shop right next door to Costello's mother's home on Third Street, once a center of bootlegging activity.

Festa told his story to Murphy and admitted that one day a young man approached him with plans for the mausoleum and asked if he could hire a contractor to build the structure. Festa saw a chance to make some money and was told by the young man that if he needed money to call a number that happened to be a direct line to Costello himself. Over a series of telephone calls, Festa said he told Costello what he needed and within hours received cash payments ranging from $3,000 to $5,000 to handle the costs of construction.

The mausoleum costs were only some of the cash transactions the agents found that were traced to Costello and his wife. Digging deeper, the agents had found a number of businesses that had generated cash for Costello, including the Beverly nightclub in Louisiana, the Wall Street real estate properties, a jukebox company, and a television distribution company. Some of Costello's investments, the agents discovered, were made in the names of others such as his brothers-in-law and his attorney George Wolf.

Costello and his wife had also spent cash well beyond their living expenses and the cost of the mausoleum. The agents discovered that Costello made an $18,000 payment in cash to buy the Sands Point house and that his wife had invested $10,000 in a jukebox company in New Orleans and loaned it $30,000, again all in cash transactions. These disbursements mounted up and convinced the IRS that the Costellos were spending money beyond what they were showing in income on their returns.

There was also another find that would prove embarrassing to Costello. The agents uncovered that he was paying $15,000 a year in living expenses—a Fifth Avenue apartment rental, car purchase, living expenses—for Thelma Martin, dubbed the gangster's "good friend" who had no visible means of support, according to Tully. Witnesses said that Costello would often visit Martin and stay for hours at a time, posing as her husband. Doing their addition, the agents believed Costello and his wife spent over a four-year period some $200,000 more than they made and *reported* in income. This led to an evasion of over $73,000 in taxes, the government charged.

The trial of Costello on the tax evasion case began on April 5, 1954, and the government needed to call over 150 witnesses in what was a herculean effort to prove its case. But before the jury was selected, the initial judge, Gregory F. Noonan had to disqualify himself because of comments he had made a year earlier when he said about Costello: "If I had my way he would now be serving his time in the most common jail we could find." Costello claimed Noonan was biased against him and although the judge insisted he wasn't still decided to drop out of the trial. Judge John F. McGohey took over.

Costello didn't skimp on his defense, hiring noted Washington D.C. attorney Edward Bennett Williams since Wolf was going to be called as a witness. Among the witnesses was Festa, the Queens stone mason, who described the secret cash deals and subterfuge he took part in over the mausoleum. Bank officials testified that Costello gave nearly $30,000 in charitable contributions over a two-year period alone. Wolf also took the stand and said that Costello dealt with him only in cash and that he put the monies in a special account from which he wrote checks to cover expenses. Other bank officials said Costello's special charity was set up with a deposit of $5,000 in his name.

On May 13, a jury of seven men and five women convicted Costello on three of the counts of the indictment covering the years 1947, 1948, and 1949 but acquitted him on the count related to the 1946 tax year. In total, the jury found Costello had evaded about $51,000 in taxes. Four days later, McGohey sentenced Costello to five years in prison and fined him $30,000, socking him also with the cost of the trial. Costello was ready for a prison sentence and promptly filed an appeal in an effort to keep from being sent back to a penitentiary.

The issues on appeal weren't frivolous. It came out in court papers that the government had not included in its net worth analysis any of the assets of Loretta Costello. Also. Costello contended that it was unfair to attribute his wife's expenses to him while at the same time not giving credit to non-taxable income she received. To Costello's lawyers, the whole idea of "net worth-expenditure" prosecution was unfair.

"The government says, in substance, that when a man spends money, the assumption is that it represents income in the same year unless the defendant comes forward and explains the expenditures. If he does not, he goes to jail," Costello argued through his lawyers.

Costello's attorneys stressed at the trial that substantial sums of money were paid out by Loretta Costello and not by her husband, with the court never receiving evidence that she did not have money of her own. The net worth theory seemed to place an almost impossible burden on a man like Costello, his attorney argued.

It would take months for the Second Circuit Court of Appeals to rule on Costello's appeal and his attorneys asked in the meantime that he be granted bail. The lawyers stressed that "it is hard to believe that bail would be denied to the defendant . . . where the defendant's name not Frank Costello. There seems to be a feeling that where Costello is concerned, constitutional rights are unimportant." The appeals court didn't buy the argument on bail and ordered Costello to stay in a local jail until the court decided his case.

Finally, on June 18, things moved in Costello's favor. U.S. Supreme Court Justice Robert H. Jackson said that his court had suddenly decided to hear four cases dealing with the net-worth theory of income tax evasion, which had been the very cornerstone of Costello's prosecution. By granting hearings in those cases, the Supreme Court was saying there is a "substantial question" about the use of the net-worth theory, said Jackson. So, while the courts were taking the time to decide how the law would be applied in a case like Costello's, Jackson granted him a $50,000 bail. This meant that even if the Second Circuit Court of Appeals shot down Costello's appeal, he could remain a free man until the Supreme Court decided the larger issue of the net-worth theory.

On April 5, 1955, almost a year after Costello was convicted on the tax case, the appeals court reversed his conviction on one count—dealing with tax year 1947—but upheld it on the two remaining counts. The result lowered Costello's fine to $20,000, but his prison sentence of five years still remained the same. It was a small victory but wouldn't prevent Costello spending at least some time behind bars.

A month later, Costello tried another tactic to stay out of jail. He had his attorneys ask the government to suspend the five-year sentence because he was simply too ill to serve it and that if he did it would be essentially a death sentence. His age and health conditions, which included heart issues, had deteriorated since he was sentenced, said Costello. Then, in a bold move, Costello offered to drop his fight against the pending denaturalization proceeding and agree to leave the country voluntarily if the government agreed.

Prosecutors didn't bite on Costello's offer, and on May 14, 1956, he surrendered to federal authorities to begin his five-year sentence. Costello bid good-bye to Loretta that afternoon and then took a taxi from his Central Park West apartment with his attorney Joseph Leary Delaney to the U.S. Courthouse at Foley Square, as Treasury Department agents followed them. At the courthouse, Costello walked into the office of the U.S. Marshals at 3:25 P.M., about thirty-five minutes early, posed for photographers and then was handcuffed for the trip to the local detention center to begin the journey to prison again.

The lawyers Costello had hired to fight for him hadn't been able to keep him out of jail, much less clear his name. He wanted to keep fighting, but the legal community seemed to think Costello was a hopeless cause. Looming ahead was the fight with the government to take away Costello's citizenship and quite possibly deport him. Wolf didn't think his client had a chance and counseled him to plead guilty and hope for leniency. Costello angrily told Wolf that if he couldn't go to bat for him he wanted to get another lawyer.

As it turned out, one of Wolf's partners was Morris Ernst, a respected lawyer who hobnobbed with civil libertarians. It was during a cocktail party in Washington D.C. for the American Civil Liberties Union that Ernst openly complained about the way Costello had become something of a pariah in New York legal circles. Within earshot was a well-known attorney named Edward Bennett Williams, who had rocketed to fame defending another pariah named Senator Joseph McCarthy, the red-baiter. According to Williams's biographer, Evan Thomas, upon hearing Ernst bemoaning Costello's situation, the Washington lawyer said "tell Wolf to call me."

As Wolf recalled, he told Costello that Williams was the best man to handle his case but bluntly told him that the legal legend would "come high" in terms of the fee he would want. Costello's response: "Let's get him, while I can still afford it."

Williams seemed to relish unpopular clients and in Costello's case he seemed to have a fascination with the old gangster's lifestyle. The "New York demimonde in the 1950's, the nightclubs populated by gamblers, professional players and show business personalities" thrilled Williams, wrote Thomas.

Williams went to work quickly and used the arcane fact that the government had used wiretaps on Costello in 1925, mixing legal evidence with illegal evidence in such a way that it was hard to isolate the good from the bad elements of the government's case regarding the naturalization issue. Williams also came up with the notion that Costello was sentenced incorrectly in the tax evasion case with too high a sentence. Costello should have been sentenced under a provision of the law that covers misdemeanors to no more than a year and a $1,000 fine, Williams said in a petition to the U.S. Supreme Court. Luck finally broke Costello's way. On March 11, 1957, the high court not only agreed to hear his appeal but granted him bail after the government couldn't come up with a reason for Costello not to be freed.

The eleven months Costello had spent in captivity had not been good for him. He claimed to have lost fifteen pounds and suffered from a cold for months. His heart was also having problems. So, after posting a bond, Costello walked out of the federal detention center in Manhattan and went home to Loretta at the apartment on Central Park West.

CHAPTER TWENTY-THREE
"SOMEONE TRIED TO GET TO ME"

WITH HIS NEWFOUND FREEDOM, Frank Costello was able to gravitate toward his old haunts and lifestyle. Costello invariably took taxis wherever he went. He could be found at the Waldorf-Astoria and the Biltmore Hotels where he would avail himself of the massage room. His favorite restaurants were numerous: Pompeii, Les Champs, the Copacabana, and the Stork Club. Costello was naturally followed by law enforcement, and the FBI files noted that while making his rounds he was "always circumspect and deferential."

But life for Costello was not going to be just socializing and eating out. The Mafia in New York City was entering a period of bloodshed. Since Costello had been away in prison and besieged by legal problems, the leadership of the family had shifted to Vito Genovese, who had originally been Luciano's number two until he had to flee the U.S. because of a murder indictment in Brooklyn. Once Genovese returned to the country after World War Two, he jockeyed for power with Costello. During the 1940s and 1950s, Costello had made some significant alliances with other Mafiosi such as Albert Anastasia, Joe Adonis, his cousin Willie Moretti, and the politically connected Anthony Carfano. Genovese had to tread carefully if he ever thought of challenging Costello.

Yet, over time Costello's allies were removed from the scene. Moretti, who Joseph Valachi said suffered from syphilis and had shown signs of being too talkative and unpredictable, was gunned down in

May 1951 in Joe's Elbow Room restaurant in Cliffside Park, New Jersey. The killing was done after Genovese planted the suggestion during a meeting with others in the crime family, saying that Moretti was a liability now, Valachi recalled. Genovese even said that if he ever lost his mind that he would want to be killed as a precaution so "as not to bring harm to this thing of ours," said Valachi.

Costello's striving to be legitimate appeared to keep him away from the volatile and dangerous world of narcotics which Genovese and others in the crime family were involved in. Genovese was clearly playing with fire in terms of drugs, something that would ultimately lead to his downfall. But against Costello, Genovese steadily seemed to be gaining the upper hand. In January 1956 another of Costello's close associates, Joe Adonis, agreed to be deported and was sent back to Italy while his wife and family remained in the U.S. Adonis had wanted to fight the government claim that he was in the U.S. illegally but decided to fold up his tent and leave to live in the relative luxury of Milan.

As Valachi remembered events, it was Genovese who believed that Costello, despite his businessman veneer, was plotting to get rid of *him*. Whatever the reason, Genovese decided to strike first.

The evening of May 2, 1957, was one of those that fit the Costello lifestyle pattern. Traveling as he did without a bodyguard, Costello met with Phil Kennedy, a former semipro baseball player who started a modeling agency, at Chandler's Restaurant on West Forty-ninth Street. News accounts said the group went to L'Aiglon on East Fifty-fifth Street to meet up with Loretta and Generoso Pope, the publisher and owner of the *National Enquirer*. Cindy Miller, a friend of Loretta's who was seven months pregnant at the time, recalled she and her husband John also met up with the group in the French restaurant. (Miller was carrying her son, also named John, who became a popular TV journalist and later a top counterterrorism official with the NYPD.) Miller remembered that she and her husband then went with Kennedy and Costello down the block for coffee and a nightcap at Monsignore after which Costello said he had to go home to field a late-night telephone call from attorney Edward Bennett Williams. So at about 10:40 P.M. Costello and Kennedy hailed a cab and traveled north to 115 Central Park West. The others made their way home separately. Both men didn't notice another black car in the vicinity that contained two men with nothing good on their minds.

Costello stepped out of the cab, bid Kennedy goodnight and proceeded to enter his building through the front door facing Central Park. Focused on getting upstairs, Costello didn't at first notice a hulking man who rushed through the door. But the big man, who held in his right hand a .38-caliber revolver, got Costello's attention by blurting out the now famous words "This one's for you, Frank" the instant before he fired a single shot. The time was 10:55 P.M.

By flinching and turning at the right moment, Costello avoided the potentially lethal trajectory of the bullet, which punctured the front of his fedora and exited out the back. The single bullet skimmed the skin on Costello's skull above the right ear and then struck the lobby wall. Miraculously, aside from a slight head wound, Costello was not seriously hurt. But Kennedy, alerted by the shot, ran back into the lobby and found Costello nursing his wound with a bloodstained handkerchief.

"Someone tried to get to me!" Costello cried out as he sat on a leather couch in the lobby.

"With his night on the town having come to an abrupt finish, Kennedy ran back outside to hail another cab," said author Larry McShane in his book *Chin: The Life and Crimes of Mafia Boss Vincent Gigante*, in describing the shooting. "He led the bleeding Costello to the street, loading him into a cab and ordered the hack to hightail it toward Roosevelt Hospital on Tenth Avenue."

The incident happened in a snap of time. The doorman told police that he had seen a limousine pull up behind the cab, which had just moments earlier let out Costello. A man rushed out and shot at Costello as he stepped into the lobby, the doorman remembered.

Cindy Miller recalled that she first learned of the shooting from a television news report and promptly called her husband John, a writer for the *National Enquirer*. John Miller rushed over to the Costello building and accompanied Loretta as she walked her two dogs in Central Park and then took Costello's wife to the hospital.

Police responded in force and took Loretta from the hospital to the local station house on West Fifty-fourth Street and later took Costello there for questioning. As more cops got involved Kennedy, Pope and others who were part of the dinner entourage that night were also pulled in for questioning. Cops also showed up at Cindy Miller's apartment and told her to go with them back to the station house for questioning, mainly to retrace where Costello had been earlier in the evening. Kennedy told investigators he got a good look at the assailant while the doorman described him as being heavy-set, about six feet tall, and wearing a dark suit and black hat.

Costello told police he didn't know who tried to kill him and that he was a man who had no enemies. The latter was untrue and Costello knew it. As described by McShane in his book, Genovese had farmed out the attempted hit to Anthony "Tony Bender" Strollo, a Genovese crime captain from Greenwich Village who conceived of a two-man team of driver Tommy Eboli and a washed-up boxer named Vincent Gigante. Costello may not have known the identities of the two men but he certainly knew who the big boss was who wanted him dead. The tipoff came from Anastasia, who had some time earlier met Costello in a restaurant and warned his friend about trying to smooth over a problem with Genovese. That veiled warning, attorney George Wolf said later, indicated to Costello that Genovese was his enemy.

It took a few weeks for detectives to arrest Gigante, who was said to have been upstate after the shooting. A Manhattan grand jury was convened, and Costello was of course called as one of the witnesses and he stuck to the story that he didn't recognize the shooter. High-ranked cops thought Costello was lying but there was little they could do to shake his story. Police also started round-the-clock coverage of Costello as a safeguard against another attempt on his life. The cops even wanted to send a security detail to go with him when he went out to the house at Sands Point.

"He said it would ruin him out there. That's tough," NYPD chief of detectives James B. Leggett told reporters. "Maybe he's going to Sands Point and if he didn't have a bodyguard what would prevent him from going to a restaurant in Queens and get shot there."

The grand jury looking into the shooting also went after something else related to Costello. The night he was wounded, cops found a list in Costello's handwriting in his jacket that listed "gross casino wins" amounting to $651,284, as well as some unexplained initials. Later, officials noted that the notations matched to the penny the winnings of the Tropicana Hotel in Las Vegas, built by Costello's old partner Dandy Phil Kastel. Investigators hauled Costello before the grand jury to ask him about the note and dollar amounts. But on the advice of Edward Bennett Williams, Costello invoked his right against self-incrimination and wouldn't say a word. Even when the prosecution said it would offer immunity to Costello if he testified about the list, he still refused to talk. Judge Jacob Schurman ruled that Costello was in contempt of the grand jury and ordered him committed to "the workhouse," which happened to be the Tombs, for thirty days. The Tombs was the infamous jail on Centre Street where all sorts of petty criminals and miscreants were held before trial or if they couldn't make bail. It was not the kind of company Costello wanted to associate with. After fifteen days he was let go.

In his biography written with Martin Gorsch, Luciano recounted that after the bungled hit, Genovese knew he was the prime suspect within the inner sanctum of the crime family. Genovese and Costello then held a meeting at the New Jersey home of Longie Zwillman to iron out some kind of compromise, said Luciano.

"Frank sent me word about it later," recalled Luciano. "Vito proposed a compromise because they had each other over a barrel after what happened. He told Frank, 'Don't do nothing.' Don't complain to nobody and most of all, don't go to Charlie Lucky with this thing, because if you do, you're gonna start a war. In that case, I promise that you'll be the first guy dead.'"

Genovese would allow Costello to retire with his gambling and real estate interests, said Luciano.

Gigante was indicted for the attempted murder of Costello, and his trial in May 1958 was an exercise in frustration for the prosecution. The doorman at the Costello apartment building, Norval Keith, admittedly had poor eyesight but swore on the witness stand that Gigante was the man he saw in the lobby fire the shot at Costello and

tell him "This is for you, Frank." But on cross-examination by defense attorney Maurice Edelbaum, Keith said that the Gigante he
saw the night of the shooting was much bigger and broader than the
defendant in the courtroom. Police believed that Gigante had gone
on a weight-loss campaign after the shooting—and also got a haircut—to hide his identity.

Costello took the stand on May 20 and gave his public version of
the shooting for the first time. But, of course, the questioning brought
out his life story as it had unfolded years earlier in the Kefauver hearings. Costello readily acknowledged his days as a bookie. When it
came time to describe the shooting, Costello said that at first he
thought the sound of the gunshot was a firecracker and didn't think
much of it until he felt blood on the side of his face.

Costello also said that he didn't catch a glimpse of anybody after
he turned his head and added that he didn't have a clue why anyone
would want to shoot him. When Edelbaum got his chance to question Costello he had him look at Gigante and asked if he knew of
any reason the defendant would want to take his life.

"No reason whatsoever," Costello answered.

Edelbaum then asked if Costello knew who pulled the trigger that
night and to tell the jury if he knew.

"Well. I'll ask you, 'Who shot me?' I don't know, I saw no one at
all," replied Costello.

"Thanks a lot, Frank," Gigante was heard to say as Costello
walked off the witness stand.

The prosecution had presented sixteen witnesses in the trial, and
the defense called just one. In the end it was apparent that the Manhattan District Attorney's Office had presented no evidence of a motive, and its single eye witness to the shooting, Norval Keith, wasn't
very persuasive. The jury got the case for deliberations late in the afternoon of May 27 and after a two-hour dinner break and more deliberations returned at 11:45 P.M. with a verdict of not guilty on the
attempted murder of Costello.

Gigante's mother Yolanda, who had been clutching her rosary,
cried out "It was the beads ! It was the beads!" to explain the verdict.
Gigante's father Salvatore began crying. Gigante himself seemed rel-

atively composed and told reporters "I knew it had to be this way because I was innocent."

In the strange ways alliances work in the Mafia, Costello seemed to actually like Gigante, at least according to the mob boss's lawyer. Wolf recalled that at some time after the trial Costello had a small gathering of people at his apartment.

"My wife and I went to dinner at Frank's apartment and there, as one of the honored dinner guests, was Vincent Gigante," recalled Wolf. "Frank was too intelligent to hold that against Vincent, who was, if anything, an errand boy sent to do a job."

CHAPTER TWENTY-FOUR
"THIS MEANS I'M NEXT"

WITH ALL THE LEGAL WORK high-powered attorney Edward Bennett Williams was doing for Frank Costello since 1957, the fees the aging gangster was paying would have likely added up to a big down payment on a nice Washington, D.C., home for the busy lawyer. Williams was, if anything, inventive in his legal strategy, filing various appeals and motions in Costello's court battles. Williams seemed to relish high-profile clients—he was also defending Teamster boss James Hoffa at the time—and he wasn't averse to taking battles all the way to the U.S. Supreme Court. By taking on Costello as a client, Williams set in motion a dizzying series of legal moves that went on for well over a year as he fought to keep his notorious client out of prison. Sometimes a scorecard was needed to sort out what was going on with Costello's cases.

Back in March 1957 Williams's argument that Costello might have been sentenced incorrectly in the income tax evasion case had led to the Supreme Court granting him bail. But in June, the high court issued a ruling that went against Costello's position. However, rather than go straight back to prison, Costello was able to remain free until at least late September after Williams asked for a postponement so that he could argue with the federal judge who heard the tax trial that the verdict should be overturned.

What Williams had in mind was another series of ingenious arguments to challenge the tax evasion conviction. He raised three points:

that the government illegally used wiretap evidence, that federal agents began watching Costello's mail, and that prosecutors screened potential jurors by secretly looking at their tax returns. These weren't insignificant issues and in October, Judge John F. X. McGohey ordered a hearing in which the prosecutors in Costello's tax prosecution were called to testify.

The former chief prosecutor, Floyd F. MacMahon who later went on to become a federal judge, admitted that the jurors were screened to find out if any had tax problems themselves and might react favorably toward Costello. Today, this potential bias would be examined when jurors are questioned before they were selected. But the secret vetting of their returns showed the length the government was willing to go to weed out anything that might give Costello an edge— including in essence carrying out tax audits of potential jurors. Another government official with the IRS told of being ordered to examine the returns and reporting back what the *New York Times* said were "irregularities and unusual deductions."

Two other prosecutors in the case, Powell Pierpoint and Whitney North Seymour Jr., who later became the U.S. Attorney in Manhattan, testified with what were called "vague" recollections about the way potential jurors were categorized in special lists. The lists were numbered from one through four, with the lowest number reflecting jurors who were probably most favorable to the government and the highest reflecting least favorable. Even the American Civil Liberties Union felt the practice was noxious and according to the *Times* "condemned" it. Williams himself stated that the practice was "a malignant growth" on the jury system, which could make people regard service as an "evil to be abhorred."

Judge McGohey had a lot to think about, and on October 22 said he was reserving his decision. But three days later Costello's world was shaken not by anything that happened in court but what transpired in the barbershop of the Park Sheraton Hotel at Seventh Avenue and Fifty-fifth Street in Manhattan. It was while he was sitting in the barber's chair, getting a haircut that Albert Anastasia, the feared Brooklyn gangster who was a close ally of Costello, was gunned down by two men. The armed pair, described by witnesses as being broad and wearing scarves over their faces, blasted away at Anastasia, striking him with five rounds, including one to the back of his head. The man from dockland known as the "Mad Hatter," fell dead to the floor as a pool of blood collected around him.

Cops found two handguns believed to have been used in the killing near the barbershop, one in a hotel corridor and the other in a trash bin at the end of a nearby subway platform. Detectives pulled in mobsters like Costello and Lansky to find out what they knew—which for the police was nothing. But privately, Costello was not only shaken with the loss of his friend, but he knew very well that he might be next. Wolf's description of the aftermath of the shooting was revealing.

"After Anastasia's murder, I was summoned within hours of the shooting," recalled Wolf. "When I arrived at Frank's apartment, I found him and Anastasia's brother Tony clutching each other and sobbing."

This was the first time Wolf saw Costello cry, and the attorney believed his client felt vulnerable in a crime war that was imminent. There would be no peaceful way of dealing with things since Costello's staunch allies had been removed by death or legal issues. Luciano was back in Italy and unable to control things. Moretti was killed in 1952. Adonis was deported back to Italy. Now, Anastasia was dead. It was just Costello now alone to face Genovese.

"There was no hope," said Wolf. "As I stood at the door of his living room, Frank looked up, saw me, and said quietly, 'This means I'm next.'"

Actually, it turned out to be Genovese who was next, although not because he lost his life. About three weeks after the hit on Anastasia, on November 14, 1957, Genovese and scores of other Mafiosi and their associates traveled to the home of Joseph Barbara Sr., in Apalachin, New York. Their presence in such large numbers caught the attention of two New York State Police troopers, Sgt. Edgar D. Creswell and trooper Vincent Vasisko. To make a long story short, while police suspected the conclave was for criminal purposes and pointed to airline and hotel reservations made under false names as evidence of secrecy, nothing was proved against those who were rounded up, and they were all let go. (Federal conspiracy charges were brought against some of the participants, but an appeals court overturned their convictions.)

Wolf later said that Costello didn't attend the Barbara event—and avoided the embarrassment and possible legal problems—because he had agreed that Genovese was to be crowned the new boss of all Mafia bosses at the meeting. But because of the bust, Costello now felt he was a marked man again.

On the legal front, Williams continued to pull rabbits out of the hat for Costello. One result was that the festering attempt by the government to denaturalize Costello was dealt a serious blow. Immigration officials claimed that Costello had lied or concealed facts on his application for citizenship back in 1925, mainly by not disclosing the way he violated the laws against Prohibition and fibbed when he said he was in real estate. The case actually went to trial when allegations were raised that police had tapped Costello's telephone during the 1926 bootlegging prosecution. Government attorneys admitted hearing the same thing but said the immigration case didn't stem from wiretap evidence.

A troubled Judge Edward Palmieri halted the trial and after reviewing some transcripts found that there had been extensive use of wiretaps beginning in the 1920s. Since Palmieri said he couldn't figure out what evidence was admissible and what was not, he granted Costello's request to dismiss the case but allowed the government time to come back to court again if there was untainted evidence.

However, Costello again went on the legal merry-go-round. An appeals court overturned Palmieri and said the judge should have given the government attorneys some time to come up with untainted evidence. The court also said the fruits of any wiretaps from 1925 to 1926 were admissible in federal court. But then the U.S. Supreme Court, which by now must have had open reservations for Costello on its dockets since Williams was so prolific in filing petitions, took up the case and reversed the appeals court, ruling that the government should have filed what was known as an "affidavit of good cause" when it sued Costello. The case was again dismissed.

Chastened, government attorneys brought a similar case in May

1958 under a different section of the immigration laws and remembered this time to file the right affidavit. The trial on the denaturalization case got started in December 1958 before Judge Archie Dawson and went into January 1959. Essentially, the government claimed Costello lied profusely on his citizenship application: claiming his occupation was real estate when in fact he was a bootlegger, that his sponsor Harry C. Sausser was of good character when he was also a bootlegger, that the only other name he ever used was Francisco Castiglia, and failing to disclose to the immigration examiner that he had been arrested four times and convicted once.

To show Costello's bootlegging past the government put his old buddy Emanuel Kessler as a witness who related how Costello trucked smuggled booze for him and told the story of the Blackwell Mansion operation in Astoria. Costello's old comments about "being in the bootlegging business" also came back to haunt him as the government brought them up again. Harry Sausser, one of the two witnesses who signed Costello's citizenship application, had died in 1926, but his daughter Helen testified about her father's bootlegging activities with Costello.

The court acknowledged that Costello did some real estate business in 1925 through his Koslo Realty Corp. but found the amount to be insubstantial. Costello presented no witnesses to rebut the government's case. The results were predictable. Judge Dawson found that for some years prior to May 1, 1925, when Costello filed his naturalization request, he had been actively engaging in bootlegging in violation of U.S. law and that his real occupation was that of a bootlegger and not in real estate. The bootlegging showed that contrary to his oath, Costello was violating the U.S. laws at will and was behaving in a way contrary to his being a "man of good moral character, attached to the principles of the Constitution of the United States."

Relying on the bootlegging evidence, Dawson didn't have to mention the other allegations about Costello concealing his criminal record and the use of other names like Frank Saverio. Costello, said Dawson, had concealed facts about himself that, had they been known in 1925, would have denied him citizenship. So, on February

20, 1959, the court granted the government's request and cancelled Costello's citizenship.

Costello wasn't in New York when Dawson yanked his citizenship because back in October, even before the immigration trial started, the old gangster decided to return to prison to serve the rest of his sentence for income tax evasion. He had no more appeals left. On October 21, what the newspapers described as a sullen Costello, suffering from a cold, surrendered in Manhattan federal court to serve what was expected to be two years and eight months in prison, taking into consideration time off for good behavior. Dressed for the occasion in a blue topcoat and blue suit and accompanied by lawyer Morris Shilensky, Costello surrendered, waving his right hand as he walked to the detention cells.

It wasn't long after Costello arrived at Atlanta federal penitentiary that he found himself in the company of old nemesis Vito Genovese. The leader of Luciano's crime clan had been indicted in July 1958 for being part of a heroin conspiracy along with Gigante, the underling who shot Costello a year earlier. A number of crime experts have long maintained that the case against Genovese was a frame up, that the main witness against him was lying about having dealt with the crime boss on the heroin deals. But Genovese was convicted and in April 1959 was sentenced to fifteen years in prison and shipped off to Atlanta, although he still remained boss of the crime family that would bear his name.

Having Costello and Genovese in the same prison could have been a volatile mix, and tension in Atlanta was high. It seemed that prisoners believed Genovese had caused Costello's tax problems and that he was ready to cause the crime boss problems. It was then that George Wolf was called to Atlanta by Costello, Wolf recalled, to help calm the situation—and in effect save Genovese's life.

Wolf gave no date for his visit to the penitentiary, but in his book, he said that the warden, whom he didn't identify, told of the looming danger. The warden said that so many inmates believed Genovese had caused Costello his tax problem and that a war was about to break out and there simply weren't enough guards to protect Genovese, remembered Wolf.

The attorney then visited Costello in a special room set aside by the warden. Costello said that indeed the situation inside the prison was dangerous and that no matter what he said to the other inmates, they didn't believe that Genovese had done nothing to cause his problem, said Wolf.

"This thing is too dangerous," Costello said, according to Wolf. "Everybody's in a panic. I pass the word myself that Vito's all right, and it don't do no good. I want us to have a meeting in the warden's office with a photographer shaking hands."

Wolf said the warden then brought him to Genovese and the two men met alone in a room. It was then that the attorney explained to Genovese what Costello had in mind and the crime boss accepted the idea of a meeting.

"George, between you and me, Frank is something," Wolf recalled Genovese telling him. "He is so smart I am always wondering what's behind everything he says and then I find he is talking straight and I'm the jackass. He even warned me about holding that meeting in Apalachin and I didn't listen."

Wolf didn't stay around for the meeting but years later saw the wisdom behind Costello's prison diplomacy. Costello not only defused the situation and possibly saved the life of Genovese but got himself protection when he got out of prison and returned to New York.

CHAPTER TWENTY-FIVE
"HE'S GONE"

FRANK COSTELLO FINALLY GOT out OF ATLANTA on June 21, 1961, for the tax case but was immediately picked up by the NYPD on some old business going back to when Vincent Gigante shot him. Back in 1957, Costello had refused to talk in the grand jury about the notes found in his pocket after he was wounded, which referred to over $650,000 in gambling winnings at the Tropicana Hotel. His clamming-up got him a fifteen-day sentence in the "work house." Clad in a suit and looking about fifteen pounds thinner, Costello was taken to Rikers Island to serve the time. It had to be a demeaning experience, as the other prisoners were common thieves and other miscreants.

The short stint on Rikers Island was really small stuff compared to the other big worry Costello had on his mind. Back in February 1957, the U.S. Supreme Court by a vote of 6 to 2 had ruled against Costello on his attempt to overturn the revocation of his citizenship. The high court agreed, in the face of all the evidence from Costello's bootlegging days, that he hadn't been truthful on his citizenship application. The justices also didn't think that he could truthfully claim that real estate was his occupation.

Costello was out of options in his effort to keep his citizenship. He also faced deportation, and the legal battle wasn't going well on that front after the Board of Immigration Appeals (BIA) said he should be booted out of the country. At least until he exhausted all his court challenges to the BIA, Costello was able to stay free on bond.

FBI surveillance reports showed that in this period after Costello got out of prison that he was "very circumspect" regarding his activities. Costello and his wife spent their days going back and forth from Manhattan to Sands Point. Cindy Miller remembers Costello liking to take walks in Central Park to watch the animals being fed in the zoo. Agents heard conflicting information about whether Costello was still active in the mob. Mob turncoat Joseph Valachi told the FBI that Costello had been "reinstated" back into Genovese's family, but agents were skeptical. Their own surveillance had not developed any significant information about Costello.

What the agents and cops did notice was that Costello continued his old pattern of taking cabs when he left his apartment late in the morning, dining in good restaurants and returning home at what was said to be sensible hours. Costello clearly wanted to keep himself above suspicion while his appeal was pending with the Supreme Court on the deportation case. While the FBI once considered Costello—because of his 1915 conviction for carrying a handgun and his association with other top hoodlums—to be dangerous, by 1963 the agency had a change of heart and considered him not a threat.

In August 1963 when Nassau County District Attorney Bill Cahn subpoenaed about twenty mobsters after Valachi had testified to Congress, Costello was on his way to his home in Sands Point when he decided to stop by the courthouse where the prosecutor had an office. As described in *Newsday*, Costello was wearing a blue suit, his hair immaculately combed, and he was smoking a cigarette when he looked at Cahn straight in the eyes.

"I was on my way to Sands Point for the weekend and I thought I'd stop by . . . I never ducked a subpoena in my life and I didn't want you to think I was ducking you," Costello, speaking in his familiar raspy voice, told Cahn.

Costello said he really couldn't answer any questions about Valachi's testimony but when asked what he was doing with himself, answered,

"I'm retired" and then left the building to get in a taxi for the trip
home.

As the year 1964 came around, Costello's world had changed
greatly. Putting aside the threat of immigration, his old friends had
disappeared, often violently. Anastasia and Moretti had been killed,
as had Anthony Carfano, an old Luciano captain who had run afoul
of Genovese and was murdered one night in 1959 as he sat in a car
with Janice Drake near Idlewild (now La Guardia) Airport. Adonis
had been deported. Luciano, the one mob boss who could have acted
as a counterweight against Genovese, had died suddenly of a heart
attack in January 1962 at the airport in Naples, Italy. Not long after
Luciano died, Costello's old gambling partner Philip Kastel committed suicide in New Orleans. Costello had his investments and
sources of legitimate income, but the old heady days of being a
mobster were gone. If the government finally had an order to deport
him, Costello might have to think about going back to his ancestral
town of Lauropoli, where his old friend "Professor" Frank Rizzo
still lived.

But, in a sudden twist of fate, on February 17, 1964, the U.S.
Supreme Court, which over the years had blown hot and cold with
Costello, gave him a final gift. In a 6 to 2 decision, the court set
aside the deportation order. The decision by Justice Potter Stewart
turned on the meaning of a phrase in the immigration law. The
wording in question stated that an alien could be deported who "at
any time after entry into the United States is convicted of two crimes
involving moral turpitude." Costello's conviction for two income
tax crimes clearly fit that definition of "moral turpitude."

However, there was a catch. Stewart wrote that those crimes didn't
help the government because they had occurred in 1954, at a time
when Costello was still a *citizen* as he had been since 1925 and not an
alien. The court said there wasn't anything in the law that showed
that Congress meant to count convictions during the period a person
was a naturalized citizen, as opposed to when naturalization was
later lost, as it was in Costello's case in 1961. The denaturalization

case was started in 1952, nearly ten years before Costello was stripped of his citizenship.

"It is the biggest victory in my life," said an effusive Costello. He might not be an American citizen, but he didn't have to leave the U.S.

For as long as he was alive, Costello could count on being under government scrutiny. For a start, the IRS and prosecutors kept surreptitiously through the 1960s pulling Costello and his wife Loretta's tax returns. The documents showed that since he was a free man Costello's main source of income was gambling, averaging about $20,000 over a three-year period from 1961 to 1963, when he reported $29,000. He had some royalties from oil leases in Oklahoma and Texas. The FBI records show that the agency was pumping Valachi for information about Costello although there was nothing that led investigators to think Costello was involved in crime family activity.

Costello was paying his taxes and had enough money to keep the apartment in Manhattan and the house in Sands Point. But there was one indication that he was feeling the need to get a bit of financial help. For that, he is said to have turned to his old friend Generoso "Gene" Pope Jr., publisher of the *National Enquirer*. According to Pope's son Paul in his book *The Deeds of My Father,* after Costello got out of prison in 1961, he visited Pope at his office in Manhattan. Both men had a long history together and it was Costello who, Paul reported, gave his father the loan to purchase the newspaper, money that had been repaid long ago.

During the meeting, Costello and Pope shared a drink and talked about old times. It was then, according to Paul, that Costello told the elder Pope that he felt he had something to do with his success.

"You did," Gene Pope answered, according to his son's account.

Costello then went on to ask Gene Pope if he would make him a partner, to give him a "little taste of the pie," as Paul recounted in his book. As much as Gene Pope knew that he owed Costello for his help, he couldn't, not in the world he was living in, make Costello a partner and told him so.

"Costello didn't have the heart to keep fighting," Paul wrote. "He was old and tired and felt embarrassed, a man who'd held lives in his hands, now begging for something that should've rightfully been his."

It is unclear if Costello ever saw Pope again after that meeting. But the so-called "Prime Minister of The Underworld" was in his dotage, an old gangster trying to keep whatever vestige of the old glory days alive, seeing a few old friends and keeping dinner dates.

Throughout the 1960s, despite regular FBI and police surveillance, law enforcement found little of substance to report about Costello. He was spotted one day in November 1964 meeting with Joseph "Socks" Lanza, the old mob boss of the waterfront, at the Waldorf-Astoria. Both men were then seen walking to Les Champs Restaurant on Thirtieth Street where the agents said "they dined leisurely," two old gangsters likely talking about the old times. After lunch, Costello went over to the Biltmore Hotel, undoubtedly to get a massage.

One indication that Costello might have had some clout and access to money was related by actor Anthony Quinn, in his co-authored autobiography *One Man Tango*. Quinn recalled how a production he was involved in around 1971 for the film *Across 110th Street,* a police-Mafia melodrama, was running into some money troubles. Quinn had what he said was an "unconventional" friendship with Costello and commiserated with him over breakfast in Rumpelmayer's café in the St. Moritz on Central Park South over the fact that a lot of money was needed to finish the production.

"How much?" Costello asked, according to Quinn.

"About a million," replied Quinn.

"Oh, that is nothing," answered Costello.

When Quinn got angry, saying that $1 million was a lot of money and that he needed it to complete the project, Costello told him to calm down and that he would give him the funding. Quinn said that he told Costello he couldn't take a check—or cash—from him and comingle it with studio funds because it would raise too many questions. Costello insisted he would make the deal for the cash on a handshake but in the end Quinn knew he couldn't take money from him and got the funding somewhere else.

FBI Agents heard that Costello might be acting as an arbiter of disputes and did try to interview Costello. In one encounter in March 1966, Costello was pleasant but on the advice of his lawyer, Edward Bennett Williams, he wouldn't say anything. "After an exchange of pleasantries, the interview was concluded," according to an FBI summary.

In July 1972, agents had a little better luck with Costello, who said he had just returned from a weekend in Sands Point. Usually, said Costello, he spent Tuesday to Friday at his apartment in Manhattan and then went back out to Long Island on Friday, returning to Manhattan on Tuesday. The agents had approached Costello because four days earlier, July 16, Thomas Eboli, one of three powerful crime-family captains who were running the Borgata after Genovese had died in prison in 1969, was shot dead after he visited his girlfriend in Brooklyn. Eboli, known as "Tommy Ryan," was a manager of boxers and at one time had squired Gigante during his brief fighting career.

Costello told the agents he didn't know Eboli in the years before he went to prison. When Costello came out of Atlanta, he said Eboli had risen in status and as he put it "grew like a mushroom." While he had met Eboli a few times, Costello said he had not seen him in person for six years. In fact, continued Costello, he had been away from people with bad reputations for years. But, when reminded by agents, Costello had to admit that he had been seen a year earlier in the presence of crime boss Carlo Gambino when he bumped into him at the Waldorf and then invited him for lunch.

These uninformative conversations, along with the uneventful life Costello appeared to be leading, finally made the FBI lose interest in him. He was considered a man of advanced age, not involved in apparent criminal activity. In October 1972, the agency placed his file in "closed status," with the option to reopen it if the situation changed. He was also now no longer considered dangerous.

Costello may have been of little help to the FBI in his conversations with them later in his life. But given the right opportunity, Costello was thinking about finally spilling the beans. At the age of eighty-two, Costello still had a sharp mind and had survived while many of his old associates had died or were consigned to prison. There was much for Costello to tell. Of course, doing so would have violated the fabled Mafia oath of *omertà*, the oath of secrecy designed to keep the organization in the shadows and away from scrutiny by outsiders. Although in later years *omertà* would be shredded by the action of many turncoats, the oath of secrecy all Mafiosi abided by was still in force—Joseph Valachi excepted.

As it turned out, writer Peter Maas, who had penned with Valachi the informant's story known as *The Valachi Papers,* was interested in Costello and the story he could tell. Fresh off his latest literary project, *Serpico*, about honest NYPD cop Frank Serpico, Maas had approached Costello, sending out feelers, prodding him. The two men engaged in a long literary courtship over a period of about five months beginning around June 1972 before Costello expressed more interest. As Maas later told *The New York Times,* Costello finally paid a visit to the author's Manhattan apartment on December 1, 1972, and for three hours both men talked.

"I told him that he was a legitimate figure in American history, and I meant it," Maas said. "There isn't a level of society that his career didn't touch."

Costello returned for more talks on December 12 and according to Maas wanted to talk—off the record—about what could be in the book. That meeting was the start of weekly meetings into late January 1973. Maas never commented about what precisely both he and Costello talked about. But after Maas died in 2001, his papers were sent to Columbia University and in one of the files is a three-page memo that outlined what Maas believed the book should contain.

As Maas envisioned things, the book would be in the third person and would be an extensive look at Costello's life, from his days in East Harlem, Prohibition, the formative days of the Mafia, and politics. Maas also wanted to draw out Costello about his relationships with mobsters like Anastasia, Adonis, Lanksy, and Luciano. Maas seemed to have enormous respect for Costello and considered him a man's man. Maas knew that Costello would be asked to give a lot in the project and whether he could do it was something only he could answer. Based on his experience writing *The Valachi Papers*, Maas was in a good position to deal with much of the history involved in Costello's life since so much would be familiar.

As the book deal came closer to reality, Maas and Costello agreed to do the interviews at the old gangster's Sands Point home. It was the setting Costello always felt comfortable with, the one closest to the life toward which he had aspired. Finally, Costello sent word that he wanted to do the project, just as he landed in the hospital with heart trouble. Costello had had problems with his heart ever since he was in prison in the 1950s and now at the age of eighty-three his physical reserve was no longer what it once was. On the morning of February 18, Maas got a call at home from Charles "The Blade" Tourine, an old Genovese crime family member who had been active in the casinos and for a time lived near Central Park.

"He's gone," Tourine said about Costello.

Frank Costello had died that morning of a heart attack at Doctors Hospital with Loretta by his bedside. Along with Costello, Maas's book project went to a final resting place in St. Michael's Cemetery.

EPILOGUE

THE WAKE FOR FRANK COSTELLO was a low-key affair at the Frank E. Campbell funeral home on Madison Avenue. Reporters were allowed inside the Williamsburg Room but were asked not to approach any of the mourners, who didn't show up in great numbers anyway. Loretta sat quietly during visitation with a lady friend. Nearby were her brother Dudley Geigerman and Philip Kennedy, the modeling agency executive who was with Costello the night he was shot by Vincent Gigante in 1957. A priest was also around and talked with some of the assembled.

Costello lay in an open walnut casket, dressed in a dark blue business suit. Loretta had apparently put out the word that she didn't want a lot of flowers, perhaps as an accommodation to her Jewish heritage, which didn't call for the profusion of floral displays commonly seen at Italian funerals. There were just what was described as a bank of white orchids, red roses, and white gladioli covering the foot of the casket. Around the casket were some floral displays of chrysanthemums, pom-poms, yellow roses, and gladioli.

The funeral was nothing like the old Mafia spectacles of the past. No long lines of limousines carried the mourners. There were no flower cars. Reporters and cameramen seemed as plentiful as those attending the rites, although on this morning no media was allowed inside. About 50 to 100 people showed up at Campbell's for the final good-bye the morning of February 21, notably restaurateur

Toots Shor. The service lasted about five minutes, with a priest recit-
ing a short prayer. Only about fifteen people traveled to St. Michael's
Cemetery.

A motorcade of the hearse, two limousines, and about a half
dozen private cars made the trip over the Queensboro Bridge to Astoria where workmen at St. Michael's Cemetery had readied the
mausoleum. Once inside the cemetery gate, the cars had only a short
distance to go to the final resting place. The casket was taken from
the hearse and placed in a protective metal liner and set between the
Ionic pillars flanking the bronze door. As Loretta, her eyes shielded
by sunglasses and with her brother Dudley next to her, looked on
mournfully, a young priest made the sign of the cross and said a
prayer. Then the mourners, one by one, placed a red carnation at the
foot of the casket.

It was as simple as that. The final rite for Costello, a man who had
risen from an impoverished family to lead the underworld and capture the imagination of the nation, was over in minutes. There was
no large crowd, no funeral spectacle. Loretta was helped back into a
limousine by her brother. Then the cemetery workers went to work.
Writer Paul Schreiber of *Newsday* captured the poignant details of
those final moments as Costello's casket went into the crypt to join
his father, mother, and sisters.

"Soon the workmen began wrestling the coffin into the mausoleum scattering the carnations. Some of them were crushed," said
Schreiber.

In the days and months after Costello's death, Loretta had to clean
up the legal messes that still followed them. Although Costello had
paid his debt to society with prison, he still left debts to the IRS,
things that his wife had to take care of. The government had claimed
there was at least $547,000 in unreported income from 1941 through
1950, on top of which the government slapped fraud penalties and
interest. Because she filed a joint return, Loretta had some responsibility for about $153,000 of the undeclared income, which she
somehow had to settle with the government. The Sands Point house
was sold by late 1975 and no doubt some of the profits went to pay
off the government. Costello's practice of dealing in cash, placing

assets in the names of others, and not keeping books and records all caught up to him and Loretta in the end. The Central Park West apartment was sold for $50,000, with virtually all of it going to the IRS.

With her brothers in New Orleans, Loretta moved down to Louisiana to be close to her family. She took a small apartment, which she tastefully furnished with a lot of photographs, fine furniture, and mirrors. As she grew older, friends and relatives said she still retained her looks. After she died Loretta was entombed in the mausoleum in 1988, her body placed in a niche right beneath Frank's. Loretta had been deeply hurt by the way Frank kept the other woman, Thelma Martin, in his life and the public way it was revealed during the tax trial. But Loretta also knew that for men like her husband, those kinds of relationships came with the territory. She accepted it and went on.

Frank Costello remains one of the most important figures in the history of the American Mafia for a variety of reasons. But in my mind what makes him preeminent among the old gangsters of that Golden Era of organized crime was the way he strived to pass as legitimate—and almost succeeded. Had Costello not lived his later years with a bullseye on his back from law enforcement and politicians, he might have been able to shake off the old taint of the mob and live like the businessman he always fancied himself to be. Costello once confided to his trusted attorney George Wolf that he always had secret dreams of better things but that he "spit" on his life, which ironically in the end had given him all he accomplished.

The late novelist and playwright Santha Rama Rau, who met Costello during a lunch at the Waldorf and became his friend, noted years after his death with a sense of understatement that "I had a very strong feeling he wanted a different kind of life than the one he lived." Rau was an unlikely acquaintance for Costello, given her success as a writer noted for her adaptation to the stage of E.M. Forester's *A Passage to India*. She found Costello a fascinating character despite his notoriety. Yet, like it or not, the life he lived gave Costello his legacy.

Had Costello morphed into complete legitimacy, he certainly might have lived his life without all the trouble which beset him. But what we know as the history of the Mafia would have been so much different. He had fame, he had charisma, all despite the fact that he was impoverished in terms of schooling that left him, as one official said, "retarded educationally." He made the cover of *Time* and *Newsweek* magazines and caused a buzz whenever he walked into the best restaurants. He also escaped physical violence, something that befell many of his criminal colleagues. Not a bad ending for a grade-school dropout. No other statesman of La Cosa Nostra ever really emerged like Costello during his day. It is a safe bet that none ever will.

NOTES

Chapter One, "Come to America"

Much of the early family history of the Castiglia family comes from materials compiled by Noel Castiglia, a first cousin twice removed of Frank Costello, who shared it with the author. Italian author Rossana Del Zio gave the author a brief tutorial about the great Italian Risorgimento during one of her visits to the United States in 2017. Historian Robert Golden, who is of Italian heritage, shared with me his knowledge of Marchioness Laura Serra, the founder of the Castiglia ancestral home of Lauropoli. Golden also shared with me the contents of correspondence he had with Costello's old friend Frank Rizzo, also of Lauropoli. George Wolf and Joseph DiMona's book *Frank Costello: Prime Minister of the Underworld*, was the source of information and quotes about Costello's petty criminal activity. Noel Castiglia was the source of information about the Polly the parrot episode and the growth of the Westport stone house and farm. Information about Giousue Gallucci and Pasquarella Spinelli, their lives, criminal careers, and deaths, came from contemporary newspaper accounts in *The New York Times, The Herald Tribune* and *The Sun,* as well as Mike Dash's *The First Family: Terror, Extortion, Revenge, Murder and The Birth of the American Mafia.* Giuseppe Selvaggi's *The Rise of the Mafia in New York*, contains references to Costello's early days on the street in East Harlem. FBI files contained some information about the early days of the Castiglia family in New York while *The Last Testament of Lucky Luciano* by Martin Gosch and Richard Hammer was the source of information about Luciano's early ties to Costello.

Chapter Two, No More Guns, Thank You

The sources of information in this chapter included recollections of Noel Castiglia and his experiences with having his ancestral background traced through Ancestry.com. The early history of the Jews in Italian government came from reports found on Wikipedia, as can the anti-immigrant statements of Henry Gannett and Theodore Bingham. Costello's early courtship of Loretta Geigerman was related to the author in part during interviews with Cindy Miller, her old friend, while Costello's comments about his wife are found in Wolf's book *Frank Costello: Prime Minister of the Underworld*. Information about Costello's wedding is contained in Wolf's *Frank Costello,* as well as in FBI files. Costello's early criminal cases are found in records unearthed as part of the government's attempt to cancel his U.S. citizenship. Wolf also described in *Frank Costello* his client's remarks about his early crimes and his aversion to carrying a firearm following his conviction in 1915. Wolf also described Costello's involvement with Henry Horowitz in the novelty business.

Chapter Three, The Boom of Prohibition

Information about the genesis of Prohibition in the U.S. and the anti-immigrant nexus can be found on the website of Kristen Kuo and Chi Chi Nwodah titled *Prohibition* found at nationalprohibition. weebly.com/immigrants.html. Prohibition history can also be found on the website *American Spirits: The Rise and Fall of Prohibition*. The bootlegging dealings and corruption allegations of George Remus are found in articles in *The New York Times*. Luciano's recollections of his early days in bootlegging with Costello and others appears in Gosch's *The Last Testament of Lucky Luciano*. Wolf's *Frank Costello* contains information about Costello's early forays in bootlegging, as do articles in *The New York Times*. J.P. Andrieux's book *Over the Side,* has information about the role of the French possessions in the smuggling of liquor into the U.S. during Prohibition. Wolf in *Frank Costello* has descriptions of Costello's early dealings with Arnold Rothstein, as does David Pietrusza in *Rothstein: The Life and Times,* and *Murder of the Criminal Genius Who Fixed the 1919 World Series.* Robert Carse in *Rum Row: The Liquor Fleet That Kept America Wet and Fueled the Roaring Twenties* has good descriptions of the impact of Prohibition on some Long Island communities and the Coast Guard vessels used to hunt bootleggers. Leonard Katz in *Uncle Frank,* describes the early liquor exchange on the streets of New York. Wolf in *Frank Costello* details Costello's day-to-day operations of the bootlegging business. Also consulted were stories in *The New York Times.*

Chapter Four, Whiskey Royalty

The details of the life of George Remus are found in articles from *The New York Times.* Jimmy Breslin's book *Damon Runyon: A Life* had details of Broadway life during Prohibition. Details of Emanuel Kessler's bootlegging operation can be found in *The New York Times* while his statements about his and Costello's interactions are found in federal court files in the case brought by the U.S. government to revoke Costello's citizenship: case Civil 133-28, *United States District Court for The Southern District of New York.* The story about Costello's hiring of Frank Rizzo as an accountant is related in Wolf's *Frank Costello.* Albert Feldman's recollections about the Astoria homes used by Costello for smuggling and Costello's use of a handgun to threaten people are found Civil 133-28, (SDNY) cited previously. Details of the Blackwell Mansion operation were found in Kessler's previously cited testimony, as well as stories in *The New York Times, The New York Tribune, New York Evening Telegram, The Brooklyn Daily Eagle* and *The Daily Star* (Queens). William Dwyer's personal history and life as a sportsman and bootlegger are found in *The New York Times.*

Chapter Five, A Woman Scorned

The story and life of Annie Fuhrmann and her husband Hans is found in numerous articles from the period published in *The Brooklyn*

Daily Eagle. The New York Times also ran some stories about the Fuhrmanns. Articles from *The New York Times* and *The Brooklyn Daily Eagle* described the violence inherent in the bootlegging racket. The Irving Wexler criminal case is described *The New York Times*.

Chapter Six, "The Greatest Roundup"

The arrests of William V. Dwyer, Frank Costello, and others in December 1925 is described in articles in *The New York Times* and *The Brooklyn Daily Eagle*. Testimony about wiretapping done at Costello's offices is found in Civil Case 113-28, previously cited. Costello's affidavit as well as that of C. Hunter Carpenter are in the file of Criminal Case C-44-488, United States District Court, Southern District of New York (1925). Details of the indictment, arraignment and preliminary court proceedings involving the case against Dwyer, Costello, and the other defendants were reported in *The New York Times*. The death of Hans Fuhrmann was reported in *The New York Times* and *The Brooklyn Daily Eagle*.

Chapter Seven, "King of the Bootleggers"

The opening statements, trial testimony, summations, as well as the verdict in the case of *U.S. v. William Dwyer et.al.* was reported in depth in *The New York Times* and *The Daily News*. Biographical material about Bruce Bielaski is contained on the web site of the Federal Bureau of Investigation, as well as in stories reported by *The New York Times*.

Chapter Eight, "Personally, I Got Drunk"

Wolf in *Frank Costello*, discussed some of the early moments in the bootlegging trial of Frank and Edward Costello. The trial was covered from opening statements, testimony, summations, verdict, and mistrial by *The New York Times* and *The Daily News*. The post-verdict activity of Costello was found in Wolf's *Frank Costello* while the controversy over Bielaski and his undercover operations was detailed in *The New York Times*. Noel Castiglia provided information about Costello's travels to the Stone House in Westport, Connecticut. Tom

Cognato provided the author details of Lucky Luciano's frustrated attempt to buy a doll for a little girl.

Chapter Nine, The Great Bloodletting

William V. Dwyer's travails with the IRS and his financial ruin were detailed in *The New York Times*. The history of what became known as the Castellammarese War can be found in DeStefano's *Gangland New York: The Places and Faces of Mob History*, as well as Selwyn Rabb's *The Five Families* and Peter Maas's *The Valachi Papers*. All three books detail some of the history of the various participants in the war, such as Al Capone, Frankie Yale, Johnny Torrio, Joseph Masseria, and Salvatore Maranzano. Nelson Johnson's book *Boardwalk Empire* details the way "Nucky" Johnson controlled Atlantic City and described events leading up to the "Seven Group" meeting of mobsters in that city in 1929. The substance of the Atlantic City meeting is described by Wolf in *Frank Costello*, while Capone's May 1929 arrest in Philadelphia and his statements to police were reported in detail in *The New York Times*.

Chapter Ten, "The Most Menacing Evil"

The finding of the Wickersham Commission and the repeal of Prohibition in 1933 were reported in *The New York Times*. Wolf in *Frank Costello* detailed how Costello got into the slot machine business in New York City. Fiorello La Guardia's political career and rise to win the mayoralty are described in Alyn Brodsky's *The Great Mayor: Fiorello La Guardia and the Making of the City of New York*. La Guardia's battle with Costello over slot machines is detailed in *The New York Times*. Huey Long's life story can not only be found on Wikipedia but in numerous articles and books, notably T. Harry Williams's *Huey Long*. Long's drunken episode in Sands Point was reported in *The New York Times*. Long and Costello's relationship over slot machines was recounted by Costello in his 1951 Senate testimony, as well as during his earlier trial for tax evasion, in which he was acquitted. The relationship between Costello and Phil Kastel can be found in Costello's 1951 Senate testimony and in a decision by the United States Tax Court in *Philip Kastel v. Commissioner* (1945). Katz's *Uncle Frank* was also consulted for details about Kastel. The business organization, ownership, and operations of Bayou Novelty Co. are described in *Kastel v. Commissioner*. The history of the Beverly casino and club are detailed in a web article at www.bestofneworleans.com. The biography of "Diamond Jim" Brocato was related to the author by his grandson Joseph Brocato and contained in a short film about him titled "In Nomine Patris: The Story of Diamond Jim Moran," produced by his late son Dr. Robert Maestri Brocato.

Chapter Eleven, "You're a Hell of an Italian"

Background on Diamond Jim Moran Brocato is found in a *New Orleans Magazine* article of October 2006 by George Gurtner. Materials on La Guardia's anti-racketeering campaign is found in his papers kept in the New York City Municipal Archives. Background and biographical material on Luciano is found in Tony Sciacca's book *Luciano: The Man Who Modernized the American Mafia* and in contemporary stories in *The New York Times*. Details of the investigation leading to Luciano's indictment, arrest, trial, and conviction by Thomas Dewey can be found in articles published in the period by *The New York Times* and in Ellen Poulsen's *The Case Against Lucky Luciano: New York's Most Sensational Vice Trial*. Information on the prosecution and murder of Dutch Schultz can be found in articles published in *The New York Times* and on Wikipedia.

Chapter Twelve, "I Know Everybody"

Biographical information on Noel Scaffa was found in an *American Weekly* article published in the *Arizona Republic* in August 1935 and written by Gene Coughlin. Background on Harry Content and his bride Margaret Hawksworth Bell is found in an article by Kevin Sheehan published in the *Albany Times Union* in August 1948. Details of the arrest and prosecution of jewel thieves Nicholas Montone and Charles Cali for the theft of the Bell jewelry can be found in *The New York Times*. FBI files on Costello contain numerous memoranda, some to director J. Edgar Hoover, about his alleged involvement in the Bell case, his indictment and subsequent non-prosecution. The FBI materials also contain summaries of Costello's statement to agents when he was arrested. *The New York Times* reported about the FBI case against Costello in the Bell case.

Chapter Thirteen, "Punks, Tin Horns, Gangsters and Pimps"

FBI files on Costello detailed some of his gambling interests outside of New York City, as well as the confidential source the FBI had with someone affiliated with the *New York Post* back in the 1930s. Information on La Guardia's campaign against the racketeers is found in his papers in the Municipal Archives. *The New York Times* reported on the failed attempt by Thomas Dewey to implicate Costello in liquor distribution rackets. *The Times* also covered the case against Tammany leader James Hines, as well as attempts by the La Guardia administration to prosecute Frank Erickson. A report on Erickson is contained in La Guardia's papers on file in the Municipal Archives. Articles in *The New York Times* were consulted for information about the trial of Costello and Kastel for income tax evasion in 1940. Katz's *Uncle Frank* and Wolf's *Frank Costello* were also consulted about Costello's slot machine business in New Orleans and his tax problems there. La Guardia's directive that police watch Costello after his acquittal in New Orleans is found in his public papers in the Municipal Archives.

Chapter Fourteen, "I Never Stole a Nickel in My Life"

Details about Costello's presence at the 1932 Democratic national convention is found in Wolf's *Frank Costello*. Background on Tammany Hall and its connection to Costello is found in Oliver E. Allen's *The Tiger: The Rise and Fall of Tammany Hall*. The trial of Tammany leader Jimmy Hines, including witness testimony and his conviction, was covered in *The New York Times*. The Herlands report is found in La Guardia's public papers. The revelations about the nomination of Judge Thomas Aurelio and Costello were covered extensively in *The New York Times,* including the initial disclosures, the political fallout, the disbarment proceedings, and the exoneration of Aurelio. Wolf described his initial meeting with Costello, his decision to represent him, and the direct aftermath of the Aurelio affair in *Frank Costello*.

Chapter Fifteen, "What the Hell Are You Fellows Doing Here?"

Historical information about the fire on the old *SS Normandie* in February 1942 can be found on Wikipedia and in *The New York Times*. There are two primary sources of information about the efforts by the U.S. government to recruit New York mobsters to help in the war effort. The most often consulted in this book was a report prepared in September 1954 by New York State Commissioner of Investigation William B. Herlands and sent to then-governor Thomas E. Dewey. A copy of the Herlands report can be found in the papers of Dewey housed at the University of Rochester. Wolf also discussed his role in the war-effort matter, including his representation of Luciano, in *Frank Costello*. Gosch's biography on Luciano was also consulted but some of Luciano's recollections seem unreliable, since he talks of "Dewey" being the prosecutor at the time when he was in fact governor.

Chapter Sixteen, Go West, Young Man

Wolf's *Frank Costello* was the source for his efforts to get Costello into legitimate businesses such as real estate on Wall Street. FBI files on Costello also had information about his 79 Wall Street venture. Information about New Jersey gambling operations involving Costello and his friends, including Joe Adonis, can be found in *The New York Times* and in Bill Friedman's *30 Illegal Years to The Strip: The Untold Stories of The Gangsters Who Built the Early Las Vegas Strip*. Information on Costello's loss of $27,000 in a cab and his effort to go to court to recover the money can be found in Wolf's *Frank Costello* and in *The New York Times*. The attempt by La Guardia to unmask Costello's alleged interest in the Copacabana and to deny the club a license was extensively reported in *The New York Times*. Biographical information about William O'Dwyer, as well as his 1945 mayoral campaign, can be found on Wikipedia and *The New York Times*. Results of the 1945 mayoral election can be found in *The Encyclopedia of New York City*, edited by Kenneth

Jackson. Oliver's *The Tiger* was also consulted for the impact of the period on Tammany Hall. Details about the release from prison and deportation of Luciano are found in the Herlands report of 1954, *The New York Times*, Sciacca's *Luciano*, Wolf's *Frank Costello* and in Gosch's *Last Testament of Lucky Luciano*.

Chapter Seventeen, Cuba Libre

Sources for information on Luciano's years in exile are Gosch's *The Last Testament of Lucky Luciano* and Gaia Servadio's *Mafioso*. For information on the Havana meeting with Luciano and others, consulted were T.J. English's *Havana Nocturne: How the Mob Owned Cuba—And Then Lost It to the Revolution*, and Allan May's web article "Havana Conference—1946 (Part Two)." Also consulted was a list from the Federal Bureau of Narcotics provided to the author by the National Archives and Gosch's *Last Testament*. Information about Frank Sinatra's trip to Cuba is found in Summers and Swan's biography of the singer, *Frank*. Bugsy Siegel's building of the Flamingo is found in Wolf's *Frank Costello*, Sciacca's *Luciano,* and Gosch's *Last Testament*. Information about Siegel's murder is contained in *The New York Times* and Sciacca's *Luciano*.

Chapter Eighteen, Tammany Tales

Works consulted for this chapter were Gosch's *Last Testament*, as well as various articles in *The New York Times* about the case to strip Irving Haim's firm of its wholesale liquor license. See also *Matter of Haim v. O'Connell*, 195 Misc. 612 (N.Y. Misc. 1948). Also used as source material on the Haim case and Costello's venture in Scotland was an article by Charles McLean published in *The Herald* of Glasgow, Scotland. Costello's denial of doing bootlegging business with Joseph P. Kennedy is found in Wolf's book *Frank Costello*. Costello's involvement in the 1949 Salvation Army dinner was detailed in various articles published at the time in *The New York Times* and in Wolf's *Frank Costello*. Material on the Ryan wiretap scandal and the 1949 mayoral election can be found in stories published in *The New York Times* and in Jackson's *Encyclopedia of The City of New York*.

Chapter Nineteen, "I'm a Neighbor of Yours"

Robert Keeler's book on the history of *Newsday*, titled *Newsday: The Candid History of a Respectable Tabloid,* gives much detail on the way Costello approached publisher Alicia Patterson socially and how the newspaper got an exclusive interview with him. Katz's *Uncle Frank* also contains some of the same information. Various stories about Costello published in June 1950 by *Newsday* were also consulted. Information about the large Guggenheim family estates of Falaise and Villa Carola can be found on Wikipedia and on websites dealing with the majestic properties of Long Island's North Shore. Costello's appearance, as well as that of Frank Erickson, in 1950 before a Senate committee looking into gambling were reported in *The New York Times*, as were events in the 1949 mayoral election.

Chapter Twenty, The Ballet of the Hands

The April 1950 murders of Charles Binaggio and Charles Gargotta in Kansas City, as well as the political ramifications, were reported in *The New York Times*. The Congressional testimony of Costello and others is contained in the *Hearings before the Special Committee to Investigate Organized Crime in Interstate Commerce, United States Senate, Eighty-First Congress (Second Session) and Eighty-Second Congress (First Session), Part 7, July 1950 to March 1951.* The so-called Kefauver hearings were extensively covered in *The New York Times* and *Newsday.* Wolf in *Frank Costello* detailed Costello's activities during the hearings. Various archived film clips of Costello's testimony can be viewed on the internet through YouTube and other websites.

Chapter Twenty-one, "Get Frank Costello"

Noel Castiglia's recollections of watching the Kefauver hearings were given to the author in email and in-person interviews in 2016 and 2017. *The New York Times* covered Costello's contempt prosecution, his conviction and surrender to jail. Wolf also wrote about the prosecution in *Frank Costello.* FBI files on Costello detailed his movements within the prison system and his activities while in custody.

Chapter Twenty-two, "Dear Frank"

The married life of Frank and Loretta Costello is discussed in Katz's *Uncle Frank*. Cindy Miller talked to the author about Loretta Costello's activities while Frank was in prison. Generoso Pope Jr's friendship with Costello and Costello's help in the purchase of the *National Enquirer* are discussed in Paul Pope's book *The Deeds of My Fathers: How My Grandfather and Father Built New York and Created the Tabloid World of Today*. FBI records on Costello detailed his prison activities, correspondence, and parole requests. Costello's release from prison was covered in *The New York Times*. Costello's civil trial, including court filings and testimony on his denaturalization case can be found in Civil Case 133-38 (USDC SDNY).

Chapter Twenty-three, "Someone Tried to Get to Me"

Willie Moretti's murder was covered by *The New York Times* and discussed by Peter Maas in *The Valachi Papers*. The attempted murder of Costello in May 1957 was discussed in Larry McShane's book *Chin: The Life and Crimes of Mafia Boss Vincent Gigante*, and Wolf's *Frank Costello*. The attempted murder was covered by *The New York Times* and numerous other newspapers and publications. Cindy Miller gave the author her recollections of the night of the attempt on Costello's life. The police investigation into the attempt on Costello's life, the arrest of Gigante, his subsequent trial and acquittal were covered by *The New York Times*. Wolf also discussed his conversations with Costello about the shooting in *Frank Costello*. Gosch in *The Last Testament of Lucky Luciano* discloses Luciano's reaction to the murder attempt on Costello.

Chapter Twenty-four, "This Means I'm Next"

The New York Times was consulted for stories about the various legal appeals attorney Edward Bennett Williams made for Costello, some successful, other not. *The Times* was also the source of material on the assassination of Albert Anastasia, as was DeStefano's *Gangland New York*. Wolf's recollections of Costello's reaction to

Anastasia's murder are found in *Frank Costello*. Details of the 1957
raid in Apalachin, New York, are found in a report prepared by
Arthur L. Reuter, acting commissioner of Investigation of The State
of New York in April 1958. Costello's immigration case, including
the trial transcripts, can be found in Civil Case 133-28 (USDC
SDNY).

Chapter Twenty-five, "He's Gone"

Costello's legal appeals to the U.S. Supreme Court, including his
loss on the citizenship case and the victory in the deportation case,
are detailed in *The New York Times*. FBI files contain information
about Costello's low-key lifestyle and absence from criminal conduct in the 1960s and 1970s. Costello's visit in 1963 to talk with
Nassau County District Attorney Bill Cahn was reported in *Newsday*. The FBI files also contain material on efforts by the agency to
interview Costello in his later years. Paul Pope's book *The Deeds of
My Father* are the source of information on the meeting between
Costello and Generoso Pope in the 1960s. Peter Maas's efforts to
write a biography on Costello in the 1970s are detailed in a 1973 article in *The New York Times*. Maas's general plans for the book are
detailed in a short memo he wrote that can be found in his papers
kept at the Columbia University Rare Books and Manuscripts Library. With the permission of his widow, Suzanne Maas, I was able
to summarize the substance of the memo for this book. Maas's comment about learning about Costello's death in a telephone call can
be found in the Biography film about Costello. Costello's death and
wake were covered by *The New York Times* and *Newsday*.

Epilogue

Costello's funeral was covered by *The New York Times* and *Newsday*. Santha Rama Rau's comments about Costello are contained in
the Biography film cited previously.

BIBLIOGRAPHY

Books and Periodicals

Allen, Oliver E. *The Tiger: The Rise and Fall of Tammany Hall.* New York: Addison-Wesley Publishing Company, 1993.

Andreas, Peter. *Smuggler Nation: How Illicit Trade Made America.* New York: Oxford University Press, 2013.

Andrieux, J.P. *Over the Side: Stories from a rum runner's files from Prohibition days in Atlantic Canada and Newfoundland.* Ontario: W.F. Rannie-Publishers, 1984.

Asbury, Herbert. *"Frank Costello: America's Number One Mystery Man." Collier's Weekly,* April 19 and 27, 1947.

Breslin, Jimmy. *Damon Runyon: A Life.* New York: Ticknor & Fields, 1991.

Brodsky, Alyn. *The Great Mayor: Fiorello La Guardia and the Making of the City of New York.* New York: Truman Talley Books, St. Martin's Press, 2003.

Carse, Robert. *Rum Row: The Liquor Fleet That Kept America Wet and Fueled the Roaring Twenties.* Mystic: Flat Hammock Press, 2007.

Cohen, Richard. *Tough Jews: Fathers, Sons and Gangster Dreams.* New York: Vintage Books. 1999.

Coulumbe, Charles A. *Rum: The Epic Story of the Drink That Conquered the World.* New York: Citadel, 2005.

Dash, Mike. *The First Family: Terror, Extortion, Revenge, Murder and the Birth of the American Mafia*. New York: Random House, Inc., 2009.

DeStefano, Anthony M. *Gangland New York: The Places and Faces of Mob History*. Guilford, Conn: Lyons Press, 2015.

Dickie, John. *Blood Brotherhoods: The History of Italy's Three Mafias*. New York: Perseus Book Group, 2014.

Downey, Patrick. *Gangster City: The History of the New York Underworld*. Fort Lee, N.J: Barricade Books, Inc. 2004.

English, T.J. *Havana Nocturne: How the Mob Owned Cuba—And Then Lost It to the Revolution*. New York: William Morrow, 2007.

Fitzgerald, F. Scott. *The Great Gatsby: The Authorized Text*. New York: Simon & Schuster, 1995.

Fried, Albert. *The Rise and Fall of the American Jewish Gangster in America*. New York: Columbia University Press. 1993.

Friedman, Bill. *30 Illegal Years to the Strip: The Untold Stories of The Gangsters Who Built the Early Las Vegas Strip*. Nevada: CreateSpace Independent Publishing Platform, 2015.

Gosch, Martin A., and Richard Hammer. *The Last Testament of Lucky Luciano*. New York: Little Brown & Company, 1975.

Hortis, Alexander C., and James B. Jacobs. *The Mob and the City: The Hidden History of How the Mafia Captured New York*. New York: Prometheus Books, 2014.

Johnson, Nelson. *Boardwalk Empire: The Birth, High Times and Corruption of Atlantic City*. Medford, N.J.: Plexus Publishing, Inc., 2002.

Kaplan, James. *Frank: The Voice*. New York: Anchor Press., 2011.

Katz, Leonard. *Uncle Frank: The Biography of Frank Costello*. New York: Drake Publishers Inc., 1973.

Keeler, Robert F. *Newsday: A Candid History of a Respectable Tabloid*. New York: Arbor House. 1990.

Kent, Joan Gay. *Discovering Sands Point: Its History, Its People, Its Places*. Sands Point, N.Y.: 2000.

Maas, Peter. *The Valachi Papers*. New York: G.P. Putnam's & Sons, 1968.

Miller, Donald. *Supreme City: How Jazz Age Manhattan Gave Birth to Modern America*. New York: Simon & Schuster, 2014.

Mockridge, Norton and Prall, Robert H. *The Big Fix*. New York: Henry Holt and Company, Inc., 1954.

Petersen, Virgil W. *The Mob: 200 Years of Organized Crime in New York*. Ottawa, Illinois: Green Hill Publishers, Inc., 1983.

Pietrusza, David. *Rothstein: The Life, Times, and Murder of the Criminal Genius Who Fixed the 1919 World Series*. New York: Carrol & Graf Publishers, 2003.

Pope, Paul David. *The Deeds of My Fathers: How My Grandfather and Father Built New York and Created the Tabloid World of Today*. New York: Rowman & Littlefield Publishers, Inc., 2010.

Poulsen, Ellen. *The Case Against Lucky Luciano: New York's Most Sensational Vice Trial*. Oakland Gardens, N.Y.: Clinton Cook Publishing Corp., 2007.

Quinn, Anthony, with Daniel Paisner. *One Man Tango*. New York: HarperCollins Publishing, 1995.

Raines, Robert K. *Hot Springs: From Capone to Costello*. Charleston, S.C.: Arcadia Publishing, 2013.

Reppetto, Thomas A. *Shadows Over the White House: The Mafia and the Presidents*. New York: Enigma Books, 2015.

Sciacca, Tony. *Luciano: The Man Who Modernized the American Mafia*. New York: Pinnacle Books, 1975.

Selvaggi, Giuseppe. *The Rise of the Mafia in New York*. Ed. and trans. William A. Packer. New York: The Bobbs-Merrill Company, Inc. 1978.

Servadio, Gaia. *Mafiosi: A History of the Mafia from Its Origins to the Present*. New York: Dell Publishing Co., Inc., 1976.

Smith, Richard Norton. *Thomas E. Dewey and His Times. The First Full-Scale Biography of the Maker of the Republican Party*. New York: Simon and Shuster, 1982.

Summers, Anthony. *Official and Confidential: The Secret Life of J. Edgar Hoover*. New York: G. Putnam's Sons, 2011.

———, and Robbyn Swann. *Frank: The Life*. New York: Knopf, 2005.

Thomas, Evan. *The Man to See: Edward Bennett Williams.* New York: Simon & Schuster, 1992.

Tully, Andrew. *Treasury Agent: The Inside Story.* New York: Simon and Schuster, 1958.

Whalen, Robert Weldon. *Murder Inc: Gangsters and Gangbusters in La Guardia's New York*: Oxford University Press, 2016.

White, Richard D. Jr. *Kingfish: The Reign of Huey P. Long.* New York: Random House Inc., 2006.

William, Dr. T. Harry. *Huey Long.* New York: Alfred A. Knopf, 1969.

Wolf, George, and Joseph Dimona. *Frank Costello: Prime Minister of the Underworld.* New York: William Morrow & Company, 1974.

Court Cases

U.S. v. Frank Costello, C141/9 (USDC SDNY) (1953)

U.S. v. Frank Costello, Civil 133-28 (USDC SDNY) (1958)

U.S. v. William V. Dwyer, et.al., Case No. A-553 (USDC SDNY) (1926)

Court Decisions

Frank Costello (Deceased) and Loretta B. Costello, Petitioners v. *Commissioner of Internal Revenue*, Respondent. Docket Nos. 48467,65107, United States Tax Court. Decision filed December 29, 1976.

Matter of Haim v. O'Connell. N.Y. State Supreme Court, 195 Misc. 612 (N.Y. Misc 1948)

Mills Novelty Co. V. Farrell, Chief of Police, 64 F.2d 476, (USCA 2nd Circuit) April 1933.

Mills Novelty Co. v. Bolan, Commissioner of Police, et al. 3 F. Supp 968 (USCD EDNY) May 1933.

Philip Kastel v. Commissioner, Docket No. 105129. United States Tax Court. 1945 Tax Ct. Memo LEXIS 44' 4 T.C.M. 1006.

The People of the State of New York, Appellant, v. 1400 Packages Containing Scotch Whiskey, etc., Respondent. 236 H.Y. 596 (Court of Appeals of New York) 1923.

United States of America, Appellee v. Frank Costello, Appellant,
221 F. 2d 668, (USCA 2nd Circuit), 1955.

Government Reports

*Hearings before the Special Committee to Investigate Organized
Crime in Interstate Commerce, United State Senate, Eighty-First
Congress (Second Session) and Eighty-Second Congress (First
Session), Part 7. July 1950 to March 1951.*

*The Activities and Associations of Persons Identified as Present at
the Residence of Joseph Barbara Sr. at Apalachin, New York, on
November 14, 1957, and the Reasons for Their Presence.* Report
by Arthur L. Reuter, Acting Commissioner of Investigation of
the State of New York, to Averell Harriman, Governor of the
State of New York, April 23, 1958.

*New York State Joint Legislative Committee on Crime, Its Cause,
Control and Effect on Society.* Report for 1970, September 1970.

*State of New York Executive Department Office of The
Commissioner of Investigation, letter report of William
Herlands dated September 17, 1954 to Governor Thomas
Dewey "on all the facts and circumstances leading to the com-
mutation of the sentence of Charles Luciano and the Granting of
Parole for Purpose of His Deportation.* The document found in
collection of Thomas E. Dewey papers at the University of
Rochester, Department of Rare Books and Special Collections.

Newspapers and Periodicals Consulted

Albany Times Union
Arizona Republic
Chicago Tribune
Daily News (N.Y.)
Daily Star (Queens)
Long Island Daily Press
Long Island Star Journal
Newsday (Long Island)
PM (N.Y.)
Rochester Democrat and
   Chronicle

Rome Daily Sentinel
   (Rome, N.Y.)
The Brooklyn Daily Eagle
The Evening World (N.Y.)
The New York Herald
The New York Sun
The New York Times
The New York Tribune
Time

Websites

www.americanmafia.com
www.bestofneworleans.com
www.biography.com
www.fbi.gov
www.findagrave.com
www.fultonhistory.com
www.germangeneology
   group.com
www.loc.gov

www.montauklife.com
www.nara.gov
www. nationalprohibition.
weebly.com/immigrants.html
www.nyc.gov
www.nexis.com
www.usinflationcalculator.com
www.wikipedia.com
www.youtube.com

ACKNOWLEDGMENTS

Writing and researching *Top Hoodlum* was a gigantic project, spanning many decades of the history of New York's organized crime scene. But luckily I had some important assistance. The first to get the nod of thanks is Noel Castiglia, who is Frank Costello's first cousin, twice removed. Noel has been an amazing student of Costello's family history as a member of the Castiglia clan and was generous in sharing with me documents and photographs that had until now been part of his private archives. By talking to members on the Castiglia family tree, Noel was able to resurrect long forgotten stories which he shared with me.

Another Costello fan who gets my thanks is Casey McBride, who curates the Facebook page "Uncle Frank's Place." Casey's lively page is dedicated to the history of Frank Costello and is a font of information and interesting photographs, some of which he helped secure for use in this book.

Nick Pileggi gets my thanks for suggesting the idea of a book about Costello and giving me the impetus to take on the project. Editor Gary Goldstein and my agent, Jill Marsal, did much to help.

The Brocato family, notably Joseph D. Brocato and Robert Maestri Brocato get my thanks for allowing use of a historic picture taken in New Orleans of their grandfather with Costello and his wife.

Two sources of information referred to me by Noel Castiglia—

Tom Cognato and Robert Golden—provided additional interesting materials as well.

Alexandra Mosca of New York and Rossana Del Zio of Rome, Italy, get a special mention for the expertise they provided. Alexandra imparted to me critical knowledge of New York cemeteries and their architecture, and was able to locate various graves. Rossano, an accomplished expert on Italian cuisine as well as organized crime, provided perspective on nineteenth century Italy and the rise of the brigands. Margaret Stacey had nice recollections of Costello from when she was a young girl.

Kevin Reilly, Carey Stumm, and Tom McAnear at the National Archives and Records Administration helped me retrieve files and information about Costello from government records.

Cindy Miller provided help with her recollections of the night Costello was shot and her friendship with him and his wife Loretta. Joel Winograd, a noted criminal defense attorney in New York, also gets my thanks. Posthumous mention has to be made of Frank Bari, an attorney who was the grandson of the late gangster and Costello friend Anthony Carfano, who over the years told me stories about Costello.

Assistance was also provided by the staffs of the New York Municipal Archives, The Historic New Orleans Collection and The University of Texas at Austin. Thanks also to author J. P. Andrieux of Canada and former *Daily News* writer William Sherman.

At *Newsday*, assistant managing editor Mary Ann Skinner not only helped get approval for me to do this book but also toiled diligently to find old photographs taken of Costello in 1950. Laura Mann of the *Newsday* library found the negatives and provided me with the necessary help in getting permission to use the images.

INDEX